Learning
from Young Children

Research in
Early Childhood Music

Edited by Suzanne L. Burton
and Cynthia Crump Taggart

Published in partnership with
MENC: The National Association for Music Education

ROWMAN & LITTLEFIELD EDUCATION

A division of
ROWMAN & LITTLEFIELD PUBLISHERS, INC.
Lanham • New York • Toronto • Plymouth, UK

Published in partnership with MENC: The National Association for Music Education

Published by Rowman & Littlefield Education
A division of Rowman & Littlefield Publishers, Inc.
A wholly owned subsidiary of The Rowman & Littlefield Publishing Group, Inc.
4501 Forbes Boulevard, Suite 200, Lanham, Maryland 20706
http://www.rowmaneducation.com

Estover Road, Plymouth PL6 7PY, United Kingdom

British Library Cataloguing in Publication Information Available

Library of Congress Cataloging-in-Publication Data

Learning from young children : research in early childhood music / [edited by] Suzanne L. Burton and Cynthia Crump Taggart.
    p. cm.
    "Published in partnership with MENC: The National Association for Music Education."
    ISBN 978-1-60709-322-0 (cloth : alk. paper) — ISBN 978-1-60709-323-7 (pbk. : alk. paper) — ISBN 978-1-60709-324-4 (electronic)
    1. Music—Instruction and study—Juvenile 2. Early childhood education. I. Burton, Suzanne L. (Suzanne Louise) II. Taggart, Cynthia Crump, 1957– III. MENC, the National Association for Music Education (U.S.)
  MT1.L516 2011
  372.87—dc22   2011010377

♾️™ The paper used in this publication meets the minimum requirements of American National Standard for Information Sciences—Permanence of Paper for Printed Library Materials, ANSI/NISO Z39.48-1992.

Printed in the United States of America

Contents

Acknowledgments   vii

Foreword   ix

PART I: UNDERSTANDING MUSICAL CHARACTERISTICS

1   Applying Brain Research to Children's Musical Experiences   3
    John W. Flohr and Diane C. Persellin

2   Language Acquisition: A Lens on Music Learning   23
    Suzanne L. Burton

3   The Role of Musical Engagement in the Musicality of
    Three-Year-Old Children   39
    Diana Dansereau

PART II: CREATING RICH LEARNING ENVIRONMENTS

4   Building Community to Elicit Responses in Early Childhood
    Music Classes   63
    Christina M. Hornbach

5   The Incorporation of Principles of the Reggio Emilia Approach
    in a North American Preschool Music Curriculum   79
    Amanda Page Smith

6   The Importance of Parents in Early Childhood Music
    Program Evaluation   95
    Shelly Cooper and Audrey Berger Cardany

7   Elementary Music Teachers' Role-Identities in and Perceptions
    of Teaching Prekindergarten Students with Special Needs   113
    Julie Derges Kastner

8   Preschool Children's Uses of a Music Listening Center during
    Free-Choice Time   131
    Wendy L. Sims, Lecia Cecconi-Roberts, and Dan Keast

9   Tonal Patterns: Providing the Vocabulary for Comprehensive
    Vocal Improvisation   141
    Krista N. Velez

PART III: MUSICAL PARENTING

10 Parents' Documentation of Their Children's Music-
    Related Behaviors   161
    *Wendy H. Valerio, Alison M. Reynolds, John Grego,
    Ching Ching Yap, and Anne McNair*

11 Music Play Zone: An Online Social Network Site Connecting
    Parents and Teacher in an Early Childhood Music Class   181
    Lisa Huisman Koops

12 Twenty-First-Century Parenting, Electronic Media, and Early
    Childhood Music Education   195
    Beatriz Ilari

PART IV: BENEFITS OF EARLY MUSIC INSTRUCTION

13 The Effect of an Age-Appropriate Music Curriculum on Motor
    and Linguistic and Nonlinguistic Skills of Children Three
    to Five Years of Age   215
    Joyce Jordan-DeCarbo and Joy Galliford

14 The Impact of a Music and Movement Program on
    School Readiness   231
    Lili M. Levinowitz

15 The Role of Early Childhood Music Class Participation in
    the Development of Four Children with Speech and
    Language Delay   245
    Cynthia Crump Taggart, Jenny Alvarez, and Kathy Schubert

16 Examining Music Experiences with Anthony, a Child Who
Has Autism 259
Wendy Valerio, Annabel Sy, Hannah Gruber, and
Claire Griffith Stockman

About the Editors 283

About the Authors 285

Acknowledgments

We would like to acknowledge several persons who were instrumental in helping this book come to fruition. First, thank you to Sue Rarus and Michael Blakeslee at MENC: The National Association for Music Education for supporting this initiative. Next, a special thanks to Korren B. Knapp for her adept assistance with figures and graphics. Finally, our gratitude goes to our review panel Diane C. Persellin, Alison M. Reynolds, and Joanne Rutkowski for reading and providing invaluable commentary on the manuscripts.

S.L.B
C.C.T

Foreword

The importance of the early music experiences of children in relation to their future music learning and development has long been recognized by the major professional music education organization in the United States, MENC: the National Association for Music Education. This has resulted in MENC's leadership and/or support for initiatives including publications, research projects, and conferences devoted to developing and promoting quality pedagogy, materials, and information for both early childhood educators and music educators. One early example is the 1985 MENC publication *The Young Child and Music: Contemporary Principles in Child Development and Music Education*, edited by Jacquelyn Boswell, which comprises the proceedings of the Music in Early Childhood Conference held at Brigham Young University in 1984. That was one of the first conferences, and thus proceedings documents, to provide a compendium of research and best-practice articles and abstracts related to music for young children. Twenty-five years later, at the University of Delaware, MENC's Early Childhood Special Research Interest Group held a conference titled "Learning from Young Children: Research in Early Childhood Music," which resulted in the current book. Although not technically a "twenty-fifth anniversary" event, it seems fitting to recognize that the 2009 conference and this book do, in essence, represent just that.

Early childhood music education research has come a long way in the past twenty-five years. The most exciting development is that more people seem to be devoting their research efforts to this area. Research related to various aspects of young children's musical characteristics, behaviors, development, and home and childcare environments, as well as issues related to their parents, teachers, and caregivers, is published regularly in all of the prominent national and international research journals. The contents of this book are a good reflection of these varied topics.

While the body of research in this field has been growing, it still seems underrepresented, given the importance of this time period in children's musical development. Although all types of research present unique challenges, research with young children is a particularly challenging undertaking, requiring creativity, patience, and persistence on the part of the researchers. Creativity must be used to devise ways to assess and interpret the responses of youngsters characterized by large individual differences, who cannot read, write, or verbalize well about music. Patience and persistence are required to obtain data often gathered in individual sessions, to transcribe and analyze recorded data, and to collect informed consent forms or data from busy parents. The pursuit of any sort of long-term or longitudinal research is difficult, given the frequent absences, irregular schedules, and often transient nature of children in childcare settings. The studies in this book, however, demonstrate that overcoming these challenges is well worth the effort.

The articles published here represent the variety of research methodologies employed and participants studied by current early childhood music education researchers. There are data obtained from infants through early elementary-age children, children with special needs, children enrolled in music classes within preschool or elementary school classrooms and outside of school settings, parents of young children, prekindergarten teachers, and music educators. The wide range of methodological paradigms includes philosophy, observation, case study, interview, survey/questionnaire, statistical analysis, mixed methods, curriculum study, content analysis, and program assessment.

Because of the range of content covered, including the varied theoretical and conceptual approaches to music education the articles reflect, this book should serve as a valuable text for use in early childhood music education courses. It also will be a useful and inspiring resource for those interested in pursuing their own research in the area of early childhood music. Perhaps this book will be inspirational enough to music education researchers that it will not take another twenty-five years before editors with a vision like that of Suzanne Burton and Cynthia Taggart will be able to identify and publish a similarly valuable and diverse collection of research studies in early childhood music education.

—Wendy L. Sims
Professor and Director of Music Education,
University of Missouri; editor, *Journal of Research in Music Education*

Part I

UNDERSTANDING MUSICAL CHARACTERISTICS

Chapter One

Applying Brain Research to Children's Musical Experiences

John W. Flohr and Diane C. Persellin

Music and the arts play an important role in human development, enhancing the growth of cognitive, emotional, and psychomotor pathways. Rich experiences with the arts at an early age provide a higher quality of human experience throughout a person's lifetime. The purpose of this chapter is to apply developments in brain research to young children's music experiences. We are at the threshold of using developing technology for studying how the brain functions and analyzing which teaching strategies are most effective with young children to maximize our efforts. Current studies hold the promise of a fuller understanding of the process of learning, guiding our profession in the development and use of more effective teaching strategies.

During the past two decades, the field of early childhood music research witnessed increased interest in brain research. With this in mind, the purpose of this chapter is to apply developments in brain research to young children's music experiences. With an emphasis on children less than six years of age, much of the presented information is also applicable to elementary students through the age of ten. The first section reviews (a) the interaction of brain research, teaching, and learning including neuromyths; (b) effect of music on structural brain changes and general intelligence; (c) plasticity; and (d) critical and optimal periods. The second section applies brain research to instructional strategies, covering topics of listening, singing, playing instruments, movement, improvisation, and imitation.

SECTION I: REVIEW OF BRAIN RESEARCH LITERATURE

Interaction of Brain Research, Teaching, and Learning

Research and theories interact to create new views of learning and education (Meltzoff, Kuhl, Movellan, and Sejnowski, 2009). Brain research, philosophical inquiry, and psychological investigations into the human mind have led to a plethora of ideas on how to teach effectively and efficiently. An example of one possible interaction stems from the recent research on brain mechanisms for music and language that appear to be comparable in general organization. "Music, like language, develops for communication, and by communication. Both depend upon functions of the brain that engage and regulate expressive movements of the body" (Flohr and Trevarthen, 2008, p. 80).

Developmentally Appropriate Practice

Before formulating guidance from brain research, it is advisable to keep developmentally appropriate practice in mind, as specified by the National Association for the Education of Young Children ([NAEYC], 2010) on its website:

1. Developmentally appropriate practice requires both meeting children where they are—which means that teachers must get to know them well—and enabling them to reach goals that are both challenging and achievable.
2. All teaching practices should be appropriate to children's age and developmental status, attuned to them as unique individuals, and responsive to the social and cultural contexts in which they live.
3. Developmentally appropriate practice does not mean making things easier for children. Rather, it means ensuring that goals and experiences are suited to their learning and development *and* challenging enough to promote their progress and interest.
4. Best practice is based on knowledge—not on assumptions—of how children learn and develop. The research base yields major principles in human development and learning. Those principles, along with evidence about curriculum and teaching effectiveness, form a solid basis for decision-making in early care and education.

One of the most rapidly developing research bases is that of brain research, which gives educators guidance regarding developmentally appropriate early childhood music education.

Children's Musical Culture

No infant or toddler is born as a musician by normal definition, although his musical expressions can be interpreted that way (McPherson, 2006). At a very early stage, just past midgestation, the fetus has capacities for perceiving and learning sounds. From three to four months of age, infants amuse themselves by rhythmically moving their bodies, waving limbs, banging objects, and clapping their hands. Phrases of baby songs are frequently grouped in stanzas of four lines forming foundations, generated in the brain, for the syntactic rules of language. Vocal imitation and vocal play when the infant is alone are more obvious and more varied at this time (Flohr and Trevarthen, 2008). Infants are born with sensitivity for the rhythmic expressive movements of other people. Neonatal vocal imitation is limited, but within a few weeks a baby can match simple vowel sounds of differing timbre as well as the rhythm of a short group of repeated sounds. Additionally, the baby is experimenting with a growing larynx (Rutkowski and Trollinger, 2004). Research on imitation in infants from the first weeks of life has shown that imitative exchange with adults (*infant mimesis*) is characterized by expressions of emotions of *interest* and *pleasure* (Kugiumutzakis, Kokkinaki, Markodimitraki, and Vitalaki, 2005). The infant's behaviors are not simply an automatic mirroring of the shape of a movement, but a means of establishing sympathetic motives, or intentions to communicate (Kugiumutzakis, 1998; Trevarthen, 2006; Trevarthen, Kokkinaki, and Fiamenghi, 1999). The exchange that infants and parents engage in together is termed *communicative musicality* (Flohr and Trevarthen, 2008).

Infants are good listeners and are attracted to subtle features of the human sounds of song or musical performance, showing certain preferences for pitch level, rhythm, and harmony that are similar to those of adult listeners (Trainor and Zacharias, 1997; Trehub, 2004). Research on baby songs, vocal chanting, and dancing games or other ritualized forms of moving and touching has indicated that every human society uses them, in some form, to stimulate play and joint participation after infants are about three months old. After three months, infants are highly attentive to rhythms of movements and rhyming of vocalization and to the emotional quality or aesthetic style of an adult's performance. Universal features of timing and modulation in infant-directed speech, baby songs, and the movements of gesture games and baby dancing confirm the intrinsic, culture-independent motive processes of both infants and adults and a fundamental rhythmic musicality, which has been inferred from the communicative behaviors of newborn infants (Trevarthen, 1999).

Flohr and Trevarthen (2008) propose that musical development in early years can best be fostered by supporting and encouraging the spontaneous vitality and inventiveness of human movement and gesture by using a child-centered approach that is intentionally open to the child's fluid experience as a naturally creative musical being. Children enjoy creation of musical forms of play for their own amusement or for sharing with other young children. This enjoyment of creating music leads to the phenomenon of *children's musical culture*, a child's way of exercising musicality and creating new forms of musical play that may not be much affected by the ideas and practices of the adult world (Bjørkvold, 1992; Flohr and Trevarthen, 2008; Moorhead and Pond, 1978). Several studies on improvisation and creativity explore children's musicality and culture creating within the child's own world of musical sounds, following ideas of Emile Jaques-Dalcroze (1921), Moorhead and Pond (1978), Flohr (1985), Kratus (1995, 2001), and others (Flohr and Trollinger, 2010).

Music and the Brain

Each part of the human body is connected to the brain, including our central nervous system and nerves. The brain also regulates release of hormones into the bloodstream. In effect, the brain is part of a much larger system that extends throughout the body.

It is important to remember that a child's brain is not the same as an adult brain. The largest growth periods of the human brain occur during the first years of life and during adolescence. While much brain development occurs in early childhood, the brain continues to change throughout life. However, the brain appears to be more malleable during the first decade of life than in adulthood. Also, positive or negative early experiences can alter both structure and function of the brain.

The brain makes connections during the prenatal period and throughout life (Gopnik, Meltzoff, and Kuhl, 1999). While some connections are found to be predetermined genetically, other connections develop from environmental influences (Flohr and Hodges, 2006). During the first decade of life, a child typically has up to twice as much neural activity and connections as adults. There is clear evidence that brain tissues and memory storing regions gain functional power and change in morphology as a result of stimulation and use (Johnson, 2005).

Synaptic Pruning

In brain development, clear additive and regressive events occur. Synapses, the connections between neurons, form in the brain and change as the young child develops, with a decrease in the level of synapses between the approximate ages of two and eight years. Evidently, the brain makes more connections than it needs. Synaptic pruning occurs as networks atrophy over time. Although there is much growth and activity during the early years, there is also evidence that there is room for change in the later years, with recent research indicating that the adult brain may be able to produce new cells (for example, in the hippocampus) (Eriksson et al., 1998; Knoth et al., 2010). Another factor involved in brain development in early childhood is the wide variability in the developmental characteristics of children. The complexity of the interaction between innate abilities and environment may also depend on the variability inherent in individual differences.

Neuromyths

Because neuroscience findings can be overstated, it is important for pedagogues and researchers to keep results of recent brain research in perspective. On the other hand, it is easy to discount neuroscience findings because of problems with the use of new technology, difficulties interpreting data, and unproven brain theory. Brain research has made large advances during the past twenty years, and these advances are promising to music education. However, research often provides more questions than answers and more fascinating "what-if" scenarios than provable learning strategies. A gulf between classroom application and research findings is not the only difficulty. Possibly biased data and what some authors call *neuromyths* complicate attempts to apply brain research to education.

Quickly developing techniques for measuring ways in which the brain changes pose another problem. In the article "Brain Imaging Skewed," Abbott (2009) wrote, "Nearly half of the neuroimaging studies published in prestige journals in 2008 contain unintentionally biased data that could distort their scientific conclusions, according to scientists at the National Institute of Mental Health in Bethesda, Maryland" (p. 1). With the complexity of brain imaging techniques (for example, EEG, PET, and fMRI), it is not surprising that vast amounts of data are sometimes misinterpreted or biased (Bennett and Miller, 2010; Vul, Harris, Winkielman, and Pashler, 2009).

The word *neuromyth* is used to describe misinformation, oversimplification, or overinterpretations of brain research findings (Goswami, 2006; Hall, 2006). Hall (2006) listed several well-known neuromyths including critical periods, localization of functions within specific areas of the brain, and left- and right-brained individuals. Neuromyths are not necessarily true or false; they present overstated or oversimplified research findings.

For instance, in brain research it is not unusual for readers and authors to confuse the terms *critical periods* and *optimal periods.* Authors often write about optimal periods as if they were critical periods. A critical period refers to the idea that there are time frames in which there will be no development or stunted development if certain stimulation is not present. An optimal period is used to refer to those periods in which development will be faster or easier (Flohr and Hodges, 2006).

Structural Changes, Localization, and Plasticity

Several studies demonstrate the types of music experiences that have an effect on the structure of the brain and demonstrate the power of music experiences on development. Unfortunately, few studies involve young children. One early study in the 1990s indicated that being actively involved in violin instruction before the age of seven changes physical development of the brain (Schlaug, Jänke, Huang, Staiger, and Steinmetz, 1995). Schlaug and others have since launched several studies of older children and adults that demonstrate how experiences change the morphology of the brain (Elbert, Pantev, Wienbruch, Rockstrub, and Taub, 1995; Gaser and Schlaug, 2003; Johnson, 2005; Norton et al., 2005). For example, professional keyboard players were found to have significantly more gray matter than amateur musicians and nonmusicians in several brain regions (Gaser and Schlaug, 2003). More gray matter and size increases in other parts of the brain are not confirmed as being advantageous for all life skills, but the finding that music experiences change morphology of the brain is important information for music teachers and parents.

Hemispheric localization was a popular idea during the 1980s and 1990s. Some educational activities were viewed as developing the right side of the brain, whereas others were focused on developing the left. The idea of hemispheric localization oversimplifies the way in which the brain processes music. Neuroimaging data suggest that neural mechanisms supporting music are distributed throughout the brain. In the *module theory*, music engages several different brain areas in a coordinated activity that activates submodules (such as musical syntax operators, timbre operators, and rhythm operators). Submodules are distributed in various regions throughout the brain. Each submodule appears to be a specialized piece of neural machinery. For a music task such as playing "Twinkle, Twinkle, Little Star" during Suzuki violin lessons, the young child's brain would integrate several submodules in a coordinated activity. There may be modules, or supermodules, or mechanisms that coordinate among different modules (Flohr and Hodges, 2006).

In the past, scientists thought that humans were born with all the brain cells they would ever have. In the past twenty years, however, research on brain plasticity, or how the physical structure of the brain changes as a result of experience, has changed the way in which researchers think of learning, growing, and developing. Plasticity refers to the notion that the brain is fluid or plastic in adaptability. After accidental brain damage, for example, the brain may reassign function from a damaged part of the brain to an uninjured area. Involvement in music may help keep the brain more fluid than if a person has no musical involvement throughout the lifespan (Caine and Caine, 1994; Thulborn, Carpenter, and Just, 1999). An ongoing study of 678 nuns indicated that rich experiences, including music, in older age help keep the brain pliable and adaptable. The nun study suggests that an adult brain can reorganize in response to positive experiences in the environment as well as negative experiences, as in cases of injury (Snowdon, 1997).

Critical and Optimal Periods—Windows of Opportunity

Critical periods, *optimal periods*, or *windows of opportunity* refer to the idea that there are set time frames in which there will be no development or stunted development if proper stimulation is not present. Both critical and optimal periods are often referred to as windows of opportunity.

A critical period can be thought of as a biological clock that opens only during a certain period of development. It is unknown presently if the critical period is due to biological clock mechanisms, the brain structures that have developed, or an interaction of the two. One example from animal research demonstrated that certain life experiences must be precisely timed to have an impact on the brain. The Nobel Prize winners Hubel and Wiesel (1970) deprived newborn kittens the use of one eye by covering it. A few months after the covering was removed, visual stimulation from the previously covered eye had no connection to the brain. A critical period in the kittens' development had been missed.

The term *optimal period* refers to those periods in which development will be faster or easier. For example, it is easier to learn to sing in tune during the ages of one to six years than at thirty-five to forty years of age. Unfortunately, authors often write about optimal periods as if they were critical periods. An optimal period and a possible critical period were observed in a study of violin training (previously referred to in the section on structural changes of the brain). In a sample of sixty musicians and nonmusicians, those who started training before the age of seven years exhibited increased corpus callosum size (Schlaug et al., 1995).

Music Enhances Cognition

Since the labeling of the "Mozart effect" in 1993, many researchers have investigated effects of music study and listening on learning (Rauscher, Shaw, and

Ky, 1993). The term *Mozart effect* was publicized and subsequently commercialized. The 1993 report contained two studies: One was conducted with college students on the short-term effect of listening to music on the outcomes of a cognitive test; the other was on the effect of piano study on young children's performance on cognitive tests. The idea, for young children, was that piano lessons (participating in an abstract, spatial-awareness task) would promote better performance in some areas of learning. Documented effects of positive gains were found in some domains of learning. Many researchers have replicated all or part of the original study (Flohr, Miller, and Persellin, 2000), and Hetland (2000), in her meta-analysis, revealed a modest effect of music training on cognitive tasks. Other researchers continue to examine the effects of music on cognition and the brain (Schlaug, Norton, Overy, and Winner, 2005). Catterall and Rauscher (2008) analyzed data from the work of Schellenberg (2004, 2005) and found that music instruction led to gains in general intelligence with a stronger effect in visual-spatial skills than verbal skills.

Positive effects from music instruction seem natural to many musicians and make sense in light of the modular theory of the brain. For example, if four areas of the brain are used during music instruction experiences, two or three of the same areas may be activated during spatial or mathematical tasks. One problem, of course, is obvious: if music shares areas of activation with other subjects, then other subjects, such as physical education, might also influence overall learning (Smith and Lounsbery, 2009). Using cognitive gains to justify music education is a tenuous position. Intrinsic benefits of music such as expressing feelings through sound provide a more solid justification (Flohr and Trollinger, 2010).

SECTION II: BRAIN-BASED INSTRUCTIONAL STRATEGIES

Do certain instructional strategies align themselves more with developments in brain research than others? Guidance from neuroscience research and national associations as well as teacher observations and assessment provide information about what works in the classroom. A teacher's effectiveness is influenced by her or his repertoire of strategies (Stronge, 2007). Using a wide range of strategies may reach more students by addressing the variety of student interests and learning styles (Persellin, 1993, 2004). Children acquire useful musical skills through quality experiences.

Listening

Listening is a fundamental music skill. Not until the late 1980s has the acquisition of music skills received notable attention from researchers and pedagogues (Haack, 1992). A significant body of literature on this topic has developed over recent years. At least three research strands support music listening and music listening activities for young children: (a) recent advances in neuroscience have yielded a better view of the human brain and given preliminary support and specificity to the idea that music has a positive effect on brain function (Flohr and Hodges, 2006); (b) studies with infants have shown positive effects of music listening including less time in a warmer or isolette, less total time in intensive care, less weight loss, fewer high arousal states, more nonstress behaviors, and positive effects on oxygen saturation levels, heart rate, and respiration (Standley, 2002, 2003); and (c) young children can discern main components of music and speech and are also adept at hearing, responding, and choosing music (Flohr, 2004; Flohr, Atkins, Bower, and Aldridge, 2000).

Infants and Listening

The advances in neuroscience have allowed investigators to test infants on their ability to attend to music and discriminate among different types of music. In one study, four- through six-month-old infants heard excerpts of Mozart minuets. Mozart's music was altered by the insertion of brief pauses at phrase points in some and at nonphrase points in others. Lights above a speaker drew the infants' attention, at which time an excerpt with either natural or unnatural breaks would begin and continue until the infants looked away. Infants were significantly more likely to look when the excerpts contained pauses at natural musical points (Krumhansl and Jusczyk, 1990).

In another study (Ilari and Sundara, 2009), three groups of five-, eight-, and eleven-month-old infants were tested to determine whether they could demonstrate listening preferences between an unaccompanied and an accompanied children's song. By monitoring head turning, results indicated that infants had a clear preference for the unaccompanied version of the song across all age groups.

Ilari, Polka, and Costa-Giomi (2002) tested thirty seven-month-old infants' long-term memory of two complex pieces of music. The infants heard the music daily for ten days followed by a two-week retention period without the music. The researchers played eight familiar excerpts mixed with eight unfamiliar pieces of music. Using the head-turning procedure, infants showed a significant preference for the familiar piece of music. The researchers also tested a control group of fifteen infants, who showed no preferences for either piece of music. These results suggest that infants in the exposure group retained the familiar music in their long-term memory. The infants could discriminate between the different excerpts of the familiar and unfamiliar pieces of music and demonstrated their preference for the familiar piece.

Listening and Young Children

Neuroscience and child development research demonstrates the value of music listening in a young child's life (Flohr, 2010). In a recent study, EEG (electrophysiological) responses were measured while four-year-old children listened to two contrasting styles of music (Flohr, Persellin, Miller, and Meeuwsen, 2011). The researchers measured relationships between listening to recorded music and cognitive abilities of four-year-old children. A total of fifty-seven preschool children were assigned to a high-scoring or low-scoring group according to their scores on a Visual Closure test (Woodcock and Johnson, 1990). Brain electrical activity classified 90 percent of children with high scores and 61 percent of low scores (for an average of 76 percent of all scores). The statistical tests do not support causality; however, data support the idea that there may be a meaningful relationship between listening to music and higher scores on the Visual Closure test. In this study and earlier studies, children's EEG data were not significantly different for two contrasting styles of music, such as Bach and rock or Vivaldi and Irish folk music (Flohr and Miller, 1995).

Instructional Applications

Infants are inherently musical and begin to form musical preferences very early in life. Parents and caregivers should be encouraged to share many different types of music with infants. Parents and music teachers should continue this throughout early childhood, as it appears that young children are open to and accepting of a wide range of musical styles. Moreover, early childhood listening research demonstrates that children are individualistic in their responses to music listening experiences (Sims, 2005, 2006).

Playing an Instrument

Audio-Motor Effects

Brain imaging studies of musicians playing their instruments show activations in motor systems. When playing an instrument, audio-motor networks are activated, which explains why it is so natural to move when playing music on an instrument. Furthermore, brain systems that link perceptual and motor areas help the two mechanisms to reinforce each other (Binkofski and Buccino, 2006; Nishitani and Hari, 2002). Motor networks link to pleasure centers in the brain (Hodges, 2010). The physical activity of making music, even at a very simple level, brings deep pleasure to young children and adults.

Active Engagement

In addition to the pleasure from playing a musical instrument, Diamond and Hopson (1998) found that learning to play a musical instrument could also increase a child's capacity for engagement or what they call "voluntary attention." Observing a young child totally engrossed in playing a drum is an excellent example of total engagement of voluntary attention.

Duke (1999) studied twenty-nine master Suzuki string teachers who worked with two or three of their young students and their parents. Thirteen expert string pedagogues evaluated videotapes of three private lessons of each student according to specific teaching behaviors such as talking, playing, modeling, and positioning the instrument. Results indicated that excellent teaching by talented Suzuki teachers is marked by active student involvement. In a study of four- to six-year-old children, researchers examined one group of children taking Suzuki music lessons and a group that was not taking music lessons outside of school (Fujioka, Ross, Kakigi, Pantev, and Trainor, 2006). Those children taking music lessons for a year improved in music listening skills and on general memory skills.

Instructional Applications

Talking about drums or showing a video of drum playing is not as effective as having students play the drums. Children benefit from many sensory-motor experiences on a variety of instruments, both small and large, as this variety requires fine- and gross-motor movements. For interested and dedicated parents and children, the Suzuki method may be an attractive method to learn to play an instrument such as the violin.

Singing

While most brain imaging research dealing with music involves studies of instrumentalists and instrumental training, several imaging studies exist that examine the relationship between brain activity and tone color in language. Investigators are currently studying whether language and singing share processing strategies in the brain (Trollinger, 2010). Singing activates the entire brain, but certain parts of it are more engaged when learning particular aspects of a song. For example, when a singer concentrates on learning the words of a song, the temporal region in the left side of the brain, where Broca's and Wernicke's areas are located, is more engaged, but when learning the melody, the right side is more engaged. This finding illustrates why music teachers sometimes teach the melody first on a neutral syllable, and then, when words are added, the melody may suffer.

Singing appears to have a positive effect on language development, speech, and comprehension. The brain behaves similarly whether one is reading aloud or singing. A study by the German researchers Jentschke and Koelsch (2009) found that highly trained boy singers had an advantage in their language perception skills related to grammar and comprehension.

Brain imaging studies of babbling infants and children show that Broca's area is more strongly activated when developing grammatical representations of language, while Wernicke's area is more activated when learning and categorizing vocabulary. The pathway between the two areas strengthens with practice, aiding comprehension and speech. Musically, the immersion approach of teaching songs works in a similar way: the more the children hear the songs, the more they will imprint the melody and words in their memories.

Instructional Applications

Research suggests that teachers should teach the words of a song first, before adding the melody OR teach the melody prior to adding the words. If the melody is taught first, simple repeated word phrases in the song could be the next step. For example, in the song "L'il Liza Jane," teach the second and fourth phrases ("L'il Liza Jane") first before teaching "I've got a house in Baltimore." Once the melody and repeated words or phrases are mastered, words to the more complex melodies could be taught as the last step before singing the entire song. Applying this strategy to teach parts of a song with either a difficult melody or difficult words may be helpful for children's learning (Trollinger, 2010). When teaching songs in which the melody is complex, brain processing can be accommodated by first teaching the melody on a neutral syllable, followed by adding verbal phrases that repeat, rather than try to teach all the words in one lesson.

Research also demonstrates that musical engagement helps students develop language-processing skills. Strategies include emphasizing words in a song or using new vocabulary. For example, when teaching a chant, the teacher might emphasize the words. To help build stronger brain connections, a simple melody can be added after the chant is learned.

Movement and Development

Recent neurological research confirms that the nervous system is richly integrated and that the brain functions as a dynamic system, transferring information at great speed, often faster than research techniques can track except locally in very limited regions or for very short periods of time. Dualistic ideas of the mind and body being separate are now replaced by the concept of body and mind working in tight reciprocal coordination in the generation of movements and consciousness.

A purpose of the brain is to put rhythmic impulses into movements of the body and to use the body to communicate these impulses and to sense them in others. Thus, the brain is, in a sense, musical before birth. The senses of touch, vibration, and hearing are present early in development. The fetus hears musical elements in the voice of the mother months before birth (usually around the twenty-sixth week) and often reacts to the rhythm of music, kicking with its legs (Flohr and Trevarthen, 2008).

In spite of their differences in size, mobility and experience, a newborn infant and an adult share a matching sense of time and the same affective values of moving. They engage one another by hearing, seeing, and touching and regulating an exchange of states of interest, intention, and emotions with intuitive ease, exhibiting intricate synchronized rhythmic activity (Trevarthen, Aitken, Vandekerckhove, Delafield-Butt, and Nagy, 2006; Trevarthen and Reddy, 2006). Both the growing cognitive powers of infants and their abilities to communicate are dependent on initiation and regulation by movements (Trevarthen, 1984; von Hofsten, 2004). From as early as six weeks, neurons of the cerebral cortex are completing postnatal proliferation of dendritic branches and the production of synaptic connections accelerates. A baby will move his head to orient to a parent's eyes as they join in turn-taking utterances of coordinated coos, prespeech lip and tongue movements, and hand gestures. From three to four months, infants amuse themselves with rhythmically moving their bodies, waving limbs, banging objects, clapping hands. Expressive movements are repeated with the three- to five-second cycle of the prelinguistic phrase, which has a variety of lively and communicative prosodic contours (Malloch, 1999; Stern, 1999).

After six months, babbling and hand banging are rhythmic, both repeating up to about three pulses per second. With exceptional learning support, a one-year-old may beat a fairly regular tempo. It has been claimed that this steady beat ability is uniquely human and an important foundation for learning the ritual forms of music (Dissanayake, 2000). Fox, Parsons, and Hodges (1998) have found that the area of the brain that controls movement is activated when humans listen to music. As a child matures, brain and body grow together. The human brain is built to move the human body. It learns from the body; it teaches the body how to deal with forces that arise in itself when it is moving, how to pick up information from the environment to guide movement toward anticipated goals, and sets the foundation for the special human dynamics of music (Flohr and Trevarthen, 2008).

Instructional Applications

Children must be given opportunities to move. Music should be taught in such a way that every young child is motivated to move, dance, clap, and pat to music. Moving is an effective way to engage children, which is necessary to ensure learning. Rote memorization, repetition, skimming of material, and drill do little to form neural connections. Moving large and small muscles through singing games and dances, and acting out stories may lead to longer-term recall (Patterson, 1997).

Engaging and Enjoyable Learning

When humans engage in pleasurable and successful learning activities, the brain rewards itself through the release of hormones such as serotonin and dopamine that are associated with feelings of satisfaction and pleasure (Braun and Bock, 2008). Involvement in musical activities changes levels of serotonin (Evers and Suhr, 2000) and dopamine (Menon and Levitin, 2005) and activates areas on both sides of the brain known to be involved in emotion, reward, and motivation (Blood and Zatorre, 2001; Blood, Zatorre, Bermudez, and Evans, 1999; Brown, Martinez, and Parsons, 2004).

Learning also activates areas that are associated with rewards and that monitor autonomic and cognitive processes. Information from an active musical experience travels from the ventral tegmental area to the nucleus accumbens and to the prefrontal cortex; this is one of several pathways activated by a rewarding stimulus such as learning and music (Hodges, 2010).

Instructional Applications

Children learn better when they are engaged and having fun, so teachers should make music class more celebratory. Those who teach young children should consider welcoming them with a favorite "Hello" song when they arrive at music class. Every effort should be made to connect music learning with warmth and joy. Teachers should congratulate children on their musical accomplishments and laugh with them over a silly song.

Children become actively engaged when given an opportunity to explore freely sound-making materials and when given guided experiences exploring sound. Teachers should create many opportunities for young children to improvise. Several techniques might include improvising responses to musical questions, giving children opportunities to create their own story songs, providing them with puppets that like to sing rather than speak, and encouraging them to create accompaniments to stories on Orff instruments. Encouraged in their ability to improvise within the parameters of musical restrictions, children are engaged and learn that their music and creativity are valued. Finally, teachers who demonstrate enthusiasm for teaching music and for working with children will promote engaging and enjoyable learning.

Imitation

Imitation is a primary way that young children learn. Humans begin to mimic as newborns and continue to do so throughout the lifespan—observing and copying actions. Good modeling of vocal sound, healthy habits when singing, playing, playing instruments, and listening are essential in the music class-room. Studies with monkeys as subjects and more recently with human sub-jects have located *mirror neurons* (Doidge, 2007; Jossey-Bass, 2008; Steen, 2007). These are neurons that fire when humans see or hear someone perform-ing an action. These neurons also fire when we perform the action ourselves. Thus, the brain has built-in mechanisms that help us learn by imitation.

Learning by imitation accelerates the learning process, because the learner does not have to start from scratch. Through imitation, humans learn what others have discovered or what the culture has learned over a long period of time in a short time span. Finally, we can learn from experts. It is difficult for a novice to imagine a finished product unless presented with a model. If the only model a beginning violinist had was her own out-of-tune scratching, she would never move toward the sound and look of an accomplished artist.

Instructional Applications

Teachers should model the behaviors that they want students to emulate. While this is self-evident, one should strive for a higher standard. It is not enough to model specific behaviors from time to time; rather, teachers should *constantly* model appropriate behaviors. Students are always observing teach-ers. It should always be a case of *do as I do* rather than *do as I say*.

CONCLUSION

Music and the arts play an important role in human development, enhancing the growth of cognitive, emotional, and psychomotor pathways. Preschools and elementary schools have an obligation to introduce children to music at the earliest possible time and to treat the arts as fundamental—not optional—curriculum areas. Rich experiences with the arts at an early age provide a higher quality of human experience throughout a person's lifetime. As a profession, we are at the threshold of using developing technology for study-ing how the brain functions and analyzing which teaching strategies are most effective with young children to maximize our efforts. These studies hold the promise of a fuller understanding of the process of learning, guiding our profession in the development and use of more effective teaching strategies.

REFERENCES

Abbott, A. (2009). Brain imaging skewed. *Nature, 458,* 1087.

Bennett, C. M., and Miller, M. B. (2010). How reliable are the results from functional magnetic resonance imaging? *Annals of the New York Academy of Sciences, 1191*(1), 133–55.

Binkofski, F., and Buccino, G. (2006). The role of the ventral pre-motor cortex in action execution and action understanding. *Journal of Physiology–Paris, 99*(4–6), 396–405.

Bjørkvold, J. R. (1992). *The muse within: Creativity and communication, song and play from childhood through maturity.* New York: Harper Collins.

Blood, A., and Zatorre, R. (2001). Intensely pleasurable responses to music correlate with activity in brain regions implicated in reward and emotion. *Proceedings of the National Academy of Sciences, 98*(20), 11818–823.

Blood, A., Zatorre, R., Bermudez, P., and Evans, A. C. (1999). Emotional responses to pleasant and unpleasant music correlate with activity in paralimbic brain regions. *Nature Neuroscience, 2,* 382–87.

Braun, A., and Bock, J. (2008). Born to learn: Early learning optimizes brain function. In W. Gruhn and F. Rauscher (Eds.), *Neurosciences and music pedagogy* (pp. 27–51). Hauppage, NY: Nova Science.

Brown, S., Martinez, M. J., and Parsons, L. M. (2004). Passive music listening spontaneously engages limbic and paralimbic systems. *NeuroReport, 15*(13), 2033–37.

Caine, R. N., and Caine, G. (1994). *Making connections: Teaching the human brain.* New York: Addison-Wesley.

Catterall, J. S., and Rauscher, F. (2008). Unpacking the impact of music on intelligence. In W. Gruhn and F. Rauscher (Eds.), *Neurosciences in music pedagogy* (pp. 169–98). Hauppage, NY: Nova Science.

Diamond, M., and Hopson, J. (1998). *Magic trees of the mind: How to nurture your child's intelligence, creativity, and healthy emotions from birth through adolescence.* New York: Dutton.

Dissanayake, E. (2000). Antecedents of the temporal arts in early mother-infant interaction. In N. L. Wallin, B. Merker, and S. Brown (Eds.), *The origins of music* (pp. 389–410). Cambridge, MA: MIT Press.

Doidge, N. (2007). *The brain that changes itself.* New York: Viking-Penguin.

Duke, R. (1999). Teacher and student behavior in Suzuki string lessons: Results from the international research symposium on talent education. *Journal of Research in Music Education, 47*(4), 293–307.

Elbert, T., Pantev, C., Wienbruch, C., Rockstrub, B., and Taub, E. (1995). Increased cortical representation of the fingers of the left hand in string players. *Science, 270*(5234), 305–7.

Eriksson, P. S., Perfilieva, E., Björk-Eriksson, T., Alborn, A. M., Nordborg, C., Peterson, D. A., et al. (1998). Neurogenesis in the adult human hippocampus. *Nature Medicine, 4*(11), 1313–17.

Evers, S., and Suhr, B. (2000). Changes of the neurotransmitter serotonin but not of hormones during short time music perception. *European Archives of Psychiatry and Clinical Neuroscience, 250*(3), 144–47.

Flohr, J. W. (1985). Young children's improvisations: Emerging creative thought. *The Creative Child and Adult Quarterly, 10*(2), 79–85.

Flohr, J. W. (2004). *Musical lives of young children.* Upper Saddle River, NJ: Prentice Hall.

Flohr, J. W. (2010). Best practices for young children's music education: Guidance from brain research. *General Music Today, 23*(2), 13–19.

Flohr, J. W., Atkins, D. H., Bower, T. G. R., and Aldridge, M. A. (2000). Infant music preferences: Implications for child development and music. *Music Education Research Reports: Texas Music Educators Association,* 2–7.

Flohr, J. W., and Hodges, D. (2006). Music and neuroscience. In R. Colwell (Ed.), *MENC handbook of musical cognition and development* (pp. 3–39). New York: Oxford University Press.

Flohr, J. W., and Miller, D. C. (1995). *Developmental quantitative EEG differences during psychomotor response to music.* Champaign, IL: ERIC Document Reproduction Service No. PS025653.

Flohr, J. W., Miller, D. C., and Persellin, D. C. (2000). Recent brain research on young children. In *Music makes the difference: Music, brain development, and learning* (pp. 37–43). Reston, VA: MENC.

Flohr, J. W., Persellin, D. C., Miller, D. C., and Meeuwsen, H. (2011). Relationships among music listening, temperament, and cognitive abilities. *Visions of Research in Music Education, 17.*

Flohr, J. W., and Trevarthen, C. (2008). Music learning in childhood: Early developments of a musical brain and body. In W. Gruhn and F. Rauscher (Eds.), *Neurosciences in music pedagogy* (pp. 53–99). Hauppage, NY: Nova Science.

Flohr, J. W., and Trollinger, V. (2010). *Music in elementary education.* Upper Saddle River, NJ: Prentice Hall.

Fox, P., Parsons, L., and Hodges, D. (1998). Neural basis of the comprehension of musical harmony, melody, and rhythm. *Society for Neuroscience Abstracts, 28,* 1763.

Fujioka, T., Ross, B., Kakigi, R., Pantev, C., and Trainor, L. J. (2006). One year of musical training affects development of auditory cortical-evoked fields in young children. *Brain, 129*(10), 2593–2608.

Gaser, C., and Schlaug, G. (2003). Brain structures differ between musicians and non-musicians. *Journal of Neuroscience, 23*(27), 9240–45.

Gopnik, A., Meltzoff, A., and Kuhl, P. (1999). *The scientist in the crib.* New York: William and Morrow.

Goswami, U. (2006). Neuroscience and education: From research to practice? *Nature, 6,* 2–7.

Haack, P. (1992). The acquisition of music listening skills. In R. Colwell (Ed.), *Handbook of research on music teaching and learning* (pp. 451–65). New York: Schirmer.

Hall, J. (2006). Neuroscience and education. *Education Journal, 84*(3), 27–29.

Hetland, L. (2000). Listening to music enhances spatial-temporal reasoning: Evidence for the "Mozart Effect." *Journal of Aesthetic Education, 34*(3–4), 105–48.

Hodges, D. A. (2010). Can neuroscience help us do a better job of teaching music? *General Music Today, 23*(2), 3–12.

Hubel, D. H., and Wiesel, T. N. (1970). The period of susceptibility to the physiological effects of unilateral eye closure in kittens. *Journal of Physiology, 206,* 419–36.

Ilari, B., Polka, L., and Costa-Giomi, E. (2002). Infants' long-term memory for complex music. *Journal of the Acoustical Society of America, 111*(5), 2456–56.

Ilari, B., and Sundara, M. (2009). Music listening preferences in early life. *Journal of Research in Music Education, 56*(4), 357–69.

Jaques-Dalcroze, E. (1921). *Rhythm, music, and education.* New York: Putnam's Sons.

Jentschke, S., and Koelsch, S. (2009). Musical training modulates the development of syntax processing in children. *NeuroImage, 47*(2), 735–44.

Johnson, M. H. (2005). *Developmental cognitive neuroscience* (2nd ed.). Malden, MA: Blackwell.

Jossey-Bass (Ed.). (2008). *The Jossey-Bass reader on the brain and learning.* San Francisco, CA: Author.

Knoth, R., Singec, I., Ditter, M., Pantazis, G., Capetian, P., Meyer, R. P., et al. (2010). Murine features of neurogenesis in the human hippocampus across the lifespan from 0 to 100 years. *PloS One, 5*(1), e8809.

Kratus, J. (1995). A developmental approach to teaching music improvisation. *International Journal of Music Education, 26,* 27–38.

Kratus, J. (2001). Effect of available tonality and pitch options on children's compositional processes and products. *Journal of Research in Music Education, 49*(4), 294–306.

Krumhansl, C. L., and Jusczyk, P. W. (1990). Infants' perception of phrase structure in music. *Psychological Science, 1,* 70–73.

Kugiumutzakis, G. (1998). Neonatal imitation in the intersubjective companion space. In S. Bråten (Ed.), *Intersubjective communication and emotion in early ontogeny* (pp. 63–88). Cambridge: Cambridge University Press.

Kugiumutzakis, G., Kokkinaki, T., Markodimitraki, M., and Vitalaki, E. (2005). Emotions in early mimesis. In J. Nadel and D. Muir (Eds.), *Emotional development* (pp. 161–82). Oxford: Oxford University Press.

Malloch, S. (1999). Mother and infants and communicative musicality. In I. Deliège (Ed.), *Rhythms, musical narrative, and the origins of human communication: Musicae Scientiae, Special Issue* (pp. 29–57). Liège, Belgium: European Society for the Cognitive Sciences of Music.

McPherson, G. E. (Ed.). (2006). *The child as musician: A handbook of musical development.* Oxford: Oxford University Press.

Meltzoff, A., Kuhl, P., Movellan, J., and Sejnowski, S. (2009). Foundations for a new science of learning. *Science, 325,* 284–88.

Menon, V., and Levitin, D. (2005). The rewards of music listening: Response and physiological connectivity of the mesolimbic system. *NeuroImage, 28*, 175–84.

Moorhead, G. E., and Pond, D. (1978). *Music of young children.* Santa Barbara, CA: Pillsbury Foundation for Advancement of Music Education.

National Association for the Education of Young Children (NAEYC), 2010. *Key messages.* Retrieved from www.naeyc.org/positionstatements/dap.

Nishitani, N., and Hari, R. (2002). Viewing lip forms: Cortical dynamics. *Neuron, 36,* 1211–20.

Norton, A., Winner, E., Cronin, K., Overy, K., Lee, D. J., and Schalug, G. (2005). Are there pre-existing neural, cognitive, or motoric markers for musical ability? *Brain Cognition, 59*(2), 124–34.

Patterson, M. (1997). *Everybody can learn.* Tucson, AZ: Zephyr.

Persellin, D. C. (1993). Responses to rhythm patterns when presented to children through auditory, visual, and kinesthetic modes. *Journal of Research in Music Education, 40*(4), 315–23.

Persellin, D. C. (2004). Foundations: Theories and approaches. In J. W. Flohr (Ed.), *Musical lives of young children* (pp. 8–15). Upper Saddle River, NJ: Prentice Hall.

Rauscher, F. H., Shaw, G. L., and Ky, K. N. (1993). Music and spatial task performance. *Nature, 365,* 611.

Rutkowski, J., and Trollinger, V. L. (2004). Singing. In J. W. Flohr (Ed.), *Musical lives of young children* (pp. 78–97). Upper Saddle River, NJ: Prentice Hall.

Schellenberg, E. G. (2004). Music lessons enhance IQ. *Psychological Science, 15,* 511–14.

Schellenberg, E. G. (2005). Music and cognitive abilities. *Current Directions in Psychological Science, 14,* 322–25.

Schlaug, G., Jänke, L., Huang, Y., Staiger, J. F., and Steinmetz, H. (1995). Increased corpus callosum size in musicians. *Neuropsychologia, 33*(8), 1047–55.

Schlaug, G., Norton, A., Overy, K., and Winner, E. (2005). Effects of music training on the child's brain and cognitive development. *Annals of the New York Academy of Sciences, 1060,* 219–30.

Sims, W. L. (2005). Effects of free versus directed listening on duration of individual music listening by prekindergarten children. *Journal of Research in Music Education, 53*(1), 78–86.

Sims, W. L. (2006). Listening to learn—learning to listen. *Early Childhood Music and Movement Association Perspectives, 1*(2), 4–5.

Smith, N. J., and Lounsbery, M. (2009). Promoting physical education: The link to academic achievement. *Journal of Physical Education, Recreation, and Dance, 80*(1), 39–43.

Snowdon, D. A. (1997). Aging and Alzheimer's disease: Lessons from the nun study. *Gerontologist, 37*(2), 150–56.

Standley, J. M. (2002). A meta-analysis of the efficacy of music therapy for premature infants. *Journal of Pediatric Nursing, 17*(2), 107–13.

Standley, J. M. (2003). The effect of music-reinforced nonnutritive sucking on feeding rate of premature infants. *Journal of Pediatric Nursing, 8*(3), 169–73.

Steen, R. (2007). *The evolving brain: The known and the unknown.* Amherst, NY: Prometheus Books.

Stern, D. N. (1999). Vitality contours: The temporal contour of feelings as a basic unit for constructing the infant's social experience. In P. Rochat (Ed.), *Early social cognition: Understanding others in the first months of life* (pp. 67–90). Mahwah, NJ: Erlbaum.

Stronge, J. H. (2007). *Qualities of effective teachers* (2nd ed.). Alexandria, VA: Association for Supervision and Curriculum Development.

Thulborn, K. R., Carpenter, P. A., and Just, M. A. (1999). Plasticity of language-related brain function during recovery from stroke. *Stroke, 30*(4), 749–54.

Trainor, L. J., and Zacharias, C. A. (1997). Infants prefer higher-pitched singing. *Infant Behavior and Development, 21*(4), 799–805.

Trehub, S. E. (2004). Music perception in infancy. In J. W. Flohr (Ed.), *Musical lives of young children* (pp. 24–29). Upper Saddle River, NJ: Prentice Hall.

Trevarthen, C. (1984). How control of movement develops. In H. T. A. Whiting (Ed.), *Human motor actions: Bernstein reassessed* (pp. 223–61). Amsterdam: Elsevier.

Trevarthen, C. (1999). Musicality and the intrinsic motive pulse: Evidence from human psychobiology and infant communication. In I. Deliège (Ed.), *Rhythms, musical narrative, and the origins of human communication: Musicae Scientiae, Special Issue, 1999–2000* (pp. 157–213). Liège: European Society for the Cognitive Sciences of Music.

Trevarthen, C. (2006). First things first: Infants make good use of the sympathetic rhythm of imitation, without reason or language. *Journal of Child Psychotherapy, 31*(1), 91–113.

Trevarthen, C., Aitken, K. J., Vandekerckhove, M., Delafield-Butt, J., and Nagy, E. (2006). Collaborative regulations of vitality in early childhood: Stress in intimate relationships and postnatal psychopathology. In D. Cicchetti and D. J. Cohen (Eds.), *Developmental psychopathology: Volume 2, Developmental neuroscience* (2nd ed., pp. 65–126). New York: Wiley.

Trevarthen, C., Kokkinaki, T., and Fiamenghi, G. A., Jr. (1999). What infants' imitations communicate: With mothers, with fathers, and with peers. In J. Nadel and G. Butterworth (Eds.), *Imitation in infancy* (pp. 127–85). Cambridge: Cambridge University Press.

Trevarthen, C., and Reddy, V. (2006). Consciousness in infants. In M. Velman and S. Schneider (Eds.), *A companion to consciousness* (pp. 41–57). Oxford: Blackwell.

Trollinger, V. L. (2010). The brain in singing and language. *General Music Today, 23*(2), 20–23.

Von Hofsten, C. (2004). An action perspective on motor development. *Trends in Cognitive Sciences, 8*(6), 266–72.

Vul, E., Harris, C., Winkielman, P., and Pashler, H. (2009). Puzzlingly high correlations in fMRI studies of emotion, personality, and social cognition. *Perspectives on Psychological Science, 4*(3), 274–90.

Woodcock, R. W., and Johnson, M. B. (1990). *Woodcock-Johnson Psychoeducational Battery—Revised.* Circle Pines, MN: American Guidance Service.

Chapter Two

Language Acquisition: A Lens on Music Learning

Suzanne L. Burton

This chapter presents a study on the application of the principles of language acquisition to music learning. I acted as a teacher-researcher, documenting three-year-old Joey's musical growth in my early childhood music class over the course of three years. I collected data through videotape, my reflective research journal, Joey's notational artifacts, and anecdotal evidence. Constant comparison of data sources gave rise to a primary theme that elucidated Joey's construction of musical meaning: Joey learned music through the recurrent process of musical immersion through active listening, intentional musical interaction and improvisation, and the modeling of reading and writing music. Developing the ability to chant rhythmically in time and sing in tune, Joey also began to understand how print music functioned. Subsequently, Joey learned how to capture his musical thoughts on paper through his own interpretation of how standard notation operates.

Modern pedagogy should . . . help us to determine how to identify and encourage the innate powers of our students' minds; to nurture what is native; to explore what it can mean to say, "Begin with where they are."

—Ann Berthoff (1981, pp. 48–49)

How do we determine what to teach in our early childhood music classes, when to teach it, and how? Perhaps the research on language acquisition holds promise for uncovering the musicality of young children. Recent research indicates that there exists a correspondence between the processes of language acquisition and music acquisition. Researchers have posited that music acquisition may be a parallel process to language acquisition (Gordon, 2004; Gruhn, 2002; Pinzino, 2007; Reynolds, Long, and Valerio, 2007). They contend that both language and music are communication systems unique to human beings (Jackendoff and Lerdahl, 2006; Patel, 2008) and that both may be acquired through normal exposure, independent of formal education (Hauser and McDermott, 2003). Reynolds and colleagues (2007) acknowledge that both language and music may be obtained aurally, orally, visually, and kinesthetically. They suggested that a child placed in particular musical conditions similar to those of language acquisition will begin to construct musical thought, eventually leading to musical independence. Because little research exists regarding the potential connection between language and music acquisition, I explored music learning within a language acquisition framework in an early childhood music class. In this chapter, I illustrate what I learned about musical development from one of my students, Joey, as he participated in the class.

CONCEPTUAL LENS: LANGUAGE LITERACY

In literate societies, language acquisition leads to the process of a person's learning to read and write language with comprehension (Clay, 1991). Researchers describe the development of language literacy as a socially dynamic, developmental, and recurrent[1] process (see figure 2.1). The young child's burgeoning understanding of language syntax, or how language works, develops through human interaction (Hirsch-Pasek, Golinkoff, and Eyer, 2003). The child, who is immersed in the language of his environment, becomes capable of expressing his thoughts through inner speech, babbling, and imitation (Clay, 1991; Madaule, 2008; Vygotsky, 1962, 1978). As a result, he develops the ability to engage in verbal interaction (conversation) with parents and caregivers who serve as language acquisition support systems (LASS) (Bruner, 1983). By engaging in early dialogue through imitation and conversation, the young child develops a functional vocabulary base. Language stimulation is one of the best predictors of later vocabulary and reading skill; the larger the vocabulary a child has, the better reader he will become (Healy, 2004).

In addition to the development of vocabulary, many other literacy-based experiences are needed for the child to bring meaning to and take meaning from print (Berthoff, 1981). Conversational interactions with significant others help the child build a vocabulary that forms the foundation for her eventual ability to read and write language with comprehension (Golinkoff and Hirsch-Pasek, 1999; Hirsch-Pasek et al., 2003; Roskos, Christie, and Richgels, 2003). As the child works with print, he is enabled to transfer meaning to and from the printed page through reading and writing (Ferreiro and Teberosky, 1996; Healy, 2004). He learns the conventions of print through

Figure 2.1.   Conceptual Lens: Language Literacy

continued literacy-based interactions with significant persons and gains book knowledge by turning the pages, becoming familiar with the top-to-bottom, left-to-right functions of reading English (Healy, 2004; Hirsch-Pasek et al., 2003; Roskos et al., 2003). When exposed to an environment filled with print, the child naturally infers meaning from print because he has become familiar with how letter combinations in print work (Ferreiro and Teberosky, 1996).

While writing is more difficult than reading, it is through writing that the child learns that print is a tool for making meaning (Roskos et al., 2003). He gradually becomes able to write and "read" his marks, ascribing meaning to them through the verbalizations of his intentions. Here, the child's verbalizations are typically richer in content than his actual writing (Roskos et al., 2003). The process of writing reinforces the process of reading, which in turn reinforces the child's vocabulary development. All of these experiences help him to make inferences and translate the written word far beyond what is written on the page (Ferreiro and Teberosky, 1996; Smith, 2004). For a child to become language-literate he must be immersed in language—preferably with a rich vocabulary, engaged in meaningful dialogue, read to regularly, and involved with forming meaning through print (Berthoff, 1981, 1982; Healy, 2004; Hirsch-Pasek et al., 2003).

THEORETICAL LENS: MUSIC LITERACY

The development of music literacy may be seen as a natural consequence of musical development when viewed through a language-acquisition lens. Hypothetically, this process is concerned with the child's musically interactive experiences that lead to his capacity to comprehend the features of tonality and meter while reading and writing music (Gordon, 2004; Pinzino, 2007). When viewed as an informal, socially dynamic, and developmental process, the child's development of music literacy begins with immersion in music that is sung, rhythmically chanted, moved to, or performed on instruments by a more experienced music maker. Through musical immer-

Figure 2.2.   Theoretical Lens: Music Literacy

sion he forms a listening foundation, which provides the underpinnings for him to express musical thoughts through musical babble and imitation. The child develops a rich musical vocabulary by engaging in musical improvisation with significant persons. As a result of these musical encounters, the child is enabled to transfer meaning to and from the printed page through reading and writing music (see figure 2.2). Listening to and engaging in musical dialogue through imitation and improvisation develop the young child's audiation, creating a foundation for his eventual ability to read and write music with comprehension.

RESEARCH STRATEGY

Research Purpose and Questions

While language literacy and music literacy are thought to be parallel processes, little research has been conducted to examine whether music literacy can be fostered through a pedagogical process similar to that used in language literacy. With this in mind, the purpose of this research was to study the music literacy development of young children. Specifically, I addressed the following questions:

1. Does the research on language literacy development have relevancy for pedagogical practice regarding music literacy?
2. What musical meanings do young children construct through their participation in a class designed to foster music literacy through a process similar to language literacy?

Research Setting and Participants

The case study reported in this chapter (Stake, 2000) was drawn from my exploratory investigation on the development of music literacy in an early childhood music class. Here, I describe the musical journey of Joey. Choosing to frame Joey's experience as a case study was not so much a choice of method,

Table 2.1. Participants in Music Literacy Classes

Year 1	Year 2	Year 3
Lab Preschool	Research Classroom	Research Classroom
N=15	N=7	N=5
15 (three years old)	5 (four years old)	1 (seven years old)
	1 (two years old)	2 (five years old)
	1 (one year old)	1 (three years old)
		1 (two years old)

but rather a choice of what to study (Stake, 2000). Joey best represented the group of children participants due to the length of his participation in the study. He also led me to a number of insights on the musical development of young children.

Joey began music classes with me at the lab preschool on the campus of my university. At the time, he was in the three-year-old preschool class. For one academic year, he participated in large and small group music classes that were held in a makeshift music area in the lab preschool's workroom. For the second year, Joey took part in music class along with six other children, three of whom had been Joey's classmates the previous year.[2] These classes were held in a classroom that also functioned as a research lab in my music building. A large, comfortable, carpeted space with a piano, plenty of room for movement, and access to all of my early childhood and general music materials, the classroom is equipped with video and audio recording capabilities and a one-way observation window. The third year of the study, five children, including Joey, continued their participation in the classes (see table 2.1).

Participant-Teacher-Researcher

Due to the continuous curricular decision-making in which I engaged and the need to be sensitive and responsive in its implementation, the nature of the study required me to be an active participant as teacher-researcher. I acted from a social constructivist (Vygotsky, 1978) orientation, taking on the role of facilitator. Accordingly, symbolic interactionism (Blumer, 1969) afforded a co-constructivist and interpretivist (Patton, 2002) lens from which to view Joey's musical growth. As explained by Blumer (1969, pp. 78–79):

"symbolic interaction" refers, of course, to the peculiar and distinctive character of interaction as it takes place between human beings. The peculiarity consists in the fact that human beings interpret or "define" each other's actions instead of merely reacting to each other's actions. Their "response" is not made directly to the actions of one another but instead is based on the meaning, which they attach to such actions. Thus, human interaction is mediated by the use of symbols, by interpretation, or by ascertaining the meaning of one another's actions. This mediation is equivalent to inserting a process of interpretation between stimulus and response in the case of human behavior.

I trusted in Joey as a co-learner and believed that our individual and collective understandings would be socially construed from our musically mediated actions and interactions.

Curricular Approach

For three years I met with the children for an average of forty-five minutes per week, implementing an emergent curriculum based on language literacy and developmental music learning (see figures 2.1 and 2.2). To inform my pedagogy, I immersed myself in research on language and music literacy development. Features of the Reggio Emilia municipal preschool system also contributed to the structure of the curriculum, its implementation, and data collection. Noted for its philosophy that children are capable and competent co-constructors of their learning, the Reggio Emilia approach emphasizes pedagogy that follows the lead of the child, the documentation of how children construct meaning, and the function of teacher as researcher (Burton, 2007; Reggio Emilia, 2009).

Since children are social beings, the use of play in musical guidance creates a situation in which optimal learning can take place (Hirsch-Pasek, Golinkoff, Berk, and Singer, 2009). Through play, young children develop their imaginations and form meaning of the abstract, changing their perceptions of reality (Vygotsky, 1978). By adopting a play-based orientation, I could balance structure with flexibility, act as a guide in the learning process, and appeal to the natural way children learn and make sense of their worlds. As I drew on the research on language literacy and considered its application to music literacy, I strove to devise playful instructional techniques to help the children express what they were learning through singing, chanting, moving, playing instruments, and reading and writing music.

As a "more able learner," I was conscious of the *zone of proximal development* (ZPD) (Vygotsky, 1978) and the need to musically challenge the children just beyond their current level of mastery. To that end, social modeling (Bandura, 1977; Haston, 2007) was another important instructional technique for demonstrating musical skills and concepts. The use of "teaching assistants," such as puppets and purposeful props, allowed me to demonstrate and model musical interaction in a playful and informal way. With little to no talking, I was able to maximize the use of musical immersion and direct the children's musical focus. Through structured guidance, I scaffolded the children's musical growth in a similar fashion as a parent or caregiver would naturally scaffold the language competency of a child.

During this study I documented Joey's musical learning through videotape, my reflective journal, Joey's notational artifacts, and anecdotes from conversations. I kept copious notes of discussions with early childhood education and early childhood music education experts, my university students, and Joey's parents regarding my observations of Joey's musical development. As a reflective practitioner, this documentation was critical to the formation of the ever-emergent curriculum.

Data Sources

Keeping triangulation in mind, the methods and types of data collected were representative of several perspectives. Primary data sources were (a) my reflective observation/planning journal, in which, after each class, I took comprehensive notes regarding Joey's participation in the class and recorded my thoughts on how to facilitate and support his musical growth. These detailed notes provided a foundation for interpretive, "thick descriptions" (Geertz, 1973, p. 6) of Joey's participation in the class; (b) artifacts of Joey's notation, which provided a window into his making of musical meaning and my instructional guidance; (c) over forty-five hours of videotape that captured the classes in real time, allowing me to revisit them and compare my journal and Joey's artifacts with the events that took place in each class; and (d) conversational notes from discussions with experts in music education and language literacy.

Trustworthiness and Credibility

Issues of trustworthiness and credibility bear on the validity of a study's findings (Lincoln and Guba, 1985). Two outside auditors, one of whom was a graduate student with experience in early childhood music instruction while the other had conducted extensive research on music acquisition, confirmed the trustworthiness of the collected data and subsequently the findings of this study. The auditors viewed video clips representative of the beginning, middle, and end of the research project. They also reviewed Joey's notational artifacts in relationship to the documentation data and video clips. Credibility of the findings was established by (a) my length of experience in the early childhood music field (seventeen years); (b) my extensive review of the literature on language acquisition, music acquisition, and play; (c) my prolonged engagement in the study, which allowed me to test emergent conceptualizations in relationship to the research questions; and (d) peer debriefing as data were collected and analyzed.

Data Analysis

Data analysis began with the first music class and continued for three years. I engaged in reflection through the constant comparison of data sources, making pedagogical decisions for the curricular direction of the class. At the end of the study I immersed myself in the data by reading through my journals, lesson plans, and notes. I examined the children's notational artifacts and viewed videotapes of the class. While reviewing and ruminating on the data, I reconstructed my pedagogical trajectory while mapping out an account of Joey's musical actions and interactions. Because I chose to frame these accounts within the conceptual lens of music literacy (see figure 2.2), data analysis was deductive. As I uncovered patterns in the ways that Joey made musical meaning, the analysis became inductive.

FINDINGS AND INTERPRETATIONS

A Recurrent Process

The primary theme that emerged from the data analysis was that, for Joey, music literacy development is a recurrent process, much like language lit-

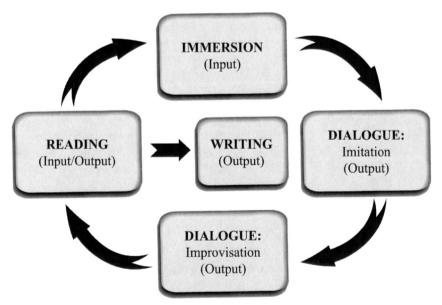

Figure 2.3. Music Literacy: A Recurrent Process

eracy (see figure 2.3). I used songs and chants without words as the basis for Joey's musical immersion. Next, I extracted melodic and rhythm fragments of this repertoire to engage him in dialogue-imitation. I provided opportunities for dialogue-improvisation, through which Joey was found to incorporate tonal and rhythm fragments acquired from dialogue-immersion and dialogue-imitation. Concurrently, I read rhythm and melody "books" to the class and modeled music writing using rhythm fragments from imitation and the rhythm books. Joey was found to incorporate these fragments into his rhythmic music writing.

Laying the Foundation: Listening

Young children are immersed in language from before birth and generally do not receive the same amount of musical exposure. Therefore, I determined that musical immersion would be the initial focus for the first semester of class. In language literacy, early childhood has been noted to be the best time for young children to learn multiple languages, suggesting that young children are quick to differentiate between the syntax of multiple languages (Madaule, 2008). Understanding same and different (classification) is an inherent part of child development (Jeppson and Myers-Walls, 2006). As such, I took these principles of discrimination-learning into consideration since young children conceptually learn what something *is* from what *it is not*. By immersing the children in multiple tonalities and meters, I was building a foundation for the audiation and differentiation of musical syntax through listening. Listening through immersion was the basis for my instructional sequence and provided a scaffold for the acquisition of musical content and development of musical skills.

Joey readily responded to the immersion activities. He moved his upper body rhythmically to the microbeat as I or rhythm puppet assistant Charlie performed rhythmic chants in duple, triple, and assymetrical meters. Joey would listen intently to me singing a song in Phrygian tonality while Chantelle, a tonal assistant puppet, would sing the resting tone or melodic fragments between repetitions of a song. Frequently, he would engage in flowing movements with his body to the songs and chants that were performed. "Joey sat next to me, I have never seen him so engaged. He moved freely to the music that I shared" (December 6, 2006—journal). On one instance of bringing out Belinda, a captivating, multicultural puppet whose role was to sing songs, "Joey ran to my side to sit close by me. Eyes peeled on Belinda, he did not move a muscle through three repetitions of my song in Lydian tonality" (October 30, 2006—video).

The First Dialogue: Conversation through Imitation

Nagy (n.d.) suggests that newborn infants are born with the capacity to interact vocally through imitation. Sensitive to the rhythm and musical qualities of language, the young child's language acquisition evolves from early imitative encounters in which she makes sounds to match the aural cues she has heard in her environment. This minimal unit of conversation captures the basic unit for bidirectional communication—the child's first conversation. These early imitative, reciprocal conversations form the basis for the acquisition of language (Speidel and Nelson, 1989).

Musically speaking, Gordon (2004) states that "the interaction of the aural and the oral is crucial for making comparisons of what is being sounded with what is being audiated" (p. 14). Through the vocal imitation of rhythm and melodic fragments, young children discriminate what they hear and audiate in relationship to what they are able to reproduce musically. I incorporated opportunities for the children to respond rhythmically through dialogue-imitation in a variety of meters and tonally through melodic patterns that outlined characteristic tones or the harmonic functions of the tonality of the song that was being sung. Joey imitated the patterns chanted by Charlie and the melodic patterns sung by Chantelle. For that first semester, Joey's rhythmic imitation was precise, and he was able to imitate four-macrobeat combinations of macro-microbeats, then subdivisions of the beat, and eventually elongations of the beat in duple, triple, and asymmetrical meters.

> When he chanted, his upper body followed with bouncing movement on the microbeat, gradually giving way to the macrobeat. Rarely did he err in his imitation of rhythm patterns. Tonally, he was generally consistent in his imitation of the resting tone and melodic patterns, although there were times that I would have to repeat my model for him. He almost always sang with accurate pitch when he took a good breath before singing. (November 17, 2006—video)

Sequencing Content

As the children's imitations became secure and I felt that they had acquired an aural foundation of tonalities and meters due to their ability to chant reliably in time and to sing in tune, I began to use rhythm and tonal syllables as a means to help them label meter and tonality of the music they were audiating. I returned to the processes of listening and dialogue, now using Gordon's beat function rhythm syllables (2007) when I chanted, and Pinzino's tonal syllables (2007) when I sang (January 23, 2007—journal).

Dialogue through Improvisation

I demonstrated dialogue-improvisation to the children by engaging in musical conversation through puppets that served as models and other props such as cell phones, microphones, and games. Through play, I was able to establish an inviting atmosphere to encourage children's improvisational interaction. Interacting in these playful encounters, Joey was comfortable improvising rhythm and melodic patterns. Surprisingly, two months after introducing both rhythm and tonal syllables, and when I had expected Joey to imitate duple meter patterns, he took the lead and initiated improvisation with rhythm syllables.

> Joey ran to the playground fence as I was leaving [the lab preschool]. "Hi Mrs. Triple Meter!" he said. I responded, "Hi Mr. Duple Meter!" He initiated a duple meter conversation with me and the children around him. He used syllables and chanted macros, micros, divisions and elongations—all in the right places! He would chant a phrase, then look at me to chant back. He engaged the four other children around him to start conversations. (April 18, 2007—journal)

The recurrent process was manifested in Joey's improvisations: melodic and rhythm fragments that Joey had acquired from immersion, that he had also chanted in imitation, made their way into his improvisations.

As noted in my journal, I found that Joey was "well versed in duple meter, but not so in triple. That is, he begins to respond in triple, then quickly moves into duple." I asked myself, "[Will a] return to immersion and imitation in those meters enable him to have greater comfort with improvising in them?" (April 25, 2007—journal). Moving back to dialogue-immersion and dialogue-imitation, I immersed Joey in triple and unusual meters. Then, we imitated patterns in triple meter with Charlie. "Giving Joey a puppet to dialogue with, I took a chance on initiating improvisation [in triple meter]; Joey began using patterns that I purposely inserted into our activities, in his improvisation" (May 2, 2007—journal).

For all of the children, melodic improvisation did not follow the same trajectory as rhythm improvisation. When I attempted to create a context for melodic improvisation, Joey responded in imitation. On one occasion, I put two hula-hoops on the floor with a cell phone in each—voila! Telephone booths! "Singing a preparatory sequence in Dorian tonality, I dialed my cell phone to 'call' Joey. Although he was in his telephone booth, he would not answer the phone. Trying again I 'dialed' Joey singing in Dorian tonality. Joey picked up the phone, 'Sorry, I don't know that language!'" From there, he engaged in imitation of melodic patterns (May 9, 2007—journal/video). I continued to work with Joey at a level that was comfortable for him, providing scaffolding opportunities for melodic improvisation. In the second year of this study,

Joey began to improvise melodically, but did not become comfortable until midway through the third year.

Familiarity with the Conventions of Print

Mills and McPherson (2006) state that "in the very beginning stages of learning to read staff notation, a young child will need to learn that music is read by moving your eyes from left to right, top to bottom on the page" (p. 159). Becoming familiarized with the conventions of musical print (in similar fashion to the written word), the young child forms meaning regarding how printed music works (Clay, 1991). In each class, I read carefully sequenced rhythm and melody books and provided books and CDs for the children to read informally while listening to my vocalizations of songs and chants (see figure 2.4).

As the rhythm books were introduced, Joey would follow the rhythm with me, pointing to the macrobeat as we chanted. While his syllables were not consistently accurate, he always chanted in time and meter. When reading melody books, Joey generally observed with interest, but did not vocalize with me as I sang. A playful technique that I used was that of a puppet, Mr. Songkeeper, and a small, child-size mailbox of which musical messages would be sent from Mr. Songkeeper to the children. The messages gave further opportunities for reading music to the children and for the children to read the messages out loud.

In the second year of music class, the children were immersed in the process of writing music through the modeling of my own process of writing of rhythm patterns. Because Joey had not yet readily engaged in tonal dialogue-improvisation and because rhythm anchors the tonal aspect of melody, I chose first to focus on writing rhythm. The patterns that I used were those with which the children had previously been saturated through listening,

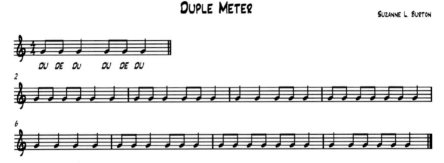

Figure 2.4. Duple Meter Rhythm Book

performed in dialogue-imitation, used in our dialogue-improvisations, and featured in the rhythm books that I read to them and that they would often read aloud to me. I modeled writing in duple and triple meters, and asked the children to dictate patterns for me to write in the meter that either they or I chose. We wrote messages for Mr. Songkeeper, carefully placing them in his mailbox, putting up the flag so he would know that he had mail. When Joey began to write his own rhythmic messages on staff paper for Mr. Songkeeper, he was found to incorporate these fragments in his music writing. Joey would gleefully come to music class with a message for Mr. Songkeeper, place it in the mailbox, turn the flag up, and await the beckoning voice of Mr. Songkeeper to request that Joey read his message to him.

Often, traditional conventions of musical print (such as time signature, filled-in note heads, the correct number of note heads and stems for a rhythm pattern, or bar lines) were not present in Joey's initial rhythm writing. Yet, when Joey read his messages, it was clear that he had conceptualized what he had put into print. Using rhythm syllables, Joey read his rhythmic messages with fluency, although his notation had approximated meaning (see figure 2.5).

At this stage of Joey's musical development, the recurrent nature of listening, dialogue-imitation, dialogue-improvisation, and reading was captured in Joey's rhythmic notation. *Reading* rhythm reinforced his process of *writing* rhythm; just as writing rhythm reinforced his process of reading rhythm. For Joey, music literacy (at least in terms of rhythmic literacy) follows a similar developmental process as language literacy, with print knowledge leading

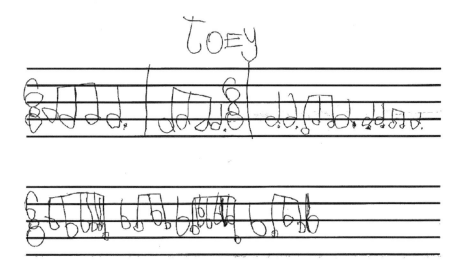

Figure 2.5. Joey's Rhythm Notation

to notation that resembles actual notation, and the ability to give rhythmic meaning to notation.

CONCLUSION

Joey's competency with rhythm developed first, whereas in the third year, he began to discriminate among and improvise within the various tonalities. His growing ability in this area is evidenced by his remark, "Ms. Suzanne, I am having trouble telling the difference between Dorian and Mixolydian!" (Joey, age 5/December 18, 2008). This leads me to wonder about possible indicators for the best time to begin modeling the writing of melody, and how to facilitate writing melody given its abstract nature. Additionally, Joey might have a natural propensity for rhythm, whereas another child may progress more quickly tonally.

While I acknowledge the limitations of a case study approach in terms of transferability to other contexts, this study presents a process that holds possibilities for pedagogical exploration. Joey's case provides an interesting study, yet at the same time yields questions about the efficacy of language acquisition as a model for structuring pedagogy toward the development of music literacy. Implementing this type of research with children in different educational contexts (early childhood, elementary school) might uncover whether the recurrent process of musical development is a phenomenon only true to Joey, or one that may further early childhood music pedagogy. In other words, would other children learn from a comparable curriculum based on this recurrent process in a similar fashion over a similar timeline? Clearly, further research into language acquisition as a construct for music learning is needed to uncover the process of becoming musically literate. As a consequence of such research, a developmental pedagogy may result that ultimately shapes musicians who are capable of expressing themselves musically through improvisation, reading music with comprehension, and capturing their musical thoughts on paper.

REFERENCES

Bandura, A. (1977). *Social learning theory.* New York: General Learning Press.
Berthoff, A. E. (1981). *The making of meaning.* Upper Montclair, NJ: Boynton/Cook.
Berthoff, A. E. (1982). *Forming, thinking, writing.* Upper Montclair, NJ: Boynton/Cook.
Blumer, H. (1969). *Symbolic interactionism: Perspective and method.* Englewood Cliffs, NJ: Prentice-Hall.

Bruner, J. (1983). *Child's talk: Learning to use language*. New York: Norton.

Burton, S. L. (2007). Diary from work-study tour of Reggio Emilia Municipal Pre-schools, Reggio Emilia, Italy.

Clay, M. (1991). *Becoming literate: The construction of inner control*. Portsmouth, NH: Heinemann.

Ferreiro, E., and Teberosky, A. (1996). *Literacy before schooling*. Portsmouth, NH: Heinemann.

Geertz, C. (1973). *The interpretation of cultures*. New York: Basic Books.

Golinkoff, R. M., and Hirsch-Pasek, K. (1999). *How babies talk*. New York: Plume.

Gordon, E. E. (2004). *The aural-visual experience of music literacy*. Chicago: GIA.

Gordon, E. E. (2007). *Learning sequences in music: A contemporary music learning theory*. Chicago: GIA.

Gruhn, W. (2002). Phases and stages in early music learning: A longitudinal study on the development of young children's musical potential. *Music Education Research, 4*(1), 51–71.

Haston, W. (2007). Teacher modeling as an effective teaching strategy: Modeling is a technique that can help your students learn effectively in many situations. *Music Educators Journal, 93*(4), 26.

Hauser, M., and McDermott, J. (2003). The evolution of a music faculty: A comparative perspective. *Nature Neuroscience, 6*(7), 663–66.

Healy, J. (2004). *Your child's growing mind* (3rd ed.). New York: Broadway Books.

Hirsch-Pasek, K., Golinkoff, R. M., Berk, L. E., and Singer, D. G. (2009). *A mandate for playful learning in preschool: Presenting the evidence*. New York: Oxford University Press.

Hirsch-Pasek, K., Golinkoff, R. M., and Eyer, D. (2003). *Einstein never used flashcards*. New York: Rodale.

Jackendoff, R., and Lerdahl, F. (2006). The capacity for music: What is it, and what's special about it? *Cognition, 100*(1), 33–72.

Jeppson, J., and Myers-Walls, J. (2006). *Child growth and development*. Retrieved from www.ces.purdue.edu/providerparent/Child%20Growth-Development/Main-CGD.htm.

Lincoln, Y., and Guba, E. (1985). *Naturalistic inquiry*. New York: Sage.

Madaule, P. (2008). *Exploring the power of listening*. Keynote speech of the Early Childhood Music and Movement Association Biennial International Conference, Providence, RI.

Mills, J., and McPherson, G. (2006). Musical literacy. In G. McPherson (Ed.), *The child as musician*. New York: Oxford University Press.

Nagy, E. (n. d.). *The first dialogue: Conversation through imitation with newborn infants*. Retrieved from www.bbsonline.org/Preprints/Arbib05012002/Supplemental/Nagy.html.

Patel, A. (2008). *Music, language, and the brain*. New York: Oxford University Press.

Patton, M. Q. (2002). *Qualitative research and evaluation methods*. Thousand Oaks, CA: Sage.

Pinzino, M. E. (2007). *Letters on music learning*. Homewood, IL: Come Children Sing Institute.

Reggio Emilia. (2009). *The municipal infant-toddler and preschool centers of Reggio Emilia.* Retrieved from http://zerosei.comune.re.it/inter/nidiescuole.htm.

Reynolds, A., Long, S., and Valerio, W. (2007). Language acquisition and music acquisition: Possible parallels. In K. Smithrim and R. Upitis (Eds.), *Listen to their voices: Research and practice in early childhood music* (Vol. 3). Toronto: Canadian Music Educators Association.

Roskos, K. A., Christie, J. F., and Richgels, D. J. (2003). The essentials of early literacy instruction. *Young Children, 58*(2), 52–60.

Smith, F. (2004). *Understanding reading.* Mahwah, NJ: Lawrence Erlbaum.

Speidel, G. E., and Nelson, K. E. (Eds.). (1989). *The many faces of imitation.* New York: Springer-Verlag.

Stake, R. (2000). Case studies. In N. K. Denzin and Y. S. Lincoln (Eds.), *Handbook of qualitative research* (pp. 435–54). Thousand Oaks, CA: Sage.

Vygotsky, L. (1962). *Thought and language.* Cambridge, MA: MIT Press.

Vygotsky, L. (1978). *Mind in society: The development of higher psychological processes.* Cambridge, MA: MIT Press.

NOTES

1. The term *recurrent* is used here to suggest a process of language and literacy acquisition that is not linear, but that loops back to earlier processes (listening, dialogue, reading/writing) in order for a person to grasp the full meaning of what was heard, verbalized, or operationalized in print.

2. I invited all of the households with three-year-olds to participate in music classes the second year at no charge. From that invitation, nine children began classes with me in the fall; two families discontinued classes due to family concerns (pregnancy and the birth of a baby), leaving seven children in the class. In year three, several children discontinued their participation because they started all-day kindergarten, which created scheduling problems.

Chapter Three

The Role of Musical Engagement in the Musicality of Three-Year-Old Children

Diana Dansereau

The purpose of this mixed-methods study was to investigate the nature and development of musicality among three-year-old children within a program of musical engagement. Forty-six children were assigned randomly to experimental and control groups. I administered Audie, a test of developmental music aptitude, and the Singing Voice Development Measure (SVDM) to all children prior to and following treatment. Children in the experimental group received thirty minutes of musical engagement each week for twelve weeks. Children in the control group did not receive these sessions. Analysis showed a significant difference (p < .01) between group means on the SVDM posttest and no significant differences (p < .05) on the music aptitude posttests. Two ancillary findings were (a) a gender difference on the SVDM pretest favoring females (p < .05), and (b) a moderate correlation (r = .352, p < .05) between tonal aptitude and SVDM posttest scores. I conducted case studies of three children in the experimental group. Within-case themes included hesitancy around singing, child-constructed patterns during classes, and music as an alternate form of communication. Cross-case themes included children's fondness for repetition and initial hesitancy toward musical expression. Qualitative and quantitative findings were converged, and the findings from each method were shown to corroborate and illuminate the findings of the other. I concluded that research-based musical engagement has a positive effect on the singing of three-year-old children. Such engagement might positively affect disposition toward music, comfort with musical expression, and prevalence of music making.

Human beings begin to process and understand music at birth, if not before (Valerio, Reynolds, Bolton, Taggart, and Gordon, 1998), and, by the time children are two years old, music is a familiar and intriguing phenomenon to them. Young children respond positively to musical activities, including singing, moving, and instrument exploration, and they spontaneously engage in music making (Campbell and Scott-Kassner, 2006). There is evidence that children ages two to five are capable of more sophisticated musical perception and behaviors than once thought, and some believe that early childhood is an optimal period for learning fundamental musical concepts and skills (Gordon, 2003; Simons, 1979). Understanding the effects of musical engagement on key aspects of young children's musicality, such as developmental music aptitude and singing voice achievement, can enable educators and caregivers to provide effective and powerful musical guidance during this important developmental period.

Researchers have studied children's singing ability for over sixty years and have found that certain elements of singing achievement, such as melodic rhythm and lyric accuracy, may be maturational (Tarnowski, 1986), and that young girls may sing more accurately than young boys (Bedsole, 1987). In addition, quality instructional techniques, such as the phrase-by-phrase method (Jacobi-Karna, 1996), solmization (Yang, 1994), and instituting small group and individual singing activities (Rutkowski, 1996), can improve the singing achievement of young children. There are conflicting findings regarding the role of text in the singing accuracy of young children. Jacobi-Karna (1996) found that four-year-olds were more accurate when singing texted songs, while Levinowitz (1989) reported that preschoolers performed an untexted song more accurately. Sullivan (2006) found that three- and four-year-old children who learned untexted songs seemed to sing and chant more often and continuously than those who learned texted songs.

In addition to studies focused on young children's singing, researchers have attempted to understand developmental music aptitude and the factors influencing aptitude. Findings indicate that developmental music aptitude can increase if young children are provided with music experiences either at home (Mallett, 2000) or in class settings (Flohr, 1981; Taggart, 1997), and that certain music experiences are particularly effective at increasing music aptitude. For example, Lange (1999) found that low-aptitude students who are taught songs without text show greater gains in aptitude than those who receive text-only instruction.

Limited research exists concerning the effect of music instruction on both the developmental music aptitudes and singing voice achievement of young children. Gawlick (2003) investigated whether home musical environment, music instruction, and/or classroom musical environment affected the developmental music aptitude and music performance of eight preschool-age children. Gawlick concluded that heredity and home musical environment may influence children's musical abilities; however, generalizations of these findings are not appropriate given the small sample size.

Rutkowski (1996) investigated the effect of individual or small-group singing activities within large-group settings on kindergarten children's use of singing voice and developmental music aptitude. There was no significant difference between the experimental and control group members' tonal aptitude posttest scores; however, significant differences were found between their singing voice achievement, with the treatment group scoring higher than the control group. A noteworthy finding of Rutkowski's study was that the control group mean singing score decreased from the pretest to the posttest, which may indicate that "ineffective instruction may actually be detrimental to children's singing-voice development" (Rutkowski, 1996, p. 362).

Although researchers have provided valuable information regarding the roles of text, gender, method of instruction (e.g., phrase-by-phrase), and context (e.g., individual or small-group singing) in children's learning of new songs, more research is needed to examine the effect of instruction on the singing achievement of preschool children. While researchers have studied the effect of music instruction on the developmental music aptitudes of early elementary-age children, such research should also be conducted on preschool-age children. The purpose of this study was to investigate the nature and development of musicality among three-year-old children within the context of a researcher-designed program of musical engagement. The program was research-based in that activities were based on the work of those who have developed research-based instructional strategies (for example, see Campbell and Scott-Kassner, 2002; Rutkowski, 1989; Valerio et al., 1998). Specific questions addressed were as follows:

1. Does research-based musical engagement affect the developmental music aptitude of three-year-old children?
2. Does research-based musical engagement affect the singing voice achievement of three-year-old children?
3. What additional aspects of a child's musicality might be influenced by research-based musical engagement?

DESIGN

A concurrent triangulation mixed-methods design (Creswell, 2003) was used, consisting of simultaneous collection of quantitative and qualitative data with equal priority of methods. Quantitative data were collected and analyzed to address research question 1, both quantitative and qualitative data were used to address research question 2, and qualitative data were used to address research question 3. I chose to converge methods for the purpose of triangulation as well as to allow for complementarity (Greene, Caracelli, and Graham, 1989), specifically for an enriched and elaborated understanding of the phenomenon of musicality in three-year-old children.

METHOD

Participants

Forty-six three-year-old children from three preschools participated in the quantitative portion of this study. There were twenty-eight males and eighteen females whose ages ranged from thirty-five to forty-seven months at the onset of the study. The children were assigned randomly into experimental (n = 24) and control (n = 22) groups. Prior to musical engagement, I administered *Audie* (Gordon, 1989) and the *Singing Voice Development Measure* (SVDM) (Rutkowski, 1990) to all of the children. I provided the children in the experimental group with thirty minutes of musical engagement once each week for twelve weeks. Children in the control group remained in their general classrooms and did not attend these sessions. All children experienced their regular classroom routines throughout the study, which contained varying amounts of musical activity, such as singing songs during morning circle time. I observed that these classroom musical activities tended not to elicit much participation or quality singing from the children. No other music classes were provided prior to or during this study in the three participating preschools.

Musical Engagement Curriculum

My musical engagement with the children consisted of informal and play-based interactions and activities that have been documented as appropriate for nurturing the musical development of very young children (e.g., Fox, 2000; Valerio et al., 1998). Specific activities were based on the work of Campbell and Scott-Kassner (2002), Rutkowski (1989), Valerio et al. (1998), and others who have developed research-based instructional strategies. My primary consideration was to provide a musically rich environment in which children could play freely, explore, and participate in a complete range of musical behaviors.

The teacher strategy was primarily one of modeling and providing opportunities for children's responses and for their initiation of further musical activity. Because of this, I use the term musical *engagement* rather than *instruction*, which implies a more formal approach. I strove to capitalize on the time allocated for musical engagement and to infuse that time with as much musical sound and interaction as possible; consequently, spoken communication was minimized during music sessions, and communication within the medium of musical sound was encouraged.

A typical session consisted of ten to twelve songs and chants, beginning with a "Hello" song and ending with a "Goodbye" song. The sessions began with songs, tonal patterns, and vocal exploration activities, followed by chants and rhythm patterns, then more singing. I sang and chanted the same material across multiple sessions, and repeated songs and chants three or four times successively within a session. Such repetition allows children to attain a high level of familiarity and comfort with musical materials and encourages comprehension of those songs and chants (Campbell and Scott-Kassner, 2006; Valerio et al., 1998). The song and chant material was presented with and without text and represented multiple musical styles, modes, and meters. The use of untexted song and chants and the ordering of the material within a session was influenced by Piaget's theory of centration and decentration, which indicates that young children focus on one salient feature of a stimulus (Flavell, Miller, and Miller, 2002). By paring down the musical elements of a song (such as removing text), children may be more likely to centrate on the melodic contour or pitch relationships of the song. Dovetailing the presentation of song and chant material may also enable children to attend to specific musical features (Rutkowski, 1989). Consequently, after singing an untexted, minor, duple meter song, I would sing an untexted, Mixolydian, duple meter song in an effort to encourage the children to attend to the changing variable of mode. I allowed a couple of seconds of silence after singing or chanting each song or pattern in order to allow the children time to audiate what had just been heard and anticipate what would follow (Valerio et al., 1998).

An activity that I included to encourage audiation involved the insertion of silences within familiar songs and chants. I would check to see if the children were successful at maintaining the song or chant in their audiation during the pause by asking the children to resume singing or chanting. Continuous and pulsating flow movements, as well as beat-centered movements, were incorporated throughout the activities.

Data Collection

All sessions were videotaped, which provided a means to analyze any effects of musical engagement on the children. SVDM and *Audie* were re-administered at the end of the treatment period, and the data were analyzed for potential statistical differences.

In addition to the quantitative methods and the qualitative analysis of videotape, I conducted case studies with three children: Sam, Maddie, and

Simon (all names are pseudonyms). Selection of these three children was based on two considerations. First, I aimed to select children who provided heterogeneity regarding music aptitude, as measured by the music aptitude pretest. Second, I endeavored to identify children whose parents and teachers would be willing and faithful participants. Initial interactions with parents as well as recommendations of preschool staff informed this decision. I observed the children closely during music sessions, conducted multiple observations in their preschool classrooms, and observed one child in his home setting, and parents and teachers shared anecdotal evidence of musical behaviors or changes in the children's musicality with me during individual semistructured interviews. Singing voice development was assessed using the *Singing Voice Development Measure* (SVDM), a nine-point scale that was developed by Rutkowski (1990) (see textbox 3.1).

Content validity was established previously for the categories of the rating scale (Rutkowski, 1986), and acceptable levels of interrater and intrarater reliability have been reported by researchers using SVDM to investigate the singing achievement of kindergarten children (Rutkowski, 1996) and children in grades 1–5 (Guerrini, 2002; Levinowitz et al., 1998). Because reliability information for SVDM was not available for use with three-year-old children, a second trained evaluator independently scored the tests administered in this study so that it was possible to establish interjudge reliability (see table 3.1).

I tested the children's singing voices individually in a quiet space within the preschools. These tests were audiotaped to allow for careful analysis after the testing session. The recordings of the singing voice pretests were analyzed, and each child was identified according to the SVDM continuum. Placement in these categories was dependent on the child's relative use of sustained tone, singing range, and ability to sing beyond the register lift (B^3-flat and above). The children were tested on SVDM after the twelve weeks of music classes using the same procedures.

Audie has been used to investigate developmental music aptitude in young children (Blesedell, 1991; Farr, 1993; Mallett, 2000; Taggart, 1997); however, moderate to low reliability levels have been reported. Mallett (2000) reported reliability for the tonal and rhythm subtests to be .36 and .53 respectively, and Taggart (1994) reported tonal subtest reliabilities of .26 (Kuder-Richardson), .53 (split-halves), and .18 (test-retest). Reliability coefficients for the rhythm subtest were .38 (Kuder-Richardson), .28 (split-halves), and .69 (test-retest). Consequently, I conducted Kuder-Richardson and split-halves reliability tests on the data collected in this study (see table 3.1). I administered *Audie* to children individually in the same space within the preschools used for SVDM. Each child and I sat together on the

Textbox 3.1. Singing Voice Development Measure

1. "Pre-Singer" does not sing but chants the song text.
   1.5. "Inconsistent Speaking Range Singer" sometimes chants, sometimes sustains tones and exhibits some sensitivity to pitch but remains in the speaking voice range (usually A^2 to C^3).
2. "Speaking Range Singer" sustains tones and exhibits some sensitivity to pitch but remains in the speaking voice range (usually A^2 to C^3).
   2.5. "Inconsistent Limited Range Singer" wavers between speaking and singing voice and uses a limited range when in singing voice (usually up to F^3).
3. "Limited Range Singer" exhibits consistent use of limited singing range (usually D^3 to F^3).
   3.5. "Inconsistent Initial Range Singer" sometimes only exhibits use of limited singing range, but other times exhibits use of initial singing range (usually D^3 to A^3).
4. "Initial Range Singer" exhibits consistent use of initial singing range (usually D^3 to A^3).
   4.5. "Inconsistent Singer" sometimes only exhibits use of initial singing range, but other times exhibits use of extended singing range (sings beyond the register lift: B^3-flat and above).
5. "Singer" exhibits use of consistent extended singing range (sings beyond the register lift: B^3-flat and above).

Adapted from Joanne Rutkowski and Martha Snell Miller, "A Longitudinal Study of Elementary Children's Acquisition of Their Singing Voices," *Update: Applications of Research in Music Education*, 22 (Fall-Winter 2003): 5–14. Used with permission.

floor, and I discreetly recorded the child's answers to the ten questions on a provided record sheet. These answers were analyzed later using a provided answer key, and each child received a score (0 to 10) indicating the number of correct responses given. The children were posttested on *Audie* after the twelve weeks of music classes.

Table 3.1. Reliability Coefficients for *Audie* and SVDM

	Audie *Tonal*		Audie *Rhythm*		SVDM
	K-R 20	Split-half	K-R 20	Split-half	Interrater reliability
Pretest	.64	.60	.60	.70	.95
Posttest	.40	.34	.57	.72	.95

ANALYSIS

Descriptive and inferential statistics were conducted on the data from the music aptitude pretests and posttests and the SVDM pretests and posttests. I used SPSS11.0.1 to conduct these analyses.

Analysis of qualitative data was an ongoing process consisting of continual reflection. Field notes were taken during all classroom observations and immediately after the home observation. I transcribed all interviews shortly after they occurred. While viewing videotapes over the course of the study, I transcribed any words spoken by me and directed to the case study participants. I also transcribed the case study participants' verbal and musical utterances and any speech by other children related to the case study participants. In addition, I made note of the case study participants' behaviors or participation in activities.

I reviewed and analyzed all data for emergent themes. I began by searching data sources for initial patterns, which led to the formation of defined codes. The data were further reviewed using these codes. Codes that emerged across multiple sources of data were identified and grouped as themes. I took care to note any data that ran contrary to the emergent themes. This method of data analysis resembles Glaser and Strauss's (1967) constant comparison method, in that coding was a process of continual reflection and was inductive in nature.

To establish trustworthiness, I spent a prolonged period of time (eighteen weeks) in the research sites with the participants, triangulated multiple sources of qualitative data, compared emerging findings from the qualitative analysis with results from the quantitative analysis to check for corroboration,

Table 3.2. *Audie* Tonal, *Audie* Rhythm, and SVDM Group Means

	Audie *Tonal*				Audie *Rhythm*				SVDM			
	Pretest		Posttest		Pretest		Posttest		Pretest		Posttest	
	M	SD	M	SD	M	SD	M	SD	M	SD	M	SD
Control	6.30	1.53	6.60	1.64	6.06	1.86	6.89	2.06	2.44	.90	2.50	.829
Experimental	6.40	1.60	7.60	1.50	6.15	1.76	7.25	2.00	2.93	1.08	3.32	.733

and submitted my themes to peer review. Three peer reviewers were given a portion of data (interview and observation transcripts) as well as initial emergent themes during week 12 of the study. One of these reviewers also served as a rater for the SVDM pretests and posttests. This review took place in a group setting and served to ensure that my interpretations resonated with the data collected and the analysis that was performed.

RESULTS

Audie and SVDM

Kuder-Richardson #20 and split-halves reliability coefficients were calculated to check the reliability of the *Audie* subtests, and interjudge reliability coefficients were calculated on the data collected from SVDM (see table 3.1). Tonal music aptitude, rhythm music aptitude, and singing voice development means for both groups increased over the course of the study (see table 3.2).

To address research question 1 ("Does research-based musical engagement affect the developmental music aptitude of three-year-old children?"), I used analysis of covariance (ANCOVA) to determine if there was a significant difference between experimental and control groups' rhythm aptitude posttest scores. Group was the independent variable (experimental and control), rhythm aptitude posttest scores the dependent variable, and rhythm aptitude pretest scores functioned as a covariate in order to control for initial differences between groups. Because the tonal aptitude data did not meet two assumptions underlying ANCOVA (linearity between the pretest and posttest, and pretest to posttest correlation), analysis of variance (ANOVA) was performed to check for significant differences between groups on the music aptitude posttest. No significant differences ($p < .05$) were found between groups on the tonal music aptitude posttest ($F = 4.06$, $df = 38$, $p = .051$), nor on the rhythm music aptitude posttest ($F = .27$, $df = 38$, $p = .607$).

To address the second research question ("Does research-based musical engagement affect the singing voice achievement of three-year-old children?"), I used ANCOVA to determine if there was a significant difference between experimental and control groups' SVDM posttest scores. Group was the independent variable (experimental and control), SVDM posttest scores the dependent variable, and SVDM pretest scores functioned as a covariate in order to control for initial (though not significant) differences between groups. A significant difference was found ($p < .01$), indicating that the mean score of the experimental group on the SVDM posttest was significantly higher than the mean score of the control group ($F = 7.81$, $df = 39$, $p = .008$). The difference in adjusted means divided by the pooled unadjusted standard deviations was .81, indicating a large effect size (Huck, 2000) and a practical as well as significant difference in singing voice achievement.

Two ancillary findings emerged from data analysis. ANOVA revealed a statistically significant ($p < .05$) gender difference on the pretest SVDM, indicating that females scored significantly higher than males. No significant gender difference was found on the SVDM posttest. A dependent t-test conducted on pretest and posttest SVDM scores of males indicated that the males improved significantly over the course of the study ($t(22) = -2.554$, $p = .018$). Changes between the pretest and posttest scores of the females were not statistically significant. The second ancillary finding was the presence of a moderate, statistically significant correlation ($r = .352$, $p < .05$) between the tonal music aptitude and singing voice development posttest scores.

Because the three case-study children also were participants in the quantitative portion of this study, I tested them using *Audie* and SVDM. Sam scored 9 on the *Audie* tonal pretest, 7 on the *Audie* tonal posttest, 7 on the Audie rhythm pretest, 7 on the *Audie* rhythm posttest, 1 on the SVDM pretest, and 3.5 on the SVDM posttest. Maddie scored 5 on the *Audie* tonal pretest, 5 on the Audie tonal posttest, 5 on the *Audie* rhythm pretest, 6 on the *Audie* rhythm posttest, 3.5 on the SVDM pretest, and 3.5 on the SVDM posttest. Simon scored 0 on the *Audie* pretests because he answered "no" to each of the questions. Gordon (1989) stated that this behavior often indicates that the "child either did not understand the directions, or is not yet ready to play" (p. 16) and suggested repeating the test at a later date. I re-administered *Audie* the following week, and Simon responded in the same manner. Simon's mother joined me during the third week to translate the test instructions into Simon's native language, but again Simon answered "no" to all of the questions. Simon received no score (due to failure to repeat the criterion song) on the SVDM pre- and posttests.

Case 1: Sam

Sam seemed eager to attend music class. Whether he truly enjoyed our time together or just craved a change in environment, when I entered his classroom he would charge up to me and ask repeatedly if it was his turn to come. Like the other children, he would then hurry down the hallway, quickly settle on the rug in the room that we used for music class, and await the first activity.

Theme 1: Hesitancy around Singing

Despite Sam's apparent enthusiasm for our classes and gregarious personality, he often exhibited uneasiness or timidity during music class, as evidenced by his actions and words (see table 3.3). Based on my review and coding of

Table 3.3.   Indications of Sam's Hesitancy toward Singing

Behaviors	Vocal Quality	Words
Left arm across eyes	Restricted singing range	Can you sing that?
Left arm across mouth	Unpleasant utterances	"No."
Rubbing eyes	("ugh"; grunting)	"I don't want to sing that."
Hands blocking ears	Chest voice employed	"I want YOU to sing it."
Hands in mouth	even in higher register	
Kicking legs	Scratchy tone of voice	
Squirming and twisting	Squealing/cooing sounds	
Curling up		
Hands over face		

the videotapes of music classes, I concluded that these apprehensive behaviors or utterances did not accompany the movement, chanting, or instrument playing activities. The only musical behavior that triggered this apprehension was singing, and his hesitancy was evident repeatedly, although decreasingly, as the study progressed.

Sam's hesitancy around singing was surprising, given a seemingly rich home musical environment that was marked by singing engagement from Sam's mother and sister. Sam's teachers incorporated music into various parts of the daily routine; however, these musical activities tended not to elicit quality singing from the children. Observations of classroom music activities highlighted the musical intensity and intimacy of our music classes. This intensity might be a possible explanation for the aversion toward singing that Sam exhibited during music class.

Theme 2: Adherence to Patterns

Sam exhibited small, self-constructed behavioral patterns across our music classes. For example, when I unpacked my guitar from its case, Sam would react by asking a question. During class 4, Sam asked, "Is that your guitar?" when I reached for my guitar case. During class 5, he asked, "Is that your big guitar?" He asked, "Is it big?" during class 6. During class 7, I reached for my guitar and Sam asked, "Is that a guitar?" During class 8, Sam asked, "Is that your big guitar?" and during class 10, he asked, "Is that your guitar?" I speculated that such patterns allowed Sam entry points into activities, opportunities for interaction, and comfort in repetition.

Based on my review of data, I concluded that Sam grew musically over the course of the study, especially related to singing and disposition toward musical activities; however, Sam's musical progress might be as appropriately attributed to his increased comfort level within our classes as to the musical engagement experiences.

Case 2: Maddie

Maddie was slow to participate in music class. She spent most of the first class observing my behaviors and those of the other children. When she was not eying her peers or me, she played with the dress-up shoes that she had brought, looked around the room, or just studied the floor. Her quietness contrasted with the other children who attempted many of the new tasks. Two primary themes emerged relative to Maddie: (a) activity-specific hesitancy and (b) a prevalence of indirect musical experiences.

Theme 1: Activity-Specific Hesitancy

Like Sam, Maddie demonstrated initial hesitancy in music class; however, Sam's hesitancy was solely toward activities involving singing, while Maddie's was directed toward novel activities. Each time a new activity was presented to Maddie, she would delay participation until she seemed comfortable with it. Typically, Maddie observed the song/activity during two different classes before engaging in that activity in the third class. Given this need for an acclimation period, Maddie seemed to crave repetitive environments. Often, she would appear bothered if there was a break in the routine and take it upon herself to ensure that pattern was restored. For example, Maddie reminded me not to forget activities or skip any children, by saying, "Are you gonna play guitar?" or "You didn't do me yet!" and "Are we gonna do the bean bags?" reminding me again, "We didn't do the guitar!" and "Tommy didn't get a turn."

An additional instance of Maddie's attempts to adhere to routine occurred after a pattern emerged related to beanbags. As soon as I passed one to each child, the children would compare their beanbags and find color matches while squealing, "We have the same!" This would usually continue until I said, "Okay, let's begin." During Maddie's ninth class, I passed out the beanbags, and no other person had a blue one. In lieu of breaking or abandoning the weekly pattern, Maddie said to me, "We have the same!" even though we did not have the same color bean bags. She seemed aware of this discrepancy, though, and after a couple of seconds of thinking pronounced to me, "We have the same color shoes!" Maddie had found a way to maintain a pattern, despite the obvious lack of similarity.

Theme 2: Prevalence of Indirect Musical Experiences

Maddie's home life presented varying models of musical engagement. Both of her parents modeled a love of listening to music, but neither parent modeled comfort with music making. Because of this, Maddie encountered a prevalence of indirect musical experiences and very few direct musical experiences at home. Her parents provided tools for music making or engagement (including instruments and recordings) but did not actually interact with Maddie in a meaningful, musical fashion.

Maddie showed progress in the quality, quantity, and ease of her singing in music class. Field notes and analysis of videotape indicated that Maddie's singing range was widened and she was able to sing over the register lift by the end of data collection. Maddie's mother also reported that she sang more frequently at home over the course of the study and her disposition toward musical expression became more positive. One notable observation was that Maddie began performing the songs from music class at home and, in so doing, infused more musical experiences into her home environment.

Case 3: Simon

Primary Theme: Importance of Music as Communication

The primary theme that emerged relative to Simon was the importance of music making as a method of communication and human interaction. I met with Simon's parents before music classes began and learned that the family had been in the United States for one year and that Simon was struggling with English.

At the beginning of our first music class, Simon avoided eye contact and sat turned away from the activity. As the class proceeded, he looked around the room and watched me, but he did not engage with or observe the other children in the class. One of the little girls made note of Simon's reluctance to participate and said to me, "Simon doesn't like to listen."

While I sang the opening song for our second class, Simon crawled around the floor, then lay on his stomach, and began rolling. He eventually rolled over to some foam toys stacked in the corner of the room and jumped on and off several of them. I said, "Simon, come sit with me." Simon sat for a few seconds, then got up and left again. Simon's seemingly off-task behavior continued throughout the class and was particularly evident during an activity involving beanbags. At one point during the activity, he burst into a couple of seconds of loud shouting and shaking his head. He then lay down, sat back up, and tossed his beanbag into the air. I said, "Don't throw it," and this time he threw it across the room with a loud grunt and chased it. This was followed by another period of jumping on and off the toys, while grunting. His behavior continued as we did an activity with the drum, and at one point, Simon let out a loud squeal, "EEEEEhhh!"

Soon after this class, I met again with Simon's parents. They had witnessed some of Simon's behavior in his classroom and were concerned. Simon's father said, "You know there are lots of things for Simon. First, [he's] bilingual . . . the other is our concern about language, social . . ." Simon's mother interjected, "developmental delay," and his father quickly responded, "We don't know that yet. . . . We will see what they say."

Because of Simon's disruptive behavior during music class, I elected to teach him individually. During our individual classes, I slowed the tempi of songs, further limited the use of speech, and pared down the number of activities, all of which helped keep Simon on task for longer periods of time; however, I noticed that he seemed content to listen to my musical expression rather than express his own musicality. I chose to limit my singing and allow him more opportunities for response. At times, I stopped singing during the cadence point of a familiarized song, which created an extended period of awkward silence. This would inevitably cause Simon to sing or chant what I had omitted, break the silence, and allow the song to continue.

Over time, Simon responded more quickly and with longer portions of the song, until he was able to sing entire songs along with me and independently. I also offered a variety of rhythm and tonal patterns for Simon to echo and echoed his patterns as well. This broadened his vocabulary of rhythmic and tonal utterances while offering him control over his own responses and some of my musical utterances. If Simon made a musical utterance at any point in our class, I would imitate it in an attempt to extend the conversation. This use of imitation as well as the insertion of silences into musical activities have been promoted by Valerio and colleagues (1998) and were also effective in eliciting responses among children as found in a study by Hornbach (2005).

The combination of the adaptation of music classes to Simon's individual needs, the limiting of my singing to allow opportunities for response, and acknowledging each of Simon's responses by emulating them led Simon to musically express himself more. Simon's initial off-task and disruptive behaviors gradually waned as his connection with the musical activities strengthened, and there was evidence that his singing range was extended. I concluded that Simon's musicality might ultimately be an important mode of personal expression, given his communication challenges and a subsequent diagnosis of significant developmental delay. For Simon, music seems to be a realm within which he can exhibit control and an area in which he can experience success.

Cross-Case Themes

Multiple themes emerged across two or more case studies. One such theme was the children's fondness for and reliance on pattern, structure, and repetition within music class. A second cross-case theme related to an initial hesitancy around music making that waned as music classes proceeded and comfort levels increased. This increase in comfort level resulted in an improved disposition toward musical activities and an increase in music making during music class for the three children in the case studies.

DISCUSSION

Although no significant differences were found between the music aptitude posttest means of the control and experimental groups, the difference in tonal music aptitude posttest means approached statistical significance ($p = .051$). This may indicate that the musical engagement in this study (twelve weeks) has the potential to affect tonal music aptitude, but was not administered for an extensive enough period or with a large enough sample to yield significant results. Although the reliability coefficients for the pretest approached those published in the *Audie* test manual (Gordon, 1989), low reliability levels were found for the posttest. Consequently, results pertaining to this subtest within this study should be interpreted with caution.

The SVDM and *Audie* mean scores of both groups increased over the course of the study. This may be due to the effects of the musical activities that were occurring in the children's classrooms or elsewhere. In addition, because the teachers were cognizant of the purpose of this study, the heightened awareness of the possible effects of musical engagement may have caused them to provide additional musical activities in the classroom.

A significant difference ($p < .01$) was found between the group means on the SVDM posttest, indicating that the musical engagement had a positive effect on the children's singing abilities. At the end of the treatment period, the mean score of the experimental group was 3.32. A 3 on the SVDM indicates a *limited range singer* who exhibits consistent use of the limited singing range (D^3 to F^3), while a 3.5 on the SVDM indicates an *inconsistent initial range singer*, who sometimes uses a limited singing range but at times uses the initial singing voice range (D^3 to A^3).

In contrast, at the end of the treatment period, the mean score of the control group was 2.5, indicating singers who waver between speaking voice and singing voice and only use a limited range when in singing voice (usually up to F^3). This increase in singing voice achievement due to musical engagement is consistent with the findings of Gawlick (2003) and Rutkowski (1996). It should be noted, though, that the Hawthorne effect may have contributed to the results, in that the experimental group participants' performance may have improved because they received special attention in the form of music classes (Gall, Gall, and Borg, 2007).

The ancillary finding of a gender difference relative to singing voice favoring females at the onset of the study is consistent with the findings of Bedsole

(1987), who studied three- and four-year-old children. Within the present study, the gender gap narrowed and was no longer statistically significant at the conclusion of the study, and the male participants improved significantly over the course of the study. This improvement may have been an outcome of the singing activities provided to the experimental group as well as the musical activities provided for all participants in their preschool classrooms. This may also have been an effect of maturation; however, a maturation effect might run contrary to the findings of Goetze (1985), Guerrini (2002), and Jordan-DeCarbo (1982), who found that early elementary-age females sang more accurately than their male counterparts. Regardless of the potential contributors to improvement, the presence of an initial gender difference among three-year-olds is noteworthy and deserving of further investigation.

The three children involved in the case studies showed development relative to various aspects of their musicality including singing voice achievement. They exhibited fondness for and reliance on pattern, structure, and repetition within music class. This finding is consistent with Hornbach (2005), who observed that such routine "may contribute to child comfort, and may elicit child joy" (p. 24). In addition, the children exhibited an initial hesitancy around music making that waned as music classes proceeded and their comfort levels seemed to increase. Sam and Simon showed an improvement in disposition toward music making, while Maddie demonstrated an increase in music-seeking behaviors and self-initiated music attempts. I concluded that research-based musical engagement had a positive effect on multiple facets of the musicality of these three children.

CONVERGENCE OF METHODS

Triangulation

The methods were converged for the purposes of complementarity and triangulation at the data analysis/interpretation stage. Through qualitative data collection and analysis, I concluded that the three children involved in the case studies made singing progress over the course of the study, and, by reviewing videotape during the study, I observed that the other children in my music classes made singing progress. These informal observations of singing voice improvement within the experimental group and the results of the qualitative portion of the study relative to singing voice were corroborated by the findings of the quantitative portion of this study, which indicated that the experimental group performed significantly ($p < .01$) better than the control group on the singing voice posttest.

One finding that emerged relative to Maddie may indicate discrepant results between the quantitative and qualitative data. While I collected sufficient qualitative evidence to conclude that Maddie's singing voice improved over the course of the study, and this finding was corroborated by the quantitative results related to the overall singing improvement of children in the experimental group, Maddie showed no gain between her SVDM pretest and posttest. This could be attributed to several factors including hesitancy toward a testing situation, or perhaps Maddie's newly acquired singing range simply was not stable enough to be evidenced during the SVDM posttest.

The ancillary quantitative finding of a moderate correlation between tonal aptitude and singing voice initially seemed to run contrary to my qualitative findings relative to Sam. Sam achieved high scores on his aptitude pretests, and then scored the lowest possible mark on his SVDM pretest, indicating that, for Sam, tonal music aptitude and singing voice as measured by SVDM were not related. Sam's SVDM pretest might not have accurately reflected Sam's singing capabilities, but rather reflected hesitancy toward singing that tended to negatively impact his singing performance.

Sam's mother's descriptions of his singing capabilities as well as my observations of Sam's singing when he believed he was unobserved contrasted with Sam's SVDM pretest. My subsequent analysis of Sam's singing capabilities, his improvement in singing tasks over the course of the study, and his improved performance on the SVDM posttest indicated that his pretest was something of an anomaly. After initially believing that Sam's case study presented divergent findings to the quantitative ancillary finding, I concluded that, in fact, Sam's actual use of singing voice and his tonal music aptitude scores corroborate the potential existence of a correlation between tonal music aptitude and singing voice.

Complementarity

Because I strove to elaborate, enhance, illustrate, or clarify the findings from one method with those of another, I also articulated a complementarity motive for mixing methods. One area in which the qualitative findings elaborated or enhanced the quantitative findings again was related to singing voice. A significant gender difference was located on the SVDM pretests, indicating that the girls were collectively singing better than the boys. Sam illustrated this phenomenon when he scored a 1 on his SVDM pretest. By studying Sam in a qualitative fashion, I concluded that Sam's poor performance on the SVDM and in music classes was likely due to hesitancy toward singing. It is impossible to conclude with any certainty why the boys did not sing as well as the girls, but the findings related to Sam provided an illustration of this phenomenon relative to one child and a potential explanation for the results.

Possibly the most useful incidence of complementarity of findings was regarding Simon. Simon's musical capabilities were unable to be measured by the testing methods used in this study; however, because of the considerable amount of qualitative data collected on Simon's musical behaviors, I have an understanding of the musical progress that he made over the course of the study and some understanding of the effect of music classes on his musicality.

IMPLICATIONS FOR EDUCATORS

The results of this study have implications for the practice of early childhood music educators as well as early childhood classroom teachers and caregivers. The data relative to singing voice may provide music educators with information that is valuable when selecting song material and providing sequential singing activities. For example, the children in this study exhibited relatively limited singing ranges—typically as narrow as D^3 to F^3, and occasionally as wide as D^3 to A^3. These ranges should be considered when choosing and introducing literature that the educator hopes children will sing. Very few children in this study were able to sing above the register lift (B^3-flat and above). Songs containing pitches over the register lift should be implemented carefully, and educators should be aware that children might initially struggle to match those higher pitches.

Qualitative data analysis indicated obstacles that stand in the way of some children's complete and carefree musical expression. Sam's case study revealed hesitancy toward singing and the negative impact on singing achievement that such an emotional obstacle can have. The presence of hesitancy reinforces the importance of musical engagement occurring within a play-based environment free from as many adult expectations as possible. Such playful engagement might encourage a child who is hesitant to attempt new activities without the fear of performance or condemnation.

Maddie's case study revealed a cautious response to new activities. Had the musical activities used in this study been presented to Maddie on only one or two occasions, it is conceivable that she would not have engaged or expressed her musicality at all during this study. Repetition seemed to provide Maddie multiple entry points into activities, the repeated experiences necessary to learn new material, and a predictable pattern and routine.

Simon had several obstacles to his musical expression including language difficulties and developmental delays. In many ways, Simon presented more obstacles to musical expression than most very young children; however, Simon was as musical and capable of musical expression as the other children in this study. As educators, we must never conclude that a child is incapable of rich musical expression; we must only keep searching for ways to reveal that musicality.

RECOMMENDATIONS FOR FURTHER RESEARCH

There is evidence from this study that research-based musical engagement has a positive effect on three-year-old children's musicality. Should this study be replicated, I recommend a longer period of musical engagement. Also, administering SVDM after a delay would provide information regarding whether musical engagement has a lasting effect on singing voice achievement. A study designed to compare the effects of the type of musical engagement implemented in this study with the effects of other approaches to early childhood music education would be useful. Finally, follow-up studies related to gender difference in singing abilities, the relationship between tonal music aptitude and singing voice, and the presence of hesitancy toward singing in young children are recommended.

REFERENCES

Bedsole, E. A. (1987). A descriptive study of the musical abilities of three- and four-year-old children. *Dissertation Abstracts International, 48*(7), 1688.

Blesedell, D. S. (1991). A study of the effects of two types of movement instruction on the rhythm achievement and developmental rhythm aptitude of preschool children. *Dissertation Abstracts International, 52*(7), 2452.

Campbell, P. S., and Scott-Kassner, C. (2002). *Music in childhood: From preschool through the elementary grades* (2nd ed.). Belmont, CA: Schirmer.

Campbell, P. S., and Scott-Kassner, C. (2006). *Music in childhood: From preschool through the elementary grades* (3rd ed.). Belmont, CA: Schirmer.

Creswell, J. W. (2003). *Research design: Qualitative, quantitative, and mixed methods approaches* (2nd ed.). Thousand Oaks, CA: Sage.

Farr, S. (1993). A comparison between home musical environment and musical aptitude in pre-K–2nd grade children. *Dissertation Abstracts International, 33*(3), 712.

Flavell, J. H., Miller, P. H., and Miller, S. A. (2002). *Cognitive development.* Upper Saddle River, NJ: Prentice Hall.

Flohr, J. W. (1981). Short-term music instruction and young children's developmental music aptitude. *Journal of Research in Music Education, 29*(3), 219–23.

Fox, D. B. (2000). Music and the baby's brain. *Music Educators Journal, 87*(2), 23.

Gall, M. D., Gall, J. P., and Borg, W. R. (2007). *Educational research: An introduction* (8th ed.). Boston: Pearson.

Gawlick, B. S. (2003). Early childhood music education in four preschool settings: The influence of classroom musical environment, music instruction, and home musical environment on young children's developmental music aptitude and music performance competence. *Dissertation Abstracts International, 64*(12), 4399.

Glaser, B., and Strauss, A. (1967). *The discovery of grounded theory.* Chicago: Aldine.

Goetze, M. (1985). Factors affecting accuracy in children's singing. *Dissertation Abstracts International, 46*(10), 2955.

Gordon, E. E. (1989). *Audie: A game for understanding and analyzing your child's music potential.* Chicago: GIA.

Gordon, E. E. (2003). *A music learning theory for newborn and young children.* Chicago: GIA.

Greene, J. C., Caracelli, V. J., and Graham, W. F. (1989). Toward a conceptual framework for mixed-method evaluation designs. *Educational Evaluation and Policy Analysis, 11*(3), 255–74.

Guerrini, S. C. (2002). The acquisition and assessment of the developing singing voice among elementary students. *Dissertation Abstracts International, 63*(1), 125.

Hornbach, C. M. (2005). Ah-eee-ah-eee-yah-eee, bum and pop, pop, pop: Teacher initiatives, teacher silence, and children's vocal responses in early childhood music classes. *Dissertation Abstracts International, 66*(9), 3246.

Huck, S. W. (2000). *Reading statistics and research.* New York: Longman.

Jacobi-Karna, K. L. (1996). The effects of the inclusion of text on the singing accuracy of preschool children. *Dissertation Abstracts International, 57*(11), 4682.

Jordan-DeCarbo, J. (1982). Same/different discrimination techniques, readiness training, pattern treatment, and sex on aural discrimination and singing of tonal patterns by kindergartners. *Journal of Research in Music Education, 30*(4), 237–46.

Lange, D. M. (1999). The effect of the use of text in music instruction on the tonal aptitude, tonal accuracy, and tonal understanding of kindergarten students. *Dissertation Abstracts International, 60*(10), 3623.

Levinowitz, L. M. (1989). An investigation of preschool children's comparative capability to sing songs with and without words. *Bulletin of the Council for Research in Music Education, 100,* 14–19.

Levinowitz, L. M., Barnes, P., Guerrini, S., Clement, M., D'April, P., and Morey, M. J. (1998). Measuring singing voice development in the elementary general music classroom. *Journal of Research in Music Education, 46*(1), 35–47.

Mallett, C. A. (2000). An examination of parent/caregiver attitudes toward music instruction, the nature of the home musical environment, and their relationship to the developmental music aptitude of preschool children. *Dissertation Abstracts International, 61*(1), 1335.

Rutkowski, J. (1986). The effect of restricted song range on kindergarten children's use of singing voice and developmental music aptitude. *Dissertation Abstracts International, 47,* 4706A.

Rutkowski, J. (1989). *The teaching of music: A curricular approach.* Unpublished manuscript, Pennsylvania State University.

Rutkowski, J. (1990). The measurement and evaluation of children's singing voice development. *The Quarterly: Center for Research in Music Learning and Teaching, 1*(1–2), 81–95.

Rutkowski, J. (1996). The effectiveness of individual/small-group singing activities on kindergartners' use of singing voice and developmental music aptitude. *Journal of Research in Music Education, 44*(4), 353–68.

Simons, G. M. (1979). A rationale for early training in music. *Education, 99*(3), 259–64.

Sullivan, K. N. (2006). The responses of preschool children to early childhood music instruction containing texted and non-texted songs and chants. *Dissertation Abstracts International, 44*(6).

Taggart, C. C. (1994). A validity study of Audie: A test of music aptitude for 3- and 4-year-old children. *Bulletin of the Council for Research in Music Education, 121*, 42–54.

Taggart, C. C. (1997). *A study of developmental music aptitude.* Paper presented at the New Directions in Music Education: Early Childhood Music Conference, Michigan State University, East Lansing, MI.

Tarnowski, S. M. (1986). Effects of single-mode versus multiple-mode group instruction on the singing accuracy of preschool children. *Dissertation Abstracts International, 47*(8), 2941.

Valerio, W. H., Reynolds, A. M., Bolton, B. M., Taggart, C. C., and Gordon, E. E. (1998). *Music play: The early childhood music curriculum guide for parents, teachers, and caregivers.* Chicago: GIA.

Yang, Y. (1994).The effects of solmization and rhythmic movement training on the achievement of beginning group piano students at the elementary school level. *Dissertation Abstracts International, 56*(1), 132.

Part II

CREATING RICH LEARNING ENVIRONMENTS

Chapter Four

Building Community to Elicit Responses in Early Childhood Music Classes

Christina M. Hornbach

With the intent of improving early childhood music education, the purpose of this qualitative study was to develop an understanding of teacher initiatives and children's responses in early childhood music classes. This study entailed naturalistic observation of the teachers (N =2) and infants/toddlers (N =14) in two early childhood music programs. Data were collected through field notes, think-aloud interviews with teachers, teacher/parent interviews, and videotape analysis; a total of six class periods, three in each setting, were observed and videotaped for future analysis. Teacher initiatives and behaviors that elicited children's responses were classified in part as (a) parent-child relationship, (b) teacher-child relationship, and (c) child as teacher. Findings revealed the following themes: (a) children respond vocally in an interactionist learning environment, and (b) the formation and nurturing of a class community is essential for encouraging children's vocal responses.

BUILDING COMMUNITY TO ELICIT RESPONSES IN EARLY CHILDHOOD MUSIC CLASSES

Vygotsky (1978) noted that typical measures of young children's mental development focus on what they can do alone, whereas "what children can do with the assistance of others might be in some sense even more indicative of their mental development than what they can do alone" (p. 85). He held that learning accompanied by social interactions exceeded learning done alone. "Music . . . is not an isolated thing; it is part of a life-process; it is separate neither from the child's consciousness nor from any aspect of his everyday life" (Moorhead and Pond, 1978, p. 48). Moorhead and Pond believed that the concept of society greatly influenced a child's actions. Music making was predicated on interactions with other children and adults in their environment. In order to maximize learning, young children need direct interaction with the subject matter and social interactions with peers, parents, and teachers.

During infancy, brain growth is fast and remarkable; the brain's neural synapses are connecting and forming lifelong cognitive processing patterns (Cohen, 2002). Consequently, early childhood brain development plays a crucial role in how people process music throughout their lives (Gordon, 2003b). A nourishing musical environment helps young children develop neural networks in their brains that strengthen their potential (musical aptitude) for future musical development and comprehension. In order to provide an appropriate musical environment, early childhood music educators must have an understanding of how children learn music; research literature and knowledgeable teachers help to provide this crucial knowledge of appropriate practice. In turn, practitioners provide models of appropriate musical interactions for parents in early childhood music classes.

MUSICAL ENVIRONMENTS

The Home

To create a musical environment for their children at home, some parents may need help in feeling comfortable singing, chanting, and moving with their child. In early childhood music classes that include parents as participants, appropriate adult/child music interactions first are modeled by the teacher, and then parents engage in music play in an informal environment, enabling parents to continue this play outside of class. Ideally, parents should be involved in class and not just serve as bystanders (Gordon, 2003b). Just as young children need to be immersed in a verbal environment to learn language, children need to be exposed to singing, rhythmic chanting, and movement to learn to be musical.

Early Childhood Music Classes

Social connections are also essential in musical maturation (Campbell, 1998; Taggart, 2003). Early childhood music classes can provide a constructive and creative musical environment that children do not experience otherwise. In this setting, it is important to elicit vocalizations from children so that the practitioner may gain an understanding of the child's musical development and gauge instruction to meet the children's musical needs.

Ideally, early childhood music classes provide rich musical and social environments. Music teachers and parents need to sing and chant to young children, just as parents interact with language with children. A social environment is imperative in stimulating language development (Haslett and Samter, 1997), and this is also true of music development. Researchers describe the vocal responses of young children to specific musical stimuli (Hicks, 1993; Moog, 1976; Reynolds, 1995; Santucci, 2002), as well as their spontaneous vocal behaviors in free musical play (Burton, 2002; Foley, 1978; Moorhead and Pond, 1978; Miller, 1986; Young, 2002). Yet there also needs to be an understanding of the particular teacher initiatives or behaviors that elicit vocal responses in young children in the social and musical environment of early childhood music classes.

CONTEXT OF THE STUDY

For this study, I chose to work with an early childhood music class at the local university's Community Music School (CMS); the class was led by my mentor, a veteran early childhood and elementary general music teacher, Dr. Ellie Michaels (a pseudonym). In addition, I also observed an early childhood music class run out of a suburban Detroit church by a colleague, Chloe Jacobson (a pseudonym). As the instrument for data collection in this participant-observation study, I chose specifically not to distance myself from the participants, but to interact with them. My experiences as a teacher and as a researcher in early childhood music provide me with a unique perspective. I have thoughts and opinions about which teacher behaviors elicit or do not elicit responses from children; I have tried out ideas in my own teaching. This is both a weakness and a strength of this study. This study may be limited by my propinquity to the research subject, but it also may be enhanced by my familiarity with the children, the early childhood music classes, and the teaching that occurs in these situations.

My research questions emerged as I taught my own early childhood music classes and tried to elicit responses from children. I wanted information about the stages of musical development of my students and what they knew, which can only be gained by engaging in teaching behaviors that elicit individual responses. I have experimented in my own teaching with trying to elicit responses from children and have discussed these ideas with my mentor and other colleagues. This study continues my search for means of eliciting responses from young children.

RESEARCH PURPOSE AND QUESTION

With the intent of improving early childhood music education, the purpose of this qualitative study was to develop an understanding of teacher initiatives that elicit children's responses in early childhood music classes. Specifically, through this study, I investigated which teacher behaviors (intentional or unintentional) precede children's (ages birth to three years) vocal responses.

METHODOLOGY

Participants

Participants in this study were the two early childhood music teachers (N = 2) and the children ($n^1 = 10$; $n^2 = 4$) involved in one class each at two early childhood music settings. Most of the children in this study ranged in age from approximately birth to three years old; one child was thirty-eight months old. The participants were predominantly Caucasian and middle class. Though there is a fee involved to attend the early childhood music classes in both settings, financial assistance is available based on need. The parents of the infants/toddlers were secondary participants.

I purposely chose both teachers for this study. I selected Ellie Michaels as a study participant because of her extensive theoretical and practical experience in early childhood music education, diverse musical and educational background, and national and international reputation as a scholar of children's musical learning. She currently teaches Early Childhood Music Methods and Elementary General Music Methods for undergraduate students at "Big 10 University," a public, research-intensive, land grant university, as well as the early childhood music classes at the university's CMS for infants, toddlers, and preschoolers.

I have had the opportunity to watch Ellie Michaels engage students of all ages in musical learning (early childhood, undergraduate students, graduate students, and practicing teachers); I find her to be caring, engaging, and challenging. Her student-centered teaching style focuses the student, either infant or undergraduate, on the content and the process of learning, which enables the student to learn and continue his/her own musical growth. It was Dr. Michaels's personality and style of teaching in the early childhood classroom, as well as her implementation of Gordon's theoretical work that specifically captured my interest for this study. Her more than fifteen years of teaching early childhood music classes combined with her extensive scholarly and curricular work in early childhood music made Dr. Michaels an ideal participant for this study.

Like Ellie Michaels, Chloe Jacobson was chosen for this study because of her teaching skills and experience. I first met her when I conducted a research project with her elementary students. Initially, I was planning just to observe Dr. Michaels and the young children at the CMS for this study. However, after observing Ms. Jacobson's teaching and interactions with elementary students, I asked her if I could come observe her work with infants and toddlers.

Ms. Jacobson began her work in early childhood music when she took an undergraduate course, Early Childhood Music Methods, with Dr. Michaels in the fall of 1994; she also participated in the university's CMS Early Childhood Music Program as a teaching assistant. She taught early childhood music in Houston, Texas, and Philadelphia, Pennsylvania, where she continued her education at Temple University working toward a master's degree in music education. At the time of the study, Ms. Jacobson taught elementary general music in the Detroit area and early childhood music classes on Saturday mornings at a satellite location of the university's CMS. Ms. Jacobson is founder and director of Little Music Makers, an early childhood music program. After viewing Ms. Jacobson teaching early childhood music classes, I felt that her elegant teaching and insights would enrich this study. Her own early childhood music teaching experience combined with her work with Dr. Michaels and other scholar-teachers of the music learning theories of Edwin Gordon made Ms. Jacobson a model participant for this study.

Both Ms. Jacobson and Dr. Michaels are currently certification teachers for the Gordon Institute of Musical Learning in Early Childhood Music. I believe including two master teachers in this study has provided a richness that would have been absent having focused on just one. It also means that the findings of this study are not teacher-specific.

Settings

The philosophy and methodology of the early childhood classes in both settings are based on the research and writing of Gordon (2003a, 2003b). Big 10 University's early childhood classes follow a curriculum developed by Dr. Ellie Michaels, professor of music education at Big 10 University and director of the Early Childhood Music Program at CMS. The curriculum is also based on the resource *Music Play* (Valerio, Reynolds, Bolton, Taggart, and Gordon, 1998). Little Music Makers, though based on the same philosophy, draws curricular materials from the work of Beth Bolton as well as from *Music Play*.

In both programs, professional musicians and teachers provide the children with exposure to an extensive music vocabulary and opportunities to play and experiment with music. By participating in regular music-making time, the children cultivate a working music vocabulary (singing, chanting, moving, and listening). At both locations, the majority of the curriculum consists of songs and chants without words, but both programs use songs and chants with words as well. Both programs require one parent/guardian to attend class, encourage parent participation, and ask parents not to force children to participate. In both settings the children come in with their parent or caregiver, sit down in a circle and sing songs, chant, move, play instruments, and interact; they "play" musically for forty-five minutes.

Early Childhood Music Classes

The early childhood classroom at Big 10 University's CMS is located at the end of a neat, carpeted hallway that includes the main office, administrative offices, music therapy room, and other music classrooms. Windows fill one wall of the early childhood classroom; they overlook the parking lot and are a frequent entertainment and gathering center for the children. This room used to be an early childhood classroom in the church; hence the windows are low and accessible. The ceiling and walls are white, plain with absolutely no adornment. The floor is blue-specked carpet that seems to hide the occasional stain well. There is no furniture except a couple of chairs by the door. The vibrancy and life that fills the room only appears when the parents and children enter. Part of one wall consists of dark wood cupboards used to store instruments, musical props, and the sound system. It is, in essence, a blank slate, perhaps only broken up by the appearance of props, such as colorful scarves, hula-hoops, and boomwhackers. During instruction, props are used primarily to focus the children's attention, though some small percussion instruments are used as well.

The environment of the Little Music Makers is similar to CMS; however, classes take place in a classroom that is rented from an active church. The classroom also has minimal furniture in it when the parents and children arrive; the instructor moves the furniture into the hallway prior to class. There is a short table in the front on which the instructor stores props and her stereo system. The classroom is more versatile than CMS's classroom, as it is used for other purposes besides the early childhood music classes. The walls similarly are barren, and there is also a large window that floods the room with light on sunny days, in addition to a small sink area. The room is carpeted and smaller than the one at CMS. Occasionally, there are random items that are left behind from previous activities that distract the children. During this study, one music class moved to a preschool room in the building, as there was an overnight retreat that needed to use the regular room. The preschool room is bright, colorful, and filled with toys and distractions. The carpet is a rainbow of colors and has a variety of game boards from various games woven in it.

Both programs are predicated on the idea that children learn music similar to the way in which they learn a language. In order to learn to speak, children informally *listen* to people talk all day long; this language learning even begins in the womb, as hearing is fully developed by the end of the first trimester. Only after listening to the language in their environment do children babble and eventually learn to speak. With music, children must listen to the sounds and syntax of the musical culture; eventually, they experiment with producing musical sounds, which is musical babble (Gordon, 2003b). As early as birth, children in both programs participate in forty-five-minute classes of informal, structured guidance in music. The teachers provide the children with exposure to an extensive music *listening* vocabulary and opportunities to play and experiment with music; in other words, children begin to engage in a dialogue in music much as they do in their native language. This generally occurs through imitation and eventually becomes an improvisatory conversation. By participating in regular music-making time, the children cultivate a working music vocabulary.

Procedure: Data Collection

This study was qualitative and descriptive in nature. There were four primary data sources: (a) field notes, (b) think-aloud interviews with teachers while viewing videotapes, (c) video tape analysis, and (d) formal and informal teacher/parent interviews. A total of six classes, three in each setting, were observed and videotaped for future analysis. I not only observed the classes that I attended, but participated as the opportunity presented itself. In this type of research methodology, it is typical for researchers to adopt both a participant and observer role (participant observations) (Bresler, 1995).

The first data source consisted of observing the preschool early childhood classes and recording naturalistic observations through field notes at the same time that the class was video-recorded. I recorded significant vocal responses by noting the time and behavior, followed by codes and/or a narrative description of the quality of the teacher/child interaction. This technique, event sampling, is an established method of observation (Bentzen, 1993). Digital photos were taken to illustrate codes or sampling at a later point. This isolated visual was not used to identify codes, but only to help organize data from the video recordings and perhaps illustrate findings for later publishing or presenting opportunities.

The second data source consisted of think-aloud interviews with the teachers. Within one week after each videotaped class session, the researcher and the instructor of the class viewed the tape together and conducted a think-aloud (Ericsson and Simon, 1993). A thinking-aloud process is one in which the subject is required to speak or express out loud thoughts that he himself had in the course of performing a task (Ericsson and Simon, 1993). The think-aloud interviews were audio-recorded and transcribed. The video was paused when the comments were lengthy; I took notes as needed.

The third data source consisted of analyzing the video material. The video recordings were viewed for event sampling and description; analysis was recorded on a videotape analysis form that was adapted from a form that Mitchell Robinson created based on the work of Miles and Huberman (1994).

The fourth data source occurred simultaneously with class observations and analysis of recordings as needed. I conducted a formal interview with the main teacher in each location using questions designed to elicit the teacher's thoughts regarding (a) teacher initiatives, (b) wait time (silence) before children's responses, and (c) children's vocal responses, as a springboard for discussion. I also conducted informal, impromptu interviews/conversations with both teachers and parents. I recorded formal interviews with teachers using a Sony M-645V Microcassette-recorder and then transcribed them. The formal interview protocol was the following: my explaining the purpose of the study, subsequent discussion, and engagement in a recorded conversation that was guided by previously determined questions. In order to improve trustworthiness, participants were asked to check the transcriptions. Informal conversations with teachers and/or parents were recorded in field notes during or immediately following the impromptu conversation; these conversations occurred at the beginning or end of classes. In addition, artifacts were copied and/or typed into word-processed documents.

Data Analysis and Results

In a participant-observation study, the aim, in part, is to be aware of the culture and environment from a participant's point of view (Hatch, 1998). This is an interpretive science, a narrative approach in which proximity and interactions with subjects are key (Graue and Walsh, 1998); there is no claim that findings are generalizable. The purpose of this research was to gain an understanding of teacher initiatives that elicited children's responses in early childhood music classes. However, themes also emerged regarding those environmental factors and relationships that helped elicit children's vocal responses and the nature of the complex interactions between a teacher and a child. Moorhead and Pond (1978) believed that music is not a solitary practice; making music is built on the intercommunication of the involved participants: teachers, children, and parents. The themes from the present study support that belief.

FINDINGS

Themes

Relationships

The nature of the *parent-child relationship*, the *teacher-student relationship*, and the *child as teacher* all elicited children's vocal responses in these two early childhood settings, emerging as primary themes of the study. In addition, a *sense of community*, another emergent theme, also elicited vocal responses in the early childhood music classrooms. Both teachers also used *touch*, which emerged as another theme, to gain a child's attention, develop the teacher-child relationship, and elicit children's responses. The parent-child and teacher-child relationships were intertwined in regard to whether a child would respond. In other words, some parents were more relaxed than others in their interactions with their children. The behavior patterns of the parent and child were formed from home environment interactions, but in each case, the teacher was found to have the unique opportunity to foster a relationship in which the child felt comfortable enough to participate.

Parent-Child Relationship as a Factor in Eliciting Vocal Responses

The parent-child relationship often had an influence on whether children responded or interacted socially. The parent/caregiver-child relationship and family life are complex ecosystems. Therefore, some children came to music class with Mom, some with Dad, some with Grandma, or some with a different caregiver every week. The children and parents used this time as playtime and musical playtime together as a dyad and also as a time to engage with a larger community and develop relationships with other children and adults.

In one particular class, a young girl who normally came to class with her mom came to class that day with her dad. "Alice" normally was the social butterfly of music class and would wander around class greeting, flirting, and interacting with other students and parents. On the day her dad brought her to class, Alice began her normal social routine, and her dad tried to pull her back into his lap. He perhaps did not know that it was developmentally and socially appropriate in this class for her to wander. Perhaps due to his unfamiliarity with the rituals and acceptable behaviors in class or his own needs, Alice's dad continued to pull Alice back on his lap when she tried to escape and go play. The teacher advised that it was fine for her to wander. Alice engaged differently in class that day. The interactions with her dad took precedence over her participation in class. Perhaps he thought he was acting in Alice's best interest by holding her back and keeping her "safe" with him; however, it overtly inhibited her participation in class and her joy, which was lacking during this class (Think-Aloud Interview, Ellie Michaels).

Children's relationships with their parents and caregivers are both complicated and varied; they also are beyond the control of the teacher. However, the influence that these fundamental relationships have on the children in class was apparent.

Teacher-Child Relationship as a Factor in Children's Vocal Responses

A comfortable, relaxed, teacher-child relationship may encourage children to respond. To this end, the teachers in this study developed an individual relationship with each child by spending time with each child as well as through various forms of exchange: facial expressions, body language, verbal encouragement, touch, and physical proximity. As a result, children began to feel more confident to try new things and explore, which is developmentally appropriate practice. "Adults play a vital socialization role with infants and toddlers. Warm, positive relationships with adults help infants develop a sense of trust in the world and feelings of competence. . . . The trusted adult becomes the secure base from which the mobile infant or toddler explores the environment" (Bredekamp, 1987, p. 5). Findings in this study showed that the teachers clearly adored children and loved being around them, which promoted an environment for the children to musically respond and in which to engage.

Developmentally appropriate practice calls for teachers to adapt instruction to the needs of the individual and the provided social construct (Copple and Bredekamp, 2009).Teachers need to recognize that every child's needs are unique. The teachers sought to identify those needs to increase social comfort, which, in turn facilitated exploration and learning. One of the teachers shared her thoughts on the teacher-child relationship:

> I want my relationship with the children to be sort of the musical equivalent of feeling free to tell me anything (laughs). With different kids, that takes different forms. With "Tigger" particularly, it's a little bit more aggressively playful, whereas, with "Bashful" it's being very gentle and loving. And every day after class I have a few minutes with Bashful when he melts onto my shoulder and tries to avoid going back to his Mom. This is not a statement on how he feels about his mom, but it is a statement of how he feels about me. (Teacher Interview, Ellie Michaels)

The teacher-child relationship was often enhanced by touch or physical proximity, though sometimes the children needed space. The National

Association for the Education of Young Children's "Guidelines for Developmentally Appropriate Practice" state that adults assist in a child's accomplishments by supplying encouragement and physical proximity (Bredekamp, 1987; Copple and Bredekamp, 2009). This was apparent in the study. When an adult is above a child, he or she may appear threatening. Therefore, the teachers got down on the floor so that they would appear smaller than the child. As a teacher, it is also important to respect a child's boundaries and need for physical space. Children often need physical space to feel safe and to assert themselves. The teachers would make an overture by tickling a toe while the child sat in the parent's lap. If the child pulled away and turned in toward the parent, the teacher knew not to come further into the child's personal space. Often, a teacher could continue to interact with the child by interacting with the parent or a nearby child. In this way, the child would approach the teacher when s/he was ready. When the teacher-child relationship was well established, the child let the teacher into his/her space and/or accepted physical touch. This physical touch might have been a tickle to the toe while the teacher was singing the resting tone or a "buzz" to the stomach. The touch may have helped the teacher ingratiate herself with the student, eliciting a verbal response. Thus, teachers in this study prioritized physical touch and developing a relationship with the children. Because each child was unique in personality and personal needs, the teachers adapted their use of facial expressions, body language, verbal encouragement, touch, and physical proximity to each child.

Child as Teacher

In these early childhood music settings, the children also functioned as the teacher; teachers often used this as an opportunity to elicit vocal responses. Children in this study often tried to control the order of songs or props, but also enjoyed being the one to give vocal or rhythmic patterns. For instance, one child was "the teacher" when he took a toy microphone and gave patterns to the teacher and his grandparents:

> The "Mad Matcher" is the "teacher." He has the microphone and is giving Chloe [teacher] patterns and offers his grandpa a turn as well. He is taking turns. He has vocally given patterns—but then it turns into a game. He is now pressing the microphone into grandpa's nose and gets up to do the same to grandma. (Video Summary Form)

The behavior of the child acting as teacher may be teacher-, parent-, or child-initiated. Several of the children took their turns as teacher by being the one who gives a rhythm or tonal pattern; basically, the children were starting the

musical conversations. When the child acted as the teacher and invited his/
her teacher or his/her parent to respond to a pattern, it automatically elicited
responses from the child in the form of the child's own initiative. When the
above student gave the teacher and his grandparents patterns, he generated or
created them from his own listening vocabulary in order to start the conversation. By initiating the musical conversation, he automatically was giving the
teacher information about his developing musical vocabulary. This technique
seemed to remove the pressure of the situation for some children. When encouraged to start musical conversations, the student seemed to feel as if it was
his/her decision whether to start the conversation or to respond, and the need
for personal control was met.

Community

In early childhood music classes, the teacher, parents, and children work
together to build an appropriate community. In both settings, there was a feeling of community and a sense that "we are all in this together." The parents
interacted with each other as well as other children.

> "Gretel" throws an egg at Chloe [teacher]; Chloe throws an egg at Gretel, who
> is in the middle of the circle with all of the eggs, and sings tonic "bum." Who
> started this game? Gretel throws one back at Chloe. "Baby" makes a vocaliza-
> tion in the background and Chloe sings "aeeh" on tonic and sends an egg again
> to Gretel. Chloe extends the game to "Sleeping Beauty" and then Gretel turns
> and includes her mother. (Video Summary Form)

Parents and children in class work to clean up props together; Gretel helps the
Mad Matcher put away the beanbag "keyboard" he has laid out on the carpet.
There was a feeling of community in both music classrooms. Children were
interacting with each other; the parents became involved and interacted with
each other's other children. As a result, they modeled this behavior to their
own children. For instance, a newborn baby's mom, who was relatively quiet
in class, chimed in when one student would not take a ride in the parachute.
She asked the child to show her baby how to take a ride in the parachute. The
child asked his caregiver to join him in the parachute and the baby's mom
showed approval (Video Summary Form). In another situation, one student
was a little rough in his physical interaction with a younger student (he was
trying to hug a much younger student who fell over from the weight of the
hug). The teacher asked the child to apologize for being rough and the child
tried to apologize to the younger child who had turned to seek comfort from
a parent. The child ended up leaning forward and kissing the other child's
bottom as she left; all of the parents laughed at this kind gesture (Video Summary Form).

Some parents were more relaxed than others in their interactions with their children, and this affected their participation in the community. In the cases in which the parents were less participatory and interactive, the teacher-student relationship was essential in order to help the child feel comfortable enough to participate and model an interactive and playful environment for the parent.

Children varied wildly in their levels of independence. Both of the classroom environments established routines and rituals that enhanced a feeling of trust and intimacy in the classroom. The routines and rituals established in these environments enabled the children to develop behavior patterns and expectations that increased their comfort levels. The routine/rituals of the classroom, child independence, and a sense of community all contributed to an educational setting in which the children felt safe and perhaps inspired to respond vocally.

Developing "community" in early childhood music classes enhanced children's participation and individual vocal responses. Each class had its own subculture, and the strength of the community grew as each class session progressed. Parents increased their interactions with other children as all people in each context became more familiar and comfortable. Finally, as the children came to know the teachers, the teachers became more approachable, so that, in time, and in their own way, the children became approachable to their teachers.

SUMMARY

In summary, the *parent-child relationship*, *teacher-child relationship*, and the *child as teacher* built the foundation for community in the early childhood music classrooms. *Community building* helped teachers elicit vocal responses from young children. The parent-child relationship and how each child functioned with his/her parent affected whether the child responded vocally and also helped to determine the child's level of comfort in the classroom. Just as the parent-child relationship was important, the teacher-child relationship affected whether children responded vocally in class. Finally, children also enjoyed taking the initiative and acting as teacher, leading vocally responsive activities.

The formation and nurturing of an interactive community was essential for a vital learning environment. Teachers developed relationships with children and children with teachers. Parents were vital to these communities: They formed relationships with other children, parents, and the teachers. For the music classes to be productive, all people involved needed to be aware that each setting was a community and be willing participants. Children responded vocally in an interactionist learning environment, and the formation and nurturing of a class community was essential for encouraging children's vocal responses.

Particular teacher behaviors enriched learning and elicited musical responses. Determining the appropriate behaviors for each class and individual students was a complex and demanding task for the early childhood music teachers. "Beyond providing direct instruction, the adult is responsible for preparing a rich and stimulating environment, asking enticing questions, and adjusting the amount of assistance according to children's needs" (Alvarez and Berg, 2002, p. 128). Pedagogical practice was determined by the teachers through their understanding of developmentally appropriate practice and current research on the musical development of young children, the enactment of pedagogical content knowledge, length of practice in the field, and teacher expertise.

These particular classes were unique subcultures that will not be replicated again. However, the findings may provide practitioners with information to inform their own teaching by trying out similar teacher initiatives to see if they elicit responses in their own teaching settings.

CONCLUSION

Music learning is enhanced when an interactionist and playful environment between children, parents, and teachers is fostered (Campbell, 1998; Taggart, 2003). The thoughts of Dewey and Piaget support the interactionist perspective (Losardo and Notari-Syverson, 2001). Teaching is not a monologue; it is process-oriented. It is active, not passive. Teachers should maximize individual and group interactions with children that are driven by the children's needs.

First, the ideal early childhood music environment is most effective when it is an interactive environment. When the stage is set, the teacher, parents, and children become co-creators in musical learning. Second, teachers should develop and value relationships and community. It is helpful to build relationships with children and a classroom community. When children feel comfortable and enjoy interacting with a teacher, they are more likely to respond to teacher's initiatives. These initiatives often come in the form of physical touch (a tickle to the toe), proximity to the student (often with the teacher in submissive, nonthreatening positions like lying down on the floor), or play. Community interactions with other parents and children also provide a social network of support for infants and toddlers in early childhood music classes. Finally, teachers must continue to find ways to elicit individual responses from children, as these responses provide information on children's musical learning and development. By establishing relationships and building community in the classroom, an interactive musical community with young children is formed that elicits and honors the vocal responses of each child.

REFERENCES

Alvarez, B. J., and Berg, M. H. (2002). Musical learning and teaching and the young child. In E. Boardman (Ed.), *Dimensions of musical learning and teaching* (pp. 121–37). Reston, VA: MENC.

Bentzen, W. R. (1993). *Seeing young children: A guide to observing and recording behavior* (2nd ed.). Albany, NY: Delmar.

Bredekamp, S. (Ed.). (1987). *Developmentally appropriate practice in early childhood programs serving children from birth through age 8.* Washington, DC: National Association for the Education of Young Children.

Bresler, L. (1995). Ethnography, phenomenology, and action research in music education. *Quarterly Journal of Music Teaching and Learning, 6*(3), 4–16.

Burton, S. (2002). An exploration of preschool children's spontaneous songs and chants. *Visions of Research in Music Education, 2,* 7–16.

Campbell, P. S. (1998). *Songs in their heads: Music and its meaning in children's lives.* New York: Oxford University Press.

Cohen, D. (2002). *How the child's mind develops.* London: Routledge.

Copple, C., and Bredekamp, S. (Eds.). (2009). *Developmentally appropriate practice in early childhood programs serving children from birth through age 8* (3rd ed.). Washington, DC: National Association for the Education of Young Children.

Ericsson, K. A., and Simon, H. A. (1993). *Protocol analysis: Verbal reports as data* (Rev. ed.). Cambridge, MA: MIT Press.

Foley, J. R. (1978). *Observing the nature of young children's musicality: An observation study of two classes in the Center for Young Children.* A seminar paper, MENC Historical Center, Special Collections in Performing Arts, University of Maryland Libraries.

Gordon, E. E. (2003a). *Learning sequences in music: Skill, content, and pattern.* Chicago: GIA.

Gordon, E. E. (2003b). *A music learning theory for newborn and young children.* Chicago: GIA.

Graue, M. E., and Walsh, D. J. (1998). *Studying children in context: Theories, methods, and ethics.* Thousand Oaks, CA: Sage.

Haslett, B. B., and Samter, W. (1997). *Children communicating: The first 5 years.* Mahwah, NJ: Erlbaum.

Hatch, J. A. (1998). Qualitative research in early childhood education. In B. Spodek, O. N. Saracho, and A. D. Pellegrini (Eds.), *Issues in early childhood educational research.* New York: Teachers College Press.

Hicks, W. K. (1993). *An investigation of the initial stages of preparatory audiation.* Doctoral dissertation, Temple University, Philadelphia, PA.

Losardo, A., and Notari-Syverson, A. (2001). *Alternative approaches to assessing young children.* Baltimore: Paul H. Brookes.

Miles, M. B., and Huberman, A. M. (1994). *Qualitative data analysis: An expanded sourcebook* (2nd ed.). Thousand Oaks, CA: Sage.

Miller, L. B. (1986). A description of children's musical behaviors: Naturalistic. *Bulletin of the Council for Research in Music Education, 87,* 1–16.

Moog, H. (1976). *The musical experience of the pre-school child* (C. Clarke, Trans.). London: Schott.

Moorhead, G. E., and Pond, D. (1978). *Music of young children: Pillsbury Foundation Studies.* Santa Barbara: Pillsbury Foundation for Advancement of Music Education.

Reynolds, A. M. (1995). *An investigation of the movement responses performed by children 18 months to three years of age and their caregivers to rhythm chants in duple and triple meters.* Doctoral dissertation, Temple University, Philadelphia, PA.

Santucci, P. (2002). *Infant responses to baritone and falsetto singing during face-to-face interactions.* Unpublished master's thesis, University of South Carolina, Columbia.

Taggart, C. C. (2003). Child-centered play in music: Developmentally appropriate practice. *Early Childhood Connections, 9*(2), 15–23.

Valerio, W. H., Reynolds, A. M., Bolton, B. M., Taggart, C. C., and Gordon, E. E. (1998). *Music play.* Chicago: GIA.

Vygotsky, L. S. (1978). *Mind in society: The development of higher psychological processes.* Cambridge, MA: Harvard University Press.

Young, S. (2002). Young children's spontaneous vocalizations in free-play: Observations of two- to three-year-olds in a day-care setting. *Bulletin of the Council for Research in Music Education, 152,* 43–53.

NOTE

This study is part of the author's dissertation, "Ah-eee-ah-eee-yah-eee, Bum, and Pop, Pop, Pop: Teacher Initiatives, Teacher Silence, and Children's Vocal Responses in Early Childhood Music Classes" (UMI No. 3189669).

Chapter Five

The Incorporation of Principles of the Reggio Emilia Approach in a North American Preschool Music Curriculum

Amanda Page Smith

The experiences of children in two preschool classes in a music curriculum that incorporated principles of the Reggio Emilia approach were examined in this study. Video recordings, transcriptions of child compositions, and field notes were analyzed through the lens of Reggio principles. Findings demonstrated that light and shadow play, two features frequently used in the schools of Reggio Emilia, enabled the children to make discoveries, empowered them to create their own learning experiences, and gave them agency over their learning and the learning of their classmates. Group composition provided a musical equivalent to the creation of murals in the visual arts domain of Reggio Emilia and enabled children to communicate musically in an expressive way. Reflective video documentation gave rise to the children as co-researchers. Age-based implications for the implementation of the Reggio approach were found to exist for music instruction.

The municipal schools in the town of Reggio Emilia in northern Italy serve as a model for progressive early childhood centers throughout the world. Hailed as the most avant-garde preschools in the world (Kantrowitz and Wingert, 1991), the schools of Reggio Emilia, Italy, are centered on the "hundred languages of children," acknowledging that all children possess multiple intelligences and multiple modes of communication and expression. The grounding vision of the Reggio Emilia approach "is based on the image of a child who has great potential for development and is the subject of rights, a child who learns and grows in relation with others, through the hundred languages of doing, being, reflecting, and knowing" (North American Reggio Emilia Alliance [NAREA], 2008).

The child is the protagonist in the Reggio Emilia approach. Learning is child-centered, and the teacher plays the role of partner or co-researcher

79

with the child. The focus is on the child's competencies rather than the child's deficiencies. The thorough and creative documentation serves as a central means of communication between the child, the teacher, and the community. In Reggio schools, the environment acts as a third teacher, meaning that the space that children, teachers, and parents create for the child's learning has significant impact on the child's work. To this effect, the schools are built with many windows to allow light to flood the learning space and shelves to creatively display objects for the children to use as tools. Many preschools in North America adopt the Reggio approach, as is shown through the large membership of schools in the North American Reggio Emilia Alliance (NAREA, 2008). Music is a vibrant feature of the schools in Reggio Emilia. However, based on publications on Reggio Emilia and my study visit to the Reggio schools, the element of music education most present in the approach is discovery[1]; there is little to no focus on musical skill building or performance. None of the municipal schools of Reggio Emilia employ a music teacher, though several *atelieristas* are employed in each school. The role of the Reggio atelierista is to prepare materials for visual arts projects, to collaborate with teachers, to work with children on their visual art projects, and to display the products and processes of the children's work for the children, teachers, and the community to enjoy. In Reggio, there is not a musical equivalent to the atelierista. Upon visiting the Reggio schools, I queried, "If discovery is the only element of music given priority in the Reggio schools, how will the children develop the skills of producing pitch and rhythm to use as tools to further discover, make, and compose music?"

RESEARCH QUESTIONS

With this overarching question in mind, I set out to examine the role of music in a North American preschool that has adopted the Reggio Emilia approach and the ways in which a traditional preschool music curriculum might be modified to incorporate elements of the Reggio Emilia philosophy. Given the varying degrees to which the Reggio Emilia philosophy can be incorporated into a North American preschool curriculum, and the broad spectrum through which the child's experience can be interpreted, a qualitative research design was appropriate for this investigation.

Two questions framed this study:

1. In what ways can key principles of the Reggio Emilia philosophy be incorporated into an American preschool music curriculum?

2. In what ways is the musical learning of a preschool child affected when a music curriculum is altered to incorporate elements of the Reggio Emilia philosophy?

GROUNDING LITERATURE

This study was informed by the findings of advocates for early childhood music education. The findings of Smith (1963), Sergeant and Roche (1973), Cohen and Baird (1990), and Rutkowski (1996) show that voice and ear training are beneficial for three- and four-year-old children. Levinowitz and colleagues (1998) found that the number of New Jersey elementary students who can sing in tune has dropped 33 percent over the last twenty years, leading her to conclude that children's musical interests should be supported in the early years in order to flourish (Hoffman, 2008).

Additionally, this study is grounded in Moorhead and Pond's (1978) studies on the spontaneous music making of children during the 1930s and 1940s. Through extensive observation of young children in a naturalistic context, Pond determined that young children's musical experiences are primarily based on the discovery of sound, and that social, environmental, and procedural conditions for children's music making should be carefully planned and observed. Further, Burton (2002) demonstrated that the spontaneous songs of young children are reflections of the child's capacity to organize musical ideas in relationship to her surrounding environments.

Based on the work of Edwards, Gandini, and Forman (1998), Malaguzzi (1998), and the NAREA (2008), the following principles of the Reggio Emilia approach have further focused this study:

1. *The child as the creator of his/her own learning.* In Reggio schools curriculum is driven by the interests of the children.
2. *The child and adult as researchers.* Rather than a prescribed lesson in which information transfers from the adult to the child, children and teachers work together to answer questions that arise through project work. Additionally, the teachers are constantly learning and evaluating as they determine where the curriculum will go based on the children's curiosities.
3. *The environment as the third teacher.* The space that children, teachers, and parents create for the child's learning has significant impact on the child's work.
4. *Documentation as communication.* Teachers creatively document the process of learning through photographs, captions, collages, and other types of visual displays.

5. *The one hundred expressive languages of children.* In the Reggio approach, it is said that children learn and communicate in one hundred expressive languages.
6. *The dialogue between child and adult.* The ongoing discourse between the child and the teacher creates a learning environment in which the children and the teacher both have input in the learning process. When the children and teacher dialogue together, whether it is spoken or another kind of expressive interaction, the teacher can also assess the value and success of the learning.
7. *Collaborative work.* Rather than focus on individual work, the Reggio approach favors collaborative projects, such as the creation of murals in the visual arts domain.

American music educators such as Andress (1998), Matthews (2000), Crisp (2007), and Crisp and Caldwell (2007) have examined opportunities for connections between music education and the Reggio approach. Andress (1998) looked to project-based music lessons as a model for this partnership and created a web of exploration based on the initiatives of the children in her class. Matthews (2000) discussed some of the challenges of approaching music education in a Reggio-influenced school environment. She considered how children "acquire" music and asked how "the student could *be* musical rather than become musical" (Matthews, 2000, p. 21). Matthews created opportunities for children to *mess around* with instruments on their own initiative, and she documented music learning by audio-recording and transcribing the children's music. Crisp (2007) combined Orff Schulwerk with the Reggio Emilia approach and contributed lesson plans as a starting point for music educators who sought to weave the two together. Crisp's lessons, *Exploring Barred Instruments with the Young Child: Lessons 1 and 2* (Crisp and Caldwell, 2007), were used in this study and will be discussed subsequently.

METHODOLOGY

Participants

Between January 21 and March 11, 2009, the children of two preschool music classes at a private school in Manhattan, New York, participated in a study that integrated elements of the Reggio Emilia early childhood approach with a traditional preschool music curriculum. With Human Subjects approval from the host school, 2 South (a class of four-and-a-half- and five-year-olds) and 3 North (a class of three-and-a-half- and four-year-olds) participated in the study. 2 South came to music class in half groups of eleven children, each half attending one thirty-minute class each week. 3 North met in a full group of fourteen children, which attended music class twice per week for thirty minutes. During the study, there were two music class periods in which the 3 North children came in half groups for fifteen minutes each.

In this study, I, the researcher, served as the music instructor and sole collector of data. I am the only music teacher at the school, and I typically teach twenty-one thirty-minute preschool music and movement classes per week. I am responsible for the design of the music and movement curriculum and lesson plans at the school; thus, the curriculum could be modified as needed for the two participating classes in order to serve the study. I also direct a graded church choir program in the same building, in which several of the children in the study classes participated. The church choirs, however, did not participate in the study.

Design and Procedure

I designed two curricula incorporating principles of the Reggio Emilia approach to early childhood education, one for each study class, in anticipation of developmental variances between the class of threes and fours and the class of fours and fives, as well as to compliment the curricular themes in the two different classrooms. The following data were collected to account for multiple perspectives: fourteen digital video-recordings of complete music class meetings, verbatim transcriptions of those video-recordings, transcriptions of three songs spontaneously composed by children, journal notes, field notes, interviews with children and one teacher, twenty photographs, and two edited videos. I analyzed the data during and after their collection. The act of carefully transcribing video footage of children, as well as interviewing the children and one teacher, provided a triangulated perspective of the data (Merriam, 1998) centering on the learning that the participants experienced (Creswell, 2009).

Trustworthiness

In this study, I used *differing perspectives*, defined by Creswell (2003) as the presentation of material that is contrary to themes presented. I considered the perspectives of Pond (1980) on the spontaneous music making of young children, and Becker (1986) and Oehrle (1991) on multicultural views of music making in an attempt to control for my own bias toward traditional Western music education. Additionally, I used *interpretive validity*, defined by Johnson (1997) as the ability of the researcher to understand and represent the attitudes and feelings of the participants in regard to the subject of the research. To achieve this, I transcribed fourteen video-recorded lessons and interpreted the data in ways that revealed the scope and breadth of the participants' experience.

Creswell (2009) points out that a researcher's *prolonged time* in a field gives validity to the study by the fact that the researcher has long-ranging perspective on the study subjects. Because I worked with the children for as many as two and a half years prior to the study and two months after the study, prolonged time in the field supports the validity in this study.

Analysis triangulation supports the trustworthiness of this study. Fourteen classes were video-recorded and transcribed verbatim. A colleague from the University of Chicago, who has a background in music performance and social work, served as an *external auditor*, which is defined by Creswell (2009) as a person "not familiar with the researcher or the project and [who] can provide an objective assessment of the project throughout the process of research or at the conclusion of the study" (p. 192). The auditor reviewed the data and verified that the codes were identified and interpreted in an appropriate way, and that they were relevant to the data collected. Additionally, the head teacher of the 3 North class performed a *member check*, which Merriam (1998) defines as taking the data and study information back to participants to confirm that the data are accurate and the interpretations are plausible. She verified that the data and its interpretations were congruent with her observations during the study.

Here, I will present an overview of the implementation of the Reggio-influenced curricula through a description of two representative projects.

Project One: 2 South

The older of the two participant classes was 2 South. This group of children was engaged and excited by the project work and the collaboration embedded in the study curriculum. Their project stemmed from a pair of lessons created by Crisp (2007) in which flashlights visually guide children through the space of the room. Later, the children transfer the movement that they use following the flashlight to finger movement on barred Orff instruments and, utilizing Magorian's (1999) poem "Night Lights," create a culminating performance that combines the spoken word, the light of the flashlights, and Orff instruments. The 2 South music lessons began with Crisp's lesson. Using the flashlights and Orff instruments, the class created a vocabulary of instrument play relating to the light's action. Children took turns using the flashlight to guide their peers as they played the instruments, acting as conductors. At this point, the project strayed from Crisp's lessons; I chose to use a different poem than Crisp suggested—one from the Siegen-Smith (1999) collection titled "Fireflies," which was written by Weil (1999).

The topic of fireflies in the poem sparked creative movement and composition in the 2 South children. I hung a scrim made from a semi-sheer curtain secured to a curtain rod in front of a small stage. Behind it, I placed a flood lamp, creating what the Reggio educators call a *provocation* for the children—the presentation of carefully selected materials and the invitation for the children to determine their use. The children explored the scrim and determined many creative ways to use it. When I asked how we could use the scrim, Benjamin said, "Lightning bugs? Pretend the flashlight's the back of the lightning bug." Amanda said, "We could turn off the lights and then somebody could go behind there and point it behind the cloth where the lightning bugs are flying." Greg got excited, saying, "Let's do that!"

In later classes, I invited the children to create a melody to accompany "Fireflies." With prompting, two children sang their ideas to me for the first and last phrases of the poem. I video-recorded this session so that I could play back their ideas, both on that day for the children to hear and later on my own in order to transcribe their compositions. To draw out the children who were not putting forth ideas for a melody, I invited each child to sit behind a barred instrument and choose notes to accompany the middle phrase, "you could read secrets under your blanket." One child carefully played the ten syllables of the middle phrase between two different bars, and this became our second phrase. The class sang their composed song together. Before the next class, I transcribed the song on staff paper so that the children could see that they had created a real composition. I reminded them of the melody, and together we practiced the song.

To bring the project to fruition, I encouraged the class to create a performance that included the singing of our song, the playing of Orff instruments, and a "play" behind the scrim. Each child took on a specific role: singer, conductor, instrumentalist, actor-playing-a-firefly, or actor-playing-a-firefly-catcher. Together, we determined a sequence for the performance and practiced it. In the final class, the children performed the piece as rehearsed for the video camera instead of a live audience. The video performance was posted on the school's website for the children and parents to view, serving as a source of documentation.

Project Two: 3 North

The 3 North class was comprised of fourteen very eager three- and four-year-olds. Their study turned out to be less of a continuous project than the 2 South study because the children were not initiating project work the way that the older children in 2 South were. Instead, I tried various approaches to weaving Reggio-inspired elements—such as composition, light exploration, and documentation—into what had been a more typical early childhood music context. The study began with an exploration of shadows. I shined a light projector against a blank wall with the lights in the room turned off and invited the children to "find their shadows." After time for shadow discovery, I guided the children in exploratory movement. They made shadows to resemble birds and connected the experience by casting bird shadows on the wall while actively listening to a recording of Saint-Saëns's *Carnival of the Animals*.

Following this activity, I invited the children to create songs about birds. Several children composed songs spontaneously, and I recorded them on digital video. Throughout the study, I sought opportunities to follow the children's interests and to see if their ideas would take us in the direction of Reggio-like project learning. However, I found that this type of collaboration was difficult for children so young. Instead, I focused on documenting music lessons as a means of combining the Reggio principle of documentation with early childhood music education. Documentation in the Reggio approach is a visually based depiction of the process of learning. This type of documentation proves to be problematic in the case of music, which is abstract, multisensory, and intangible. To address the need for sound and motion in documentation, I video-recorded most lessons and transcribed three songs that were composed by individual children. Experimenting with a process that came about in a discussion with Suzanne Burton on February 18, 2009, I used iMovie to edit one of the lessons into a fourteen-minute film and then invited the children to watch. The children enjoyed watching themselves and their friends on film. As they watched, I recorded all of their comments. Among many comments from the children, Rajiv said, "That's me!" Wendy asked, "Where's me?" Ellie said, "You'll just have to wait and see, right, Mrs. Smith?" While watching footage of the children making shadows, Oliver noticed, "Brent just bumped Ellie's shadow."

After transcribing their comments about the film, I edited their comments into the video as subtitles at the moments in which they were spoken. I also posted a description of one of the study's *Carnival of the Animals* lessons on the school's website, along with pictures of the lesson. The edited video was presented on the school website along with the performance video of the 2 South class's culminating experience. This new form of documentation captured the process of the children's learning: their experiences and comments, and shared their competencies with the community, aligning well with the principles of Reggio Emilia.

THEMES

Through this study, I sought to explore the ways in which key principles of the Reggio Emilia philosophy could be incorporated into an American preschool curriculum, and to examine the ways in which the musical learning of preschool children was affected by the incorporation of this philosophy into a music curriculum. Whereas findings from qualitative research are not generalizable, findings from this study may have features of transferability.

Developmental Differences between Age Groups

Because of important differences in the development of children aged three to five years, I found that the degree to which the Reggio philosophy might be incorporated into a music classroom could vary widely. Many of the Reggio principles, including the *child as the creator of his own learning*, the *child and adult as researchers*, the *dialogue between child and adult*, and *collaborative work*, imply a significant degree of collaboration and self-regulation on the part of the child. Therefore, I experienced more success developing emergent curriculum and project work with the older of the two study classes.

Project work proved to be a challenge with the 3 North group of three- and four-year-old children in their first year of formal schooling. While Helm and Katz (2001) found that children as young as three are capable of engaging in meaningful project work, Katz and Chard (1994) assert that the social and emotional development involved in many aspects of project work may not progress at a rapid rate in children until the age of four or older. I found that foundational music experiences and discovery-based learning were more appropriate for the three- and four-year-old age group.

However, the group of four- and five-year-old children in the 2 South class had success in a curriculum that called for collaboration with the teacher and with other children. They were able to listen and dialogue, and were responsive to the needs of the group. For the younger children in 3 North, building a foundation for discussion, exploration, collaboration, respect, and research may enable them to more successfully participate in Reggio-influenced experiences when they are four and five years old.

Environment as the Third Teacher

The incorporation of shadow play and light play honors the Reggio principle that the *environment serves as the third teacher*. The aesthetic draw of shadow and light play helped me to create an environment that was engaging, inspiring children's creativity. These forms of play provided the children with opportunities to discover, study, and construct their own understandings about movement, space, and light, thus enabling them to act as agents of their own learning. This finding is supported by Bruner (1991), who observed that learning does not occur in isolation, but within social and environmental contexts. Shadow play and light play, by their nature, occur in a social context that additionally aids in the child's learning experience. Vygotsky (1986) observed that children's learning is enhanced by collaboration with skilled peers. Collective creative movement in the context of shadow play served as another mode of expression honoring the *hundred languages of children* in the Reggio Emilia approach.

Composition

For the children of 2 South and 3 North, composition served as one of *the hundred languages of children* by acting as a mode of expression that was different from speech, movement, or visual communication. Musical composition in the music classroom provided an opportunity for the children to take ownership of their musical learning. In this study, the fact that the children's spontaneous song creations possessed meter, mode, and text showed that they had internalized Western musical form. This is supported by Burton (2002), who found that young children's spontaneous songs were informed by their environments. By being given the opportunity to create their own music, the children were enabled to be the creators of their own learning. Additionally, composition in this context allowed me, the teacher, to act as a researcher. By analyzing the children's compositions, I could assess their musical understanding and learn more about the children's musical development.

Compositional expression was also achieved in the study through creative movement in dance and shadow play, in which the children were the creators of their own learning. Additionally, group composition united the children of the 2 South class, demonstrating the collective expressive competencies of a class. In this way, group composition could be considered the musical equivalent of the visual art mural: a commonly used form of group-work in the Reggio culture.

Video Documentation

Video documentation of music classes served Reggio principles by making the competencies of the children known to the community and by providing the opportunity for the children and the teacher to be researchers. Because the visual arts are prominent in Reggio schools, visual documentation is prominent. Due to the multisensory nature of music and movement, visual documentation is not sufficient for the recording and sharing of musical experiences. In this digital age, video documentation is not only possible, it is accessible, and many avenues for sharing video documentation are now available. Using video documentation in this study, I was able to examine the spontaneous songs of the children and transcribe them. Audio documentation could also be used for this purpose.

However, video documentation allowed for the addition of sight, enabling me to know which child was singing and to observe and study nonverbal expressions of the child composer and those children who were listening. Video documentation allowed the children to act as researchers as they watched themselves and made comments about their understanding of their participation. Showing footage of the children *to* the children themselves and allowing them time to reflect on it provided an additional layer of documentation to the children regarding their own work. Vygotsky (1986) demonstrates the value of providing a scaffold within the zone of proximal development in which the child may construct understanding. In the present study, the video of the children in their music class provided a structure through which the children could understand their learning and build on it.

The 2 South class created a multifaceted performance around the topic of Weil's poem "Fireflies" in which the children played instruments, sang an original composition, and created a shadow play behind a scrim. Rather than share this performance with a live audience, which may have added a degree of pressure to the experience, disrupting the emergent process, and which would have been a challenge because of space issues with the instruments and the scrim, the performance was video-recorded. These videos, which could be viewed on the school website, enabled parents to see the process of their children's musical learning, as well as to appreciate their children's creative competencies through performance.

DISCUSSION AND IMPLICATIONS

Documentation

Video and Internet documentation served as an effective way to display the process of music learning and make the children's competencies known. For young children ages three and four, video or audio recording of spontaneous singing proved to be a successful way to incorporate composition into the class. In a typical preschool music context, these songs may be transcribed and later sung to the children to validate their work and to lead to further learning. Children ages five and older were able to begin group composition with my facilitation. These children were capable of considering the contributions of others and were able to build on each other's creative ideas. As a facilitator, the music teacher in a typical preschool music class could begin with a simple text, such as a short poem, and ask the children to offer ideas of how the text could be sung. The teacher could record or quickly notate the children's musical phrases and make decisions about which fragments would work together.

The Music Atelierista

The implementation of a music curriculum that incorporates elements of the Reggio Emilia approach could require a time commitment far greater than that required for a traditional preschool music program. Some preschool music teachers lead as many as ten different classes of children per week. Creating the opportunity for an emergent curriculum implies a significant amount of preparation and follow-up for the music teacher. By nature, each class's emergent curriculum will be different based on where the children decide to take their project. For each class, the music teacher would need to discuss project opportunities with each head teacher prior to the start of the curriculum, and the music teacher would need to follow up with those head teachers as determined by the nature of the project. Depending on the direction of the project, the music teacher may also need to do significant preparatory work and research to find and provide the necessary materials to implement the project.

A great deal of time is involved in organizing the process of video-recording, observing the videos of students, organizing the video material, transcribing compositions, and editing clips for documentation purposes. The process of documentation alone could easily double a music teacher's preparatory time. Though extremely worthwhile, the integration of concepts of the Reggio Emilia approach warrants consideration of the realities of its application in the North American preschool.

One solution to this dilemma might be to create a position for a *music atelierista* to support the work of the music teacher. Similarly to the atelierista in the Reggio schools, who works with small groups of children in an art studio, a music atelierista would work with small groups of children in their classroom or in the music room. The atelierista would supplement the group music experience. This may provide a way for children to shape the direction of their own learning without having to compete for a chance to contribute among a large number of classmates. This approach would be more individualized, allowing children with less dominant personalities to determine the direction of their learning without being swayed by the teacher or peers. A music atelierista could also take part in communicating with classroom teachers about project work, and organizing and creating documentation. An ideal music atelierista would be a teacher trained in music with the capability to guide children in the development of their musical skills, one who also has the capacity to prepare and organize multimedia documentation.

IMPLICATIONS FOR FURTHER RESEARCH

Because of the musical value of early childhood music education and the popularity and success of the Reggio Emilia approach to early childhood education, further research on the relationship between the two would be valuable for the early childhood education community. Topics for further research might include the following: (a) the developmental appropriateness of collaborative music making among different ages of preschool children as it relates to the Reggio approach, (b) the impact of a Reggio-inspired music curriculum in various socioeconomic cultures, (c) the effect of empowering and facilitating children to take responsibility for the documentation of a Reggio-inspired music curriculum, (d) assessment of children's musical development prior to and after their immersion in Reggio-inspired music curriculum, and (e) an examination of the value of musical documentation for classroom teachers and parents.

CONCLUSION

Within the one hundred languages of children, music holds a prominent place. A vehicle for children's self-expression, discovery, experimentation, research, collaboration, reflection, and for their doing, being, and knowing, music as taught in North American preschools can be inspired and informed by the Reggio Emilia approach. As Sergio Spaggiari (2007), director of Early Childhood Education for Reggio, said, "You don't begin to build a building on the sixth floor. Similarly, you wouldn't teach children without giving them a strong educational foundation in the first six years." Children deserve a rich foundation in musical education during the valuable years of early childhood, and the influence of Reggio Emilia on that education can lead to learning that is filled with great beauty and meaning.

REFERENCES

Andress, B. (1998). Where's the music in "the hundred languages of children?" *General Music Today, 11*(3), 14–17.

Becker, J. (1986). Is western art music superior? *Musical Quarterly, 72*(3), 341–59.

Bruner, J. (1991). The narrative construction of reality. *Critical Inquiry, 18*(1), 1–21.

Burton, S. (2002). An exploration of preschool children's spontaneous songs and chants. *Visions of Research in Music Education, 2*. Retrieved from www-usr.rider.edu/~vrme/v2n1/index.htm.

Cohen, A. J., and Baird, K. (1990). Acquisition of absolute pitch: The question of critical periods. *Psychomusicology, 9*(1), 31–37.

Creswell, J. W. (2003). *Research design: Qualitative, quantitative, and mixed methods approaches* (2nd ed.). Thousand Oaks, CA: Sage.

Creswell, J. W. (2009). *Research design: Qualitative, quantitative, and mixed methods approaches* (3rd ed.). Thousand Oaks, CA: Sage.

Crisp, B. (2007). *Exploring our roots, expanding our future: Exploring barred instruments with the young child* (Vol. 2). Retrieved from www.mmbmusic.com.

Crisp, B., and Caldwell, L. (2007). Orff-Schulwerk and the Reggio approaches are interwoven successfully. *The Orff Echo, 39*(3), 26–30.

Edwards, C., Gandini, L., and Forman, G. (1998). Introduction: Background and starting points. In *The hundred languages of children: The Reggio Emilia approach; Advanced reflections* (2nd ed., pp. 5–26). Greenwich, CT: Ablex.

Helm, J. H., and Katz, L. (2001). *Young investigators: The project approach in the early years.* New York: Teachers College Press.

Hoffman, S. (2008). *Music Together as a research-based program.* Retrieved from www.musictogether.com.

Johnson, R. B. (1997). Examining the validity structure of qualitative research. *Education, 118*(3), 282–92.

Kantrowitz, B., and Wingert, P. (1991). The best schools in the world. *Newsweek* [Online]. Retrieved from www.newsweek.com.

Katz, L., and Chard, S. (1994). *Engaging children's minds: The project approach.* Norwood, NJ: Ablex.

Levinowitz, L. M., Barnes, P., Guerrini, S., Clement, M., D'April, P., and Morey, J. M. (1998). Measuring singing voice development in the elementary general music classroom. *Journal of Research in Music Education, 46*(1), 35–47.

Magorian, M. (1999). Nightlights. In N. Siegen-Smith (Ed.), *A pocketful of stars: Poems about the night.* New York: Barefoot Books.

Malaguzzi, L. (1998). History, ideas, and basic philosophy. In C. Edwards (Ed.), *The hundred languages of children: The Reggio Emilia approach; Advanced reflections* (2nd ed., pp. 49–97). Greenwich, CT: Ablex.

Matthews, C. L. (2000). No known destination: Pre-primary music and Reggio Emilia. In *Spotlight on early childhood music education* (pp. 20–22). Reston, VA: MENC.

Merriam, S. B. (1998). *Qualitative research and case study applications in education.* San Francisco, CA: Jossey-Bass.

Moorhead, G. E., and Pond, D. (1978). *Music of young children.* Santa Barbara, CA: Pillsbury Foundation for Advancement of Music Education.

North American Reggio Emilia Alliance. Home page. (2008). Retrieved from www.reggioalliance.org.

Oehrle, E. (1991). An introduction to African views of music making. *Journal of Aesthetic Education, 25*(3), 163–74.

Pond, D. (1980). The young child's playful world of sound. *Music Educators Journal, 66*(7), 38–41.

Rutkowski, J. (1996). The effectiveness of individual/small-group singing activities on Kindergarteners' use of singing voice and developmental music aptitude. *Journal of Research in Music Education, 44*(4), 353–68.

Sergeant, D. C., and Roche, S. (1973). Perceptual shifts in the auditory information processing of young children. *Psychology of Music, 1*(1), 39–48.

Siegen-Smith, N. (Ed.). (1999). *A pocketful of stars: Poems about the night.* New York: Barefoot Books.

Smith, R. B. (1963). The effect of group vocal training on the singing ability of nursery school children. *Journal of Research in Music Education, 11*, 137–41.

Spaggiari, S. (2007, March 26). Reggio for childhood and education. Lecture presented at the Center Loris Malaguzzi, Reggio Emilia, Italy.

Vygotsky, L. S. (1986). *Thought and language* (2nd ed.). Cambridge, MA: MIT Press.

Weil, Z. (1999). Fireflies. In N. Siegen-Smith (Ed.), *A pocketful of stars: Poems about the night*. New York: Barefoot Books.

NOTE

1. The researcher defines music discovery as the experience of music from the natural impulse of the child without the imposition of formal structure, musical skills, or group singing.

Chapter Six

The Importance of Parents in Early Childhood Music Program Evaluation

Shelly Cooper and Audrey Berger Cardany

The underlying goal of this study was to examine if an early childhood music program was aligned with its basic goals—outlined by the program's creators—so that instruction could be improved to better serve the needs of the children and parents attending the program. Using data from a parent survey, the authors examined parents' perspectives regarding the program that included (a) program and instructor, (b) free play, (c) group activities, (d) song starters, (e) resource pages, and (f) student observers and interns. In addition to providing basic demographic information, parents' perspectives on the program were sought through an invitation to respond to open-ended comments or to make suggestions regarding the program.

Questions regarding the overall attitude toward the program resulted in high scores—evidence that the program was successful in reaching families. Free play was ranked higher by the parents of the younger children (ages two and three). Parents' answers to questions regarding group activities suggest that music teachers should consider planning for and providing materials for free musical play, as well as providing adults with guidelines regarding what to expect from their children. Open-ended responses revealed that parents witnessed the benefit of music experiences in themselves and their children. This survey addressed the unique aspects of music learning in early childhood, particularly regarding the role of parents and adults. The authors note that curricular change and refinement will not occur without ongoing program assessments.

Assessment is an integral component of teaching and learning. Because of the developmental nature of how young children learn and their limited ability to reflect on their work, assessment of early childhood music learning often is linked to program evaluation. Thus, adults, particularly parents and teachers, must interpret children's music behaviors and learning outcomes (Rauscher,

95

2000, p. 49). To that end, the researchers of this study evaluated the early childhood music program *Musical Play at the UA* through a parent survey.

PROGRAM EVALUATION

Program evaluation provides integral data on a specific program; yet few examples of school music program evaluations exist (Colwell, 2002). School music program evaluations consist of regular assessment that provides evidence to shape instruction, satisfy accountability requirements, and provide progress to parents (Radocy and Boyle, 1987). Steps for music program evaluation outlined by Bates (1985) include articulating program objectives, collecting relevant data, interpreting data, and implementing steps for improvement. The central aim of a school music program evaluation is improving the program through use of assessments of student music learning outcomes. "The controlling idea underlying the entire program is the development of musicianship and musical responsiveness" (Bates, 1985, p. 24).

Evaluating Early Childhood Music Programs

The evaluation of a music program for young children must not be confined to music learning outcomes because of the holistic nature of young children's learning. Children between the ages of two and five operate in what Gordon (2003) describes as the developmental music aptitude period. "Music aptitude is a measure of children's potential to learn music; it represents 'inner possibilities'" (p. 13). "A preplanned scope and sequence does not mean the imposition of a rigid program on these children; rather, the sequence must reflect a carefully thought out, interactive approach that involves much free-choice play. As we plan we must know that one never arrives at the perfect curriculum model, for constant change and refinement are the very nature of curriculum" (Andress, 1989, p. 27). Berger and Cooper (2003) agree with Andress and suggest "continually aligning and adjusting teaching actions to the process; consistently assessing current curriculum, classroom environment, and student needs; and providing ample and appropriate opportunities for free musical play" (p. 163). A music educator must make a conscious decision every time a song or movement activity is presented.

Curricular change and refinement will not occur without ongoing program assessments. "Sound assessment of young children is challenging because they develop and learn in ways that are characteristically uneven and embedded within the specific cultural and linguistic contexts in which they live" (Copple and Bredekamp, 2009, p. 22). Input from families, therefore, is essential for assessing children's progress, even though assessment of young children may rely heavily on narrative observations of children, assessment of developmental music aptitude, and collections of children's representative work. "Teachers solicit parents' knowledge about children's learning and developmental progress and incorporate this information into ongoing assessment and evaluation strategies" (p. 176). Developmentally appropriate practice for assessing young children's learning must include parental participation.

The National Association for the Education of Young Children (NAEYC) promotes what Copple and Bredekamp (2009) identify as "and/both thinking" (p. 49). Instead of limiting choices by arguing either one approach or the other, program directors must recognize the complexity and interrelationship of early childhood practice, and therefore challenges are best addressed by adopting and/both thinking. Consequently, teachers should evaluate a child's individual progress and study musical outcomes as a result of music experiences and instruction, *and* should study the parents' perceptions of their children's progress and success in music settings that include aspects of meeting children's social and emotional needs. Surveying parents is a valid evaluation tool, serving as an "unobtrusive measure that does not call for the direct attention and cooperation of the student" (Boyle, 1989, p. 24). This study aligns with one of the core values of the NAEYC's work by recognizing the need for "reciprocal relationships between practitioners and families," as through the creation of these "collaborative partnerships with families" practitioners can better understand the children's progress and development (Copple and Bredekamp, 2009, p. 23).

Lehman (1989) notes that "the curriculum, the schedule, the quality and quantity of instructional materials and equipment, and the facilities all contribute in important ways to program quality" (p. 26). Parent scrutiny of these program environmental aspects remains of particular importance due to the relationship between children's developmental music aptitudes and their participation in a rich musical environment. "The sooner children begin to enjoy a rich music environment, the sooner their music aptitude will begin to move upward toward its birth level, and the closer it will come to reaching and remaining at that level throughout life" (Gordon, 2003, p. 14).

The program objectives for *Musical Play at the UA* include enhancing children's music learning in an indirect and developmentally appropriate manner and were outlined at the inception of the early childhood music program (2001/2002). Objectives include (a) reaching families, (b) following children's skill development, (c) meeting children's and parents' musical needs, and (d) encouraging and facilitating at-home music making (Berger and Cooper, 2003).[1] Reaching families is a stated goal based on the accepted premise of parents as essential to the young child's learning process. NAEYC promotes the building of "reciprocal relationships with families" through mutual respect, collaborations, and parents serving in decision-making roles (Copple and Bredekamp, 2009, p. 23). "For children, the teachings of their parents will always be core" (Pestalozzi, 1974, p. 26). Vygotsky (1987) recognized the child's need for adult assistance in his articulation of a *zone of proximal development* (ZPD), which included the child's developmental functions that cannot yet be accomplished without the aid of others. Gordon (2003) highlighted the importance of parents in the music learning of young children, stating that "the home is the most important school that young children will ever know, and children's parents are the most important teachers they will ever have" (p. 3). In addition, many researchers recognize the influence of home environment on children's music aptitude (Brand, 1985; Kirkpatrick, 1962; Mallett, 2000; Marjoribanks and Mboya, 2004; Reynolds, 1960; Thames, 1979).

Music experiences in early childhood lay the foundation for later music learning. As parents witness children's enjoyment with music and interest in music experiences, they may become impelled to provide quality music experiences (Cardany, 2004). Custodero and Johnson-Green (2003) noted that parents' past music experiences influence how and what musical experiences they provide for their children. Guerrini (2005) stated that parental motivation to provide a rich musical environment likely does not depend on parents' music aptitude, but results "because of parents' own emotional response to things musical; that is, that they enjoy music and are affected by it in a positive manner" (p. 32).

The musical experiences provided in early childhood music programs have far-reaching effects on how parents and other adults in attendance interact with young children. Therefore, it makes sense to (a) include parents in early childhood music programs, (b) assess how well the parents' musical needs are being met, and (c) evaluate the program's effectiveness in *sending music home.*

De Grätzer (1999) studied *Playing Music with Mum or Dad*, a music program for parents and their three-year-old children in Argentina, and found that parent and child communication was enhanced through participation in the program. Through the program evaluation, it became clear that music teachers had difficulty helping parents support and participate in their children's music learning, and de Grätzer concluded that young children needed an adult's help to acquire necessary skills in music. "If the adult in question is the only music teacher, there is not much parents can do to give certain continuity to the musical activity at home, since they are not completely familiar with the repertoire of games and songs used in the classroom"

(p. 48). De Grätzer recognized the parents as "very alert to their own musical development" (p. 60), and that adults learned to reverse their negative experiences concerning music learning in the past as a result of attending the music classes with their children.

Sichivitsa (2007), in a study of students' motivation in music, stated that, if parents value music, they would be more likely to support their children's music education in the future. In additon, deVries (2009) surveyed parents of children ages five and under enrolled in preschools and found a lack of parental knowledge about music. Parents also reported a "lack of time to engage in music-making on a regular basis" (p. 395). When parents and children learn songs together and interact with adults in guided and free musical experiences, those kinds of musical expressions and engagements are less likely to remain "what we do in music class" and may find their place in everyday parent-child interactions and children's free play at home. It follows, then, that a program goal for an early childhood music program should include sending music home.

Using content analysis, Sims and Udtaisuk (2008) studied the music content in three parenting magazines in the United States. They found limited music-specific content and noted, "[T]here was little in these magazines to inform or motivate parents to provide the truly rich musical home environment that music educators seek to encourage" (p. 23). They stated that the messages parents receive in these magazines about music for their children are primarily utilitarian, with little mention of children's music development.

The parent survey of the program *Musical Play at the UA* is an essential assessment component of this program's evaluation because of parents' vital role in children's music learning, their provision of a rich musical environment, and their role as observers and interpreters of children's music making. This parental survey of *Musical Play*'s alignment to its articulated goals addresses these unique aspects of music learning in early childhood. Since the program had functioned at its current location for more than two years, an evaluation of this type was deemed necessary to examine whether the program was fulfilling—from the parents' perspectives—the four key elements as articulated by the program creators.

Musical Play at the UA Program Overview

The mission of the *Musical Play at the UA* program states:

> The *Musical Play* program is designed to assist children ages 2 to 5 and their parents. The program creators sought to help families build a repertoire of songs and activities for everyday living and to encourage musical play at home. The program includes developmentally appropriate songs, materials, and activities

and incorporates a wide variety of topics, presentations, and interactions. The songs and activities presented contribute to the well being of children, both cognitively and emotionally. Music centers form a basis of the program, as the program was designed to incorporate musical free play. The centers are the vehicles for engaging children in thinking and playing with music. Through these centers, parents may learn new ways to play musically with their children. The child's acquisition of musical skills, within this rich environment, empowers and enhances personal and musical expression, as well as aids in language acquisition and coordination development. (Cooper and Cardany, 2008, p. 4)

During each session of the program, children and parents attend ten weekly forty-five-minute classes. The classes are designed to accommodate the needs of various age groups (such as children ages two to three and children ages four to five), although at times an older or younger sibling will attend a different age class for parental convenience. The classes are formatted to follow a four-part structure: (a) opening free play, (b) guided group activities, (c) free play, and (d) guided group activities.

Undergraduate students—two or three per session—have opportunities to intern during the classes. Their involvement includes interacting with parents and children, setting up the classroom environment, and assisting with distributing materials during class (scarves, drums, bells, and so forth). Within the study period, a few interns led activities during group instruction. In addition to the interns being present in the classes, it is common to have one or two music education students observe a class from the perimeter of the room as part of their undergraduate methods course requirements.

Free Musical Play

Music educators and early childhood educators recognize the importance of play and its ability to influence child development (Berger and Cooper, 2003; Ellis, 1973; Singer, 1973; Vygotsky, 1987; White, 1959), but when immersed in a playful music environment, what do parents think? Taggart (2000) states that "even within group activities, children must be allowed to listen, watch, and musically explore as they wish" (p. 24) and suggests that the aspects of free musical play enhance group activities. But do parents understand the importance of musical exploration? Addison (1990) posits that if our teaching methods "are made accessible and attractive, we shall carry our parents with us" (p. 141). This illuminates the need for instructional effectiveness, student engagement, and parent-teacher communication to garner parent support and understanding, especially in the area of musical play.

Teachers need to know the children they teach to engage them in learning and discovery, with the key being the ability to find the right balance of education, engagement, and playfulness. The focus of *Musical Play at the UA* is to allow multiple opportunities for musical play. The program has similar aims to *Playing Music with Mum or Dad* (de Grätzer, 1999), such as helping parents extend music activities in the home and supporting parent's musical development and enjoyment as they participate in the program with their children so that they may "regain the pleasure of playing" (p. 50).

METHODOLOGY

The purpose of this study was to evaluate the program *Musical Play at the UA*, specifically to determine the program's alignment with articulated goals by surveying parents. Using data information from the parent survey (see figure 6.1), the authors examined parents' perspectives on various aspects of the program. The Likert-type questions asked parents to respond to degrees of agreement/disagreement (5 = strongly agree; 4 = agree; 3 = neutral; 2 = disagree; 1 = strongly disagree) for the following categories: (a) overall experiences with the program and instructor; (b) free play; (c) circle/group activities; (d) song starters (manipulatives such as instruments, props, or puppets used during group activities, then given to families to promote music making in the home); (e) resource pages; and (f) university student interns and observers. Each of the categories contained between five and seven questions.

In addition to the Likert-type questions, parents were asked to provide basic demographic information and respond to open-ended questions such as the following: (a) How did you learn about the program? (b) What was your child's favorite music center? (c) What was your favorite music center? (d) Did you bring siblings to participate? This survey also addressed whether parents witnessed the benefit of music experiences in themselves and their children. Parent perspectives on the program were sought through an invitation to respond to open-ended comments or to make suggestions regarding the program.

Surveys were distributed to current program participants at the final class period of the ten-week session and were mailed to participants from the three prior ten-week sessions, for a total of four consecutive sessions. Parents anonymously returned their surveys through the U.S. postal service using enclosed, self-addressed, stamped envelopes with the university address listed as the return address. Although fifty-two families participated in the program during those four semesters, some parents had multiple children enrolled, some had enrolled in multiple sessions, and not all parents returned their surveys. Therefore, twenty-six completed surveys were returned for a 50 percent response rate. The surveys from the twenty-six families represented thirty-four children (twenty boys and fourteen girls). Of the returned surveys, the twenty-six families were distributed across the semesters as follows: (a) spring 2007, six families; (b) fall 2007, five families; (c) spring 2008, five families; and (d) fall 2008, fifteen families. Of the twenty-six families, two families attended three consecutive semesters, and three families attended two consecutive semesters. The surveys represented thirteen two-year-old children (38 percent), nine three-year-old children (26 percent), six four-year-old children (18 percent), and six five-year-old children (18 percent).

RESULTS

As discussed earlier, the parent surveys were designed to elicit responses in the following categories: (a) program and instructor, (b) free play, (c) group activities, (d) song starters, (e) resource pages, and (f) student observers and interns. The results from each category will be discussed below.

The parent responses for the first six questions (category 1: program/instructor) regarding their overall experiences with the program and the instructor's ability to be a positive role model and knowledgeable educator had an average score of 4.80. This indicates a high level of support for the program and instructor. Open-ended responses regarding the program and instructor indicated that the program was considered to be well run and professional. Many parents considered the program fee reasonable and expressed how much their child enjoyed/loved the class. The pacing was considered smooth and age appropriate: "I appreciated that you let my 2 yr. old be a 2 yr. old." Others considered class time well managed, as it "always started and ended on time." Recommendations or criticisms of the program mainly centered on the time of day of the class, with parents preferring morning sessions (the current program only offers late afternoon sessions), and taking the time to introduce all participants (instructor, interns, parents, children) during the first class.

Category 2 questions focusing on free play tended to be ranked higher by the parents of the younger children (mean = 4.92), and, in fact, were ranked higher than any other category for this age group. Parents of the older children rated their support of free-play activities as somewhat less valuable than the younger children, with a mean of 4.42. Parent responses for category 3 (group activities) indicated that those with four- and five-year-old children rated it slightly lower (4.5) than those of two- and three-year-old children (4.62). Open-ended responses regarding free play included support and enjoyment of the centers. The music center that focused on drums was the favorite center for children and parents, with the puppets and music play tables (a table with four instruments built into the table top: drum, cymbal, xylophone and xylopipe, with removable multicolored maracas and mallets) ranking second and third, respectively. One parent indicated that play tables were the most enjoyable "because we could interact together."

The questions for categories 4 (song starters) and 5 (resource pages) were designed to elicit information about whether those items were a catalyst for at-home music making. The "song starters" are music manipulatives, such as an instrument or puppet, that "correlate with songs and activities from group sessions and are intended to encourage musical play at home" (Cooper and Cardany, 2008, p. 6). Parents of two- and three-year-old children rated song starters the same as those of four- and five-year-old children with a mean score of 3.8 and 3.85, respectively. Parents indicated that they enjoyed the music instruments (shakers, rhythm sticks, etc.) as the most preferred song starters. Several parents requested that song starters include CDs of the songs used within group activities.

The resource pages provide parents with information, such as authors of children's books, composers of listening selections, and instructions for fingerplay or movement activities. Responses for resource pages showed that the parents of four- and five-year-old children rated the resource pages slightly lower than the parents of younger children with mean scores of 3.4 and 3.72, respectively. One parent suggested having the resource pages sent by e-mail or made available online rather than provided as papers at the end of each session.

Survey data contained numerous parent comments, with only three parents (12 percent) not providing any answers for the open-ended questions. Several themes emerged. Sample open-ended responses indicating the success of the program in promoting at-home music making included the following:

- "[M] sang more outside of class than she ever has."
- "I think the class was a very positive thing for us to do together. [A] sings all the time at home now."
- "[B] loved the classes and still talks about them."
- "The songs were very fun and we sang them throughout the week. [L] even started making up his own lyrics to some of them."
- "I feel that it helped my child in three things (specific—plus many others): 1. early literacy 2. preparation for school (group environment) 3. love of music—he's learning mariachi at his elementary school now."

Ten families revealed within the open-ended questions that they brought another family member and/or friend—either child or adult—to attend a session during the ten-week program.

As this early childhood music program is also used as a teaching/observation environment for preservice teachers, the researchers wanted to know if the students' presence was a deterrent to the children's or the parents' music making. Category 6 (student interns/observers) questions addressed this issue, with parents of the youngest children rating the inclusion of student interns and observers with a mean score of 4.2. The parents of the older class rated the interns and observers slightly lower with a mean score of 3.92. Sample open-ended comments about the interns included "I felt the student interns were a huge plus—always so pleasant, cheerful and helpful," and "The teaching assistants did a great job of helping the kids feel welcome and involved." Although parents of the older class rated interns and observers slightly lower, no surveys included negative remarks that may have provided insight for the parents' ratings.

DISCUSSION AND IMPLICATIONS

This study addresses music learning in early childhood, particularly regarding the roles and perceptions of parents and adults, through a parental survey. The survey results from this study allowed the researchers to examine the extent of parental interest and their opinions regarding the various types of music activities experienced, the available resources, and the use of student interns and observers. Parents were central to the program assessment, because they are a vital part of the young child's music learning experiences. The NAEYC supports assessments that address the individual child's abilities, "but also what children can do with assistance from other children or adults" (Copple and Bredekamp, 2009, p. 22). Including parents in evaluations of programs for young children is part of the NAEYC's core values for early childhood education. Input from families should be "part of the program's overall assessment strategy" (p. 22).

The *Musical Play at the UA* program provides the environment for parents to watch their child's participation, music-making experiences, and musical experimentation. The first set of questions provides the overall attitude toward the program, which resulted in high scores as evidence that the program was successful in reaching families, which is one of the program's initial goals.

Free play was ranked higher by the parents of the younger children (ages two and three). This high ranking may suggest emergent parental understanding of the developmentally appropriate practice of musical play, and—in this program—specifically free play. The parents supported a program that provided music centers and encouraged parent engagement, and they recognized the value in these types of activities, especially for younger children. Many parents commented on the music play tables as the most enjoyable because they were opportunities for the parent-child dyad to interact.

The group activities provided parents the songs, fingerplays, and movement activities to extend musical interactions beyond classroom time. The answers in this section also provided information regarding whether the program as a whole and teachers individually responded to the musical skill development levels of young children. Adults may expect adult-like music behaviors from young children. Yet, through this survey, the parents indicated an awareness of their children's musical skill-development levels. Sample open-ended responses included:

- "I love it that you have all the instruments in the back because if my children's interest in group activities disappears they can go there for a few minutes and then return to the group activities without pressure."
- "It was great watching my children 'unfold' and participate more and more with each weekly session."
- "We enjoyed the energy, variety."

Parents' answers to questions regarding group activities suggest that music teachers should consider planning for and providing materials for free musical play as well as providing adults with guidelines regarding what to expect from their children. The typical teacher-facilitated music circle time activities remain important for amassing songs and developing musical behaviors, but not to the exclusion of children's opportunities to engage in free musical play and "unfold," as one parent noted.

Sichivitsa (2007) noted that children rely on parental and teacher feedback to evaluate their own musical abilities. This provides further evidence of the importance of program evaluation, as teachers and administrators need to know if parents are *seeing* and *hearing* their children's musical development. Focusing solely on a child's musical development might not be enough for retention in a music program or to prompt further interest in music. Teachers could represent the epitome of highly effective music instruction at this level through play, and children could excel musically, but in order for the child to think *I'm a good music maker*, the parents need to recognize the growth and provide essential feedback.

Researchers have noted the importance of parental involvement in music programs as well as the effect of parent-child relationships (Brand, 1985; Gordon, 2003; Zdzinski, 1996). Song starters and resource pages can foster a similar music environment in the home and are key components of this program. Some parents articulated their enjoyment of interacting with their children through the music play tables. This type of parent-child communication bonding through music is supported by de Grätzer (1999). Ten families shared that they brought another family member and/or friend to the music session(s), indicating a shared sense of family and community. Therefore, teachers working in settings that include both parent and child can further support family bonding by providing music instruction that includes multiple and continuous opportunities for parent and child interactions.

The parents' open-ended remarks reflected a high level of parent support for the program. These types of insights, feelings, and intuitions shared by parents can inform teachers. Music teachers desire to teach to the music development of the child and the parent, but the parents in this study articulated that nonmusical aspects of the classes are important as well.

Parents who recognize their children's musical interest or abilities may become more musically involved and grow to value the role of music in their children's lives, despite minimal previous interest in or support of music. In a study of 130 collegiate choir members, Sichivitsa (2007) found that parental support of music had a significant impact on college students' self-concepts in music. Although the students in Sichivitsa's study were college age, the results emphasize an important cycle. Custodero and Johnson-Green (2003) found that musically experienced parents were more apt to sing and provide other musical experiences for their young children. Music educators who teach early childhood must be concerned with the music development of the child and the music development and experiences of the parent. "A child's circle of influence begins in the home" (Lum, 2007, p. 18). Thus, early childhood music programs should constantly focus on interaction between the parent-child dyad to help empower the parents to feel confident in sharing music experiences with their children at home.

As a result of the information gleaned from parent surveys, the current program will continue to provide many opportunities for music play. More centers with an "interactive component" for parent and child were created and incorporated. The program facilitator is providing "Suggestions for Further Reading" as an added component to the resource pages—reading suggestions that address and highlight the importance of free music play and the importance of family music making.

Addison (1990) asserts that it "behooves teachers with an interest in music to find out something of what parents think about music's place in the curriculum" (p. 133). Likewise, it behooves teachers to discover parents' thoughts about music programs designed for their children. Further research is needed on program evaluation in early childhood music education through the collection of observational data and the examination of lesson plans and the corresponding activities that are presented. *Musical Play at the UA* fo-

"MUSICAL PLAY AT THE UA"

Thank you for participating in Musical Play! To help the program better serve you and future participants, please complete this survey and return it in the self-addressed-stamped envelope provided.
Thank you! ☺

Statement	Strongly Agree	Agree	Neutral	Disagree	Strongly Disagree
My overall experience with *Musical Play* was positive, and I would recommend the program to my friends.					
I have recommended *Musical Play* to my friends.					
The registration fee for the 10-week session was priced appropriately.					
Instructor treated me with respect.					
Instructor understood the needs and abilities of preschool children.					
Instructor was a positive, musical role model.					
Free Play					
There were a variety of age-appropriate musical instruments and centers.					
There was an adequate amount of musical instruments and centers to accommodate all participants involved.					
The musical instruments and centers allowed interaction between you and your child.					
The musical instruments and centers promoted interaction between you and your child.					
The musical instruments and centers provided during free play are an asset to the program.					
Circle/Group Activities					
The circle/group activities kept my child's interest.					
The circle/group activities provided an adequate variety of movement opportunities.					
The circle/group activities provided an adequate variety of singing opportunities.					
The circle/group activities provided an adequate variety of opportunities for playing instruments.					
Books used within circle/group activities are an asset to the program.					

Figure 6.1a.   Parental Survey

Statement	Strongly Agree	Agree	Neutral	Disagree	Strongly Disagree
Song Starters					
The song starters were used at home.					
The song starters prompted music-making outside of the *"Musical Play"* class. (e.g., home, car, etc.)					
My child plays with the instruments provided as song starters.					
My child uses the "song cards" provided as song starters.					
My child uses the animals provided as song starters.					
My child uses the scarf provided as a song starter.					
My child enjoyed the weekly "color pages."					
Resource Pages					
The resource pages were used at home.					
The resource pages prompted music-making outside of the *"Musical Play"* class. (e.g., home, car, etc.)					
My child showed interest in the resource pages.					
I used the resource pages to remember songs and activities.					
I used the CD with music for movement activities with my child. (If applicable – some sessions did not receive a CD)					
UA Student Interns/Observers					
The University of Arizona student interns were an asset to the program.					
The University of Arizona student interns were helpful to me and my child(ren).					
The University of Arizona student interns were a distraction to me and my child(ren).					
Individuals who came to observe class sessions inhibited my music making.					
Individuals who came to observe class sessions inhibited my child's music making.					

Figure 6.1b. Parental Survey

1. Age of child(ren) enrolled _____

2. If applicable: Ages of sibling(s) attending but not enrolled _____

3. Sessions enrolled (Please check all applicable)

       Spring 2007 _____   Fall 2007 _____

       Spring 2008 _____   Fall 2008 _____

4. How did you learn about the program?

5. Did you bring another family member and/or friend (either child or adult) to attend a session with you and your child?   Yes _____   No _____

6. My child's favorite music center was

7. My favorite music center was

8. Additional Comments/Suggestions:

    Optional: Name _____

Figure 6.1c.   Parental Survey

cuses on the need for parents to be involved with their child(ren) so that they can scaffold their child's music learning (Gordon, 2003; Pestalozzi, 1974; Vygotsky, 1987). Would a program that does not require parental involvement yield similar results?

"If music educators can take into account what children know, want and like it is likely that what is taught would be more readily assimilated by the children" (Lum, 2007, p. 19). Parents' assessments of their preschool children's likes and dislikes—with regard to music activities—can inform the teacher to formulate appropriate content for the curriculum. "Each child is a mosaic of sorts, with colorful pieces contributing in complex ways to form the whole of his physical, social, intellectual, and emotional selfhood" (Shehan-Campbell, 1998, p. 222). The evaluation of early childhood music programs enables early childhood music teachers to contribute to each young child's budding musical mosaic.

REFERENCES

Addison, R. (1990). Parents' views on their children's musical education in the primary school: A survey. *British Journal of Music Education, 7*(2), 133–41.

Andress, B. (1989). Music for every stage: How much? What kind? How soon? *Music Educators Journal, 76*(2), 22–27.

Bates, D. A. (1985). Program evaluation in music. *Canadian Music Educator, 26*(4), 22–32.

Berger, A., and Cooper, S. (2003). Musical play: A case study of preschool children and parents. *Journal of Research in Music Education, 51*(2), 151–65.

Boyle, J. D. (1989). Perspectives on evaluation. *Music Educators Journal, 76*(4), 22–25.

Brand, M. (1985). Development and validation of the home musical environment scale for use at the early elementary level. *Psychology of Music, 13,* 40–48.

Cardany, A. (2004). Music education for preschool children: Perspectives and experiences of parents. *Dissertation Abstracts International, 65*(11), 4141. (UMI No. 3152384).

Colwell, R. (2002). Assessment's potential in music education. In R. Colwell and C. Richardson (Eds.), *The new handbook of research on music teaching and learning* (pp. 1128–58). New York: Oxford University Press.

Cooper, S., and Cardany, A. B. (2008). Making connections: Promoting music making in the home through a preschool music program. *General Music Today, 22*(4), 4–12.

Copple, C., and Bredekamp, S. (2009). *Developmentally appropriate practice in early childhood programs serving children from birth through age 8.* Washington, DC: National Association for the Education of Young Children.

Custodero, L. A., and Johnson-Green, E. A. (2003). Passing the cultural torch: Musical experience and musical parenting of infants. *Journal of Research in Music Education, 51,* 102–14.

de Grätzer, D. P. (1999). Can music help to improve parent-child communication? *International Journal of Music Education, 34,* 47–56.

deVries, P. (2009). Music at home with the under fives: What is happening? *Early Child Development and Care, 179*(4), 395–405.

Ellis, M. J. (1973). *Why people play.* Englewood Cliffs, NJ: Prentice Hall.

Gordon, E. E. (2003). *A music learning theory for newborn and young children.* Chicago: GIA.

Guerrini, S. C. (2005). An investigation of the association between the music aptitude of elementary students and their biological parents. *Update: Applications of Research in Music Education, 24*(1), 27–33.

Kirkpatrick, W. C. (1962). Relationships between the singing ability of prekindergarten children and their home environment. *Dissertation Abstracts International, 23*(3), 886.

Lehman, P. R. (1989). Assessing your program's effectiveness. *Music Educators Journal, 76*(4), 26–29.

Lum, C. H. (2007). Children's musical surroundings: What can children tell us about music education? *Orff Echo, 39*(4), 17–20.

Mallett, C. A. (2000). An examination of parent/caregiver attitudes toward music instruction, the nature of the home musical environment, and their relationship to the developmental music aptitude of preschool children. *Dissertation Abstracts International, 61*(4A), 1335.

Marjoribanks, K., and Mboya, M. (2004). Learning environments, goal orientations, and interest in music. *Journal of Research in Music Education, 52*, 155–66.

Pestalozzi, H. (1974). *How Gertrude instructs her children* (H. Norden and R. Norden, Trans.). New York: Philosophical Library.

Radocy, R. E., and Boyle, J. D. (1987). *Measurement and evaluation of musical experiences*. New York: Schirmer Books.

Rauscher, F. (2000). Is assessment in music appropriate in the early childhood years? In *Spotlight on early childhood music education* (pp. 49–51). Reston, VA: MENC.

Reynolds, G. E. (1960). Environmental sources of musical awakening in preschool children. *Dissertation Abstracts International, 21*(5), 1214.

Shehan-Campbell, P. (1998). *Songs in their heads: Music and its meaning in children's lives*. New York: Oxford University Press.

Sichivitsa, V. O. (2007). The influences of parents, teachers, peers, and other factors on students' motivation in music. *Research Studies in Music Education, 29*, 55–68.

Sims, W. L., and Udtaisuk, D. B. (2008). Music's representation in parenting magazines: A content analysis. *Update: Applications of Research in Music Education, 26*(2), 17–26.

Singer, J. L. (1973). Theories of play and the origins of imagination. In J. L. Singer (Ed.), *The child's world of make-believe* (pp. 1–26). New York: Academic Press.

Taggart, C. C. (2000). Developing musicianship through musical play. In *Spotlight on early childhood music education* (pp. 23–26). Reston, VA: MENC.

Thames, M. L. (1979). Effects of parental background on parental attitudes toward elementary music. *Dissertation Abstracts, 40*(10A), 5358.

Vygotsky, L. S. (1987). *The collected works of L. S. Vygotsky: Volume 5, Child psychology* (M. J. Hall, Ed.; R. W. Rieber, Trans.). New York: Plenum.

White, R. F. (1959). Motivation reconsidered: The concept of competence. *Psychological Review, 66*, 297–333.

Zdzinski, S. F. (1996). Parental involvement, selected student attributes, and learning outcomes in instrumental music. *Journal of Research in Music Education, 44*, 34–48.

NOTE

1. In 2002 the first sessions of *Musical Play*—co-created by Audrey Berger Cardany and Shelly Cooper—were held on the Arizona State University main campus. *Musical Play at the UA* now serves as one of the University of Arizona School of Music Education Outreach programs under the direction of Shelly Cooper. For more information on *Musical Play at the UA* and to view pictures of children and parents participating in the program, please visit www.cfa.arizona.edu/musiceducation/out reach/musical-play-at-the-ua.

Chapter Seven

Elementary Music Teachers' Role-Identities in and Perceptions of Teaching Prekindergarten Students with Special Needs

Julie Derges Kastner

This study describes the perceptions and role-identities of two elementary general music teachers who taught prekindergarten music classes to students with special needs in order to explore whether the participants viewed their roles and skills as different from those of elementary music teaching. Data collection included observations, field notes, anecdotal evidence from informal conversations, and individual interviews, which were later transcribed. The data were coded and analyzed for emerging themes, which were (a) teacher roles, (b) teaching influences, (c) flexibility, and (d) communication and collaboration. The music teachers viewed aspects of their prekindergarten teaching as distinct from their elementary teaching. They created musical and nonmusical roles, used flexibility as a teaching strategy, and communicated with other adults as they met the needs of their prekindergarten students. Discussion and suggestions for future research also are provided.

I knew that I would always do elementary music. I didn't quite know that I would have so much early childhood and so much of the special needs area. That's something I had to learn along the way.

—Sharon, preK music teacher

ROLE-IDENTITY CONSTRUCTION

Music education and sociology researchers have explored the identities and role-identities of preservice and practicing teachers in general education and music education (Bernard, 2004; Bouij, 2004; Brewer, 2009; Conkling, 2004; Draves, 2010; Frierson-Campbell, 2004; Isbell, 2008; McCall and Simmons, 1966) and have found that individuals construct role-identities within their unique settings and in relation to others (McCall and Simmons, 1966). The concept of role-identities was developed by George J. McCall and J. L. Simmons as a theory within the sociological theory of symbolic interactionism, which posits that individuals construct meaning through interactions with others. Specifically, a role-identity is defined as "the character and the role that an individual devises for himself as an occupant of a particular social position" (McCall and Simmons, 1966, p. 67). Role-identities do not stem from the individual alone, but are created and supported as a result of their interactions within a particular social context, such as the individuals and school characteristics that flow through a "person's life stream" (p. 69).

Much of the research on role-identity has focused on preservice music teachers. Researchers have found that preservice music teachers often describe their role-identities as having separate roles of teacher and musician (Bouij, 2004; Brewer, 2009). Brewer (2009) found that preservice music teachers credited success to individual "personal qualities and knowledge" (p. 75). In addition, Draves (2010) described the importance of the relationships between preservice music teachers and their cooperating teachers in positive role-identity development. Frierson-Campbell (2004) looked at the role-identities of experienced elementary music teachers and found that many teachers credited their success to personal traits, like "flexibility, love of music teaching and/or children, patience, and stubbornness" (p. 17) as well as professional traits.

Beyond exploring role identities, other researchers have examined the construction of music teacher identities (Bernard, 2004; Conkling, 2004; Isbell, 2008). Conkling (2004) described the "identity stories" of three representative cases and found that preservice teachers develop their understanding of both teaching and being a teacher through their student teaching. Isbell (2008) surveyed 578 preservice music teachers regarding their occupational identities and socialization. Findings from his survey supported other research indicating that preservice music teachers have separate identities as musicians and teachers. Isbell also found that preservice music teachers' identities as teachers were further divided into their self-perceptions and their perceptions from others. Bernard (2004) described the musician-teacher identities of practicing elementary general music teachers and found that teaching music is itself identity construction; however, the approach and findings of this study have been met with criticism (Roberts, 2006).

While no previous research has explored the role-identities of music teachers working with students with special needs, researchers have explored teacher attitudes (Sideridis and Chandler, 1995; Wilson and McCrary, 1996) and perceptions of preservice teachers (Hourigan, 2009) toward this population. In particular, music teachers' attitudes toward teaching these students improved after receiving training or an orientation of terms and concepts unique to teaching special learners (Hourigan, 2009; Wilson and McCrary, 1996). None of the above studies, however, pertained specifically to elementary music teachers who teach prekindergarten (preK) music classes to children with special needs. More research is needed to discover whether or how elementary music teachers develop teaching strategies and role-identities specific to their contexts. Therefore, the purpose of this study was to explore the perceptions and role-identities of two elementary general music teachers, as well as the factors and influences in their prekindergarten music teaching of students with special needs.

METHOD

Participants

Participants in this study were two elementary music teachers in a small Midwestern city. Using a "purposeful sampling strategy" (Creswell, 2007), the participant selection was limited to experienced elementary music teachers who also taught preK music classes to students with special needs as a part of their district's requirements. The two participants were recommended by university faculty as excellent educators and thoughtful individuals who would provide meaningful data. They provided a case in which there was an "opportunity to learn" (Stake, 1995, p. 6). I had met one of the participants, Christine Davis (pseudonym), when I was the assistant teacher for an early childhood music class that she attended with her child and through our mutual participation in local Orff-Schulwerk and Music Learning Theory chapter meetings. I met the other participant, Sharon Summers (pseudonym), by observing a student teacher working in her classroom. The two participants are both well-respected, experienced elementary and early childhood music teachers, each of whom possesses more than twenty years of teaching experience. My previous interactions with these teachers, along with my mutual experience in teaching early childhood music, helped me to establish a rapport with the participants that allowed them to openly share their experiences.

Sharon Summers

Sharon Summers epitomized the words *resourceful* and *nurturing* in her teaching. When I knocked on her classroom door, Sharon promptly opened it and propped it open with a hefty microphone stand. Just as she used the microphone stand to serve as a makeshift doorstop, Sharon had learned to utilize a variety of objects, ideas, and individuals in her twenty-seven years of teaching to create the best possible experience for her students. After quickly greeting me, Sharon then noticed a woman passing by in the hallway. The women exchanged waves, and then Sharon said, "Excuse me. I need to give somebody a hug" (Field notes, November 4, 2009). Sharon cared deeply about all of the students and faculty at her school, which she exhibited in that moment by taking the time to comfort a colleague. Sharon had been in her current position for twenty-five years, twenty in which she taught preK music. Sharon taught five classes of preK music, including one class at Christine's school.

Christine Davis

When I met Christine for my first observation, she greeted me with a quick hug and then stood at the door of her room; she had little time to spare in her packed schedule. As we talked, she looked down the hallway as she waited for her next class. As a music teacher, Christine maintained focus on her students, and she constantly reflected on her teaching in an effort to continuously refine her craft. At the same time, Christine possessed a wonderful sense of humor and was quick to laugh at a classroom situation or herself.

Christine had taught elementary music for twenty-three years and preK music for eight years. She had previously taught preK music for one year at a school district prior to coming to her current school, where she had been for the past seven years. In her current position, Christine only taught part-time, and she taught one of the two preK music classes in her building. Christine shared that preK music teaching had been a required part of the position when she began. She believed that her previous year of teaching early childhood music helped her to be selected for the position: "I think the fact that I had that preschool under my belt was a factor in getting this job" (Interview 1, October 29, 2009).

Setting

Although the district had multiple elementary schools, only Christine and Sharon taught in schools that had preK music classes; the majority of these were held in Sharon's school. Sharon also traveled to Christine's school to teach an additional preK class, which would have otherwise overloaded the maximum amount of teaching allowed in Christine's schedule. Though they saw their preK classes for thirty minutes twice a week (which was the same amount as their elementary classes), the district did not have an early childhood music curriculum.

The preK students in the district were three- and four-year-old children who had been diagnosed as having a special need. According to Christine and Sharon, the special needs of their students ranged across a variety of disorders, including speech and language, autism spectrum disorder, and other various physical and cognitive impairments. In the preK classes, there were two to three teaching assistants (TAs), who attended music classes and assisted the participants. Although the National Association for the Education of Young Children (NAEYC, 2009) defines early childhood as children from birth to age eight, Christine and Sharon consistently referred to their preK music classes as "early childhood" music, in opposition to their elementary music classes, which were those from kindergarten to grade 5.

Originally, I had intended to work with elementary music teachers who taught preK classes of typically developing children. However, after my initial meeting with the participants, I learned that all of the preK students in these settings had a special need. Although I had not planned on describing a teaching context comprised completely of students with special needs, I felt that perspectives of these exemplary teachers were still worthy of study. Since this is a case study with two participants, the results of this study are not generalizable. However, there may be elements of transferability to the unique contexts of other music teachers and music-teacher educators.

Data Collection

Data were collected from four sources: individual interviews, observations, field notes, and anecdotal evidence. The interviews were comprised of two audio-taped interviews conducted individually with each participant. I e-mailed the interview questions to the participants in advance so that they could reflect on their answers prior to the interviews. The initial interview with Christine took place in her home before any observations and with Sharon the day following my first observation in her classroom. The second interviews took place after completing all of the observations. Each interview averaged sixty minutes in length. The interviews were recorded using *GarageBand* on my laptop computer. As advocated by Creswell (2007), I conducted the interviews using semistructured techniques, which allowed me to seek clarification or to delve further into the participants' answers. The interviews were then transcribed.

Observations occurred as the participants taught their preK music classes. I observed two preK music classes with Christine Davis and four with Sharon Summers. While Christine only taught one section of preK music, Sharon taught multiple sections. The classes I observed with Sharon occurred on two occasions of back-to-back preK music classes, totaling four sections. During the observations, I acted primarily as an observer, which allowed me to take descriptive field notes. Occasionally I acted as a participant in the musical activities as the children interacted with me at various times during the music classes. Data collection also included anecdotal evidence that occurred through the informal conversations held with the participants before and after the interviews and classroom observations.

Data Analysis and Verification

I manually coded and analyzed the interview transcripts, observation field notes, and anecdotal evidence for emerging themes. In coding the data manually, I first read the data multiple times. I then took sections of text from the transcripts or field notes and assigned a code "linked to the processes of thinking and interpreting" the text's meaning (Emerson, Fretz, and Shaw, 1995, p. 146). I reviewed the codes for possible connections and relationships and then combined these codes into four emergent themes.

In order to ensure trustworthiness, I employed data triangulation, peer review, and member checks. Data triangulation occurred through the collection of multiple forms of data, as described above, in order to find "corroborating evidence" (Creswell, 2007). Peer review took place through the assistance of two experienced music education researchers, who reviewed the data and codes and provided feedback, which helped to refine my labels for the codes. I conducted member checks: participants reviewed the interview transcripts and made changes according to their suggestions to reflect an accurate presentation of their thoughts (Creswell, 2007). I was able to provide trustworthiness in the results by collecting multiple forms of data, and also by having the participants, in addition to researchers unaffiliated with this project, review aspects of the data.

FINDINGS

Four themes emerged from the data as the participants described aspects of the role-identities in their preK teaching: *teacher roles, teaching influences, flexibility,* and *communication and collaboration.* The participants had developed multiple roles in teaching their preK students, including teaching roles, social modeling roles, and language modeling roles. They described their *teaching influences* as stemming from a variety of sources and individuals that were not always specific to teaching early childhood music. They often described and demonstrated *flexibility* as an essential strategy for teaching preK music. Finally, the participants both felt that *communication and collaboration* with preK classroom teachers, teaching assistants, and other support personnel were important in helping them meet the needs of their preK students with special needs.

Teacher Roles

The participants described roles that pertained to teaching music and helping their preK students develop social skills and vocabulary. Sharon stated:

> I would say that my role is *many*. You wear many, many hats [*she smiles*]. You are musician; you are mom; you are grandma [*smiles*], if you are old enough! And lately it seems like I am! [*she chuckles*] You are mentor; you are helper; you are everything; sometimes you're nurse; sometimes you're social worker. (Interview 2, November 12, 2009)

As evidenced by Sharon's quote, the participants felt a responsibility to not only be musicians and mentors to students, which are two roles typically associated with being a music teacher. They also felt called to assume roles that are less connected to teaching music, like the caring nature of a family member, nurse, and social worker, to their preK students.

Music Teacher Roles

Sharon, who taught many sections of preK music, described her teacher identity more holistically, as though her preK teaching identity was assimilated into her overall teaching identity: "First and foremost, you're the music teacher, okay? But . . . you are a teacher of *children*" (Interview 2, November 12, 2009). In this statement, Sharon made broad descriptions of her role as a teacher. Although I had asked her to specifically describe her role as an *early childhood* music teacher, she did not identify any specific differences between the roles in her preK and elementary music teaching.

On the other hand, Christine viewed her preK teaching as a separate role within her overall music teacher identity:

> I was thinking that, in a way, it's funny that early childhood and fifth grade [*she gestures to the left and right to show the two ends of the age range*] share a job, in that I'm more of a facilitator in those two places, where I put the music out there then see what they give me back. In fifth grade, it's that you want *them* to be independent and kind of take control of where the music goes, and in early childhood, it's more that you're waiting for a response for them, from them, to see where you go. (Interview 2, November 12, 2009)

Christine viewed her musical role with preK students as a facilitator. With her preK students, she had to serve as a musical catalyst for their responses: "In early childhood, I'm pretty much the music maker, and if anybody else joins in, that's just a *gem* [*smiles and throws hands out*], but there's no expectation on them for what they give me" (Interview 1, October 29, 2009).

Throughout my observations, I noticed the participants serving as the *primary music makers* and as musical models who facilitated an environment that encouraged student responses. Additionally, they expressed a desire to provide a model that exposed their preK students to new music. This included exposure to traditional songs that the children may not have heard at home as though they were "plugging in the gaps in their [musical] experience" (Christine, Interview 1, October 29, 2009). They also wanted to provide exposure to many different musical characteristics, as when Sharon explained that she had been "steeping them in minor" for a month by singing many songs in that tonality (Field notes, November 4, 2009).

Role Diversity

Both participants felt that they acquired nonmusical teaching roles as a part of their preK music teaching. Sharon expressed a desire to provide a *social model* for her students, which stemmed both from the students' young age and their special needs. Sharon took every opportunity to model appropriate social norms, like taking turns or saying "thank you" to a dancing partner. At the end of one class, she told students who did not have a turn in an activity to "put your turn in your pocket," as she pretended to put something in her own pocket (Field notes, November 4, 2009). While providing a role model for taking turns takes place in many elementary music classrooms, Sharon shared this technique as important to her perception of her preK teaching. As with the music teacher roles, Sharon perceived the *social model* role as an assimilated part of her whole teacher identity, rather than as a separate role-identity for teaching prekindergartners.

Sharon and Christine were aware of the need to provide a *language model* in their classrooms, since many of their preschool students had language delays: "[A]s a *model* for those kids, they need to hear language, too" (Christine, Interview 2, November 12, 2009). Christine shared that "since that population has trouble with speech, the times that I'm most *thrilled* are when something comes out. Sometimes it's singing, but just to get a response where there never was one" (Interview 1, October 29, 2009). One of her favorite memories of her early childhood teaching was when a child spoke a word for the first time. Sharon succinctly explained the diversity of their preK teaching roles by saying that they had to be "music [teachers]-slash-parents-slash-social workers" (Interview 1, November 5, 2009), demonstrating her simultaneous expression of a variety of roles.

Teaching Influences

Sharon and Christine described factors that influenced the way that they taught their preK music classes. They explained how they constantly sought out information from a variety of resources to help them with their teaching. Sharon listed one of her strengths in teaching preK as "seeking out anything and everything I can, musically. Going across different areas and not sticking with one" (Interview 2, November 12, 2009). In particular, they both described the influence of their methodological training and participation with their own children in early childhood music classes.

Methodological Training

While Sharon did not have undergraduate training in early childhood or preschool teaching, Christine learned about early childhood teaching through one of her college methods classes:

> My undergraduate methods teacher formed a preschool lab for our methods class as a way of watching *her* work with students and also a chance for us to work with students. So early on, before I even *became* a teacher, I had experience with preschool-age [children]. (Interview 1, October 29, 2009)

Observing her college professor and teaching preschool-age children as a preservice teacher gave Christine an initial socialization into early childhood music. Christine shared this information in her interview as a part of her teaching experience, but did not mention it when I asked her about influences on her preK teaching. This suggests that Christine did not perceive her undergraduate experiences as a strong influence in her preK teaching, which may have been due to the gap between her undergraduate coursework and the time when she began teaching preK music.

Upon starting their preK music teaching, Christine and Sharon independently sought out methodological training. Both completed a Music Learning Theory (MLT) certification course in early childhood music. Concepts and terms from this methodology, such as *variety of tonalities and meters* and *moving with flow* occurred often in their observations and interviews (see Gordon, 2003). Several times throughout the interviews, the participants mentioned that they valued the knowledge they learned from the professor in their MLT course, and they described Orff conferences and workshops as other influential methodological resources. Sharon expressed, "Well, I would have to say that I was a so-so early childhood teacher until . . . I took Music Learning Theory . . . but also ETM [Education Through Music] . . . and the Kindermusik and Musikgarten [workshops]" (Interview 2, November 12, 2009). She also observed music therapy sessions in order to learn more about working with students with special needs.

Sharon attributed her MLT professor as having the greatest impact on her preK teaching, but perceived her teaching as an interplay of elements from all of her methodological training: "They all have common threads, and if you can take those common threads, I *really* believe it can be combined and done. I really do" (Interview 1, November 5, 2009). Methodological training gave Sharon and Christine information that helped them with their teaching and gave them confidence. As Christine stated, "I feel more confident now about where to go . . . I know even when I'm not sure about it, I have resources that I can check" (Interview 1, October 29, 2009).

Motherhood

Christine and Sharon also described participation in early childhood music classes with their own children as an influence on their preK teaching. Coincidentally, they both began teaching preK music at the same time they became mothers. Sharon participated with her child in a Kindermusik class and shared, "That was the first time I had been exposed to something, maybe, more formal or something different. So I incorporated some of those things in [to my teaching]" (Interview 1, November 5, 2009). Christine shared, "Then, my own children attending preschool music classes had a big impact on me. I could model as a teacher how they were teaching, but also, I got to see first-hand my own child's development in that situation" (Interview 1, October 29, 2009).

Participation in these classes enabled Christine to understand better her students' responses by relating them to her own child's responses: "With [*names her child*], who in class, never responded [musically], I think *that* gives me more confidence with the early childhood students that don't make a response [in my class]" (Interview 1, October 29, 2009). Sharon described her preK teaching as a "unique thing," and that learning about it was an "ongoing process" (Interview 2, November 12, 2009). By seeking training specific to early childhood music and participating in early childhood music classes with their children, Christine and Sharon learned about the nature of teaching early childhood music and committed themselves to improving their preK teaching skills.

Flexibility

In teaching their preK music classes, the participants found that flexibility was a necessary factor for success. While elementary music teachers may consider flexibility as a factor for successful teaching in all grade levels, similar to Frierson-Campbell's participants (2004), Sharon and Christine specifically stated the importance of this trait in their early childhood music teaching. Sharon listed her ability to be flexible as one of the specific strengths of her preK teaching. Christine stated, "You just kind of roll with whatever they give you" (Interview 2, November 12, 2009). Christine described how she had to work at being flexible:

> It was hard for me at first, because maybe I'm more controlling than I want to admit! I'm not a good improviser, or I don't feel comfortable in that role. I think about all the things that happen and plan every second of it, and you just can't with them, and things go so much better if you don't . . . if you're willing to . . . be flexible and roll. But I like how that has really made me focus on the [preK] kids themselves and their music making. (Interview 1, October 29, 2009)

Christine attributed the need for more flexibility in her preK teaching to the lack of a district-provided early childhood curriculum:

> With the older kids, well, I have a curriculum. I don't have a set curriculum with early childhood, so it's pretty much up to me, and . . . the kids dictate, pretty much, where I'm going to go. I'm basing what comes next on *their* response. (Interview 1, October 29, 2009)

Christine had age-appropriate musical objectives in her preK music classes, but did not feel bound by the district curriculum. Rather, the lack of a district curriculum allowed her the flexibility to let her preK students explore music and participate in their own musical enculturation. According to NAEYC guidelines (2009), Christine should have a structured curriculum for preK; re-gardless, her statement reveals sensitivity toward the needs of this age group and the use of flexibility as a teaching strategy.

I observed ways in which the teachers responded to students' actions and adapted their lesson plans to accommodate students' needs. They were flex-ible with their pacing as they gauged the level of interest in each activity and paused their instruction to allow students to explore instrument parts, like guitar tuning pegs or Native American drumming mallets.

On one occasion, Christine sang a Thanksgiving song about turkeys, in which the students could "shake their tail feathers." One student rocked from side to side, lifting his feet off the ground as he shifted his weight, rather than shaking his hips as Christine had modeled. Christine acknowledged him, saying, "I love your rocking," and began to rock too, though this was not a part of her original activity. Soon all of the children were rocking. At first, Christine tried to have him stand on her feet as she rocked so that he could feel the beat. When that did not work, she held his hands and rocked with him, causing his rocking to settle with hers into the steady beat. She and the teaching assistants then rocked to the beat with every child before ending the activity (Field notes, November 11, 2009). As exhibited in their teaching and through their self-perceptions, the participants demonstrated a distinct flexibility in their preK teaching that was different from the flexibility needed for teaching elementary general music.

Communication and Collaboration

Communication and collaboration emerged as themes, as the participants' positive interactions with other adults helped them to better understand their students and develop their teaching skills. Sharon described this as "vital," saying, "I can't do this job without the back and forth communication," and that it spanned musical and social topics (Interview 2, November 12, 2009). They also communicated and collaborated with a variety of individuals concerning their preK teaching.

Music Teachers

Sharon and Christine regularly communicated with each other and with other music teachers in the district. Christine communicated with other early childhood music teachers about pursuing more early childhood training, and she felt that having a colleague with similar training made for a richer experience because she had "someone to bounce ideas off of" (Interview 1, October 29, 2009). Christine and Sharon also communicated with each other about the school district's lack of an early childhood music curriculum and about accommodating students' particular special needs:

> Sharon . . . helped me kind of figure out what my expectations were. . . . [For example] we have a boy. . . . She had him in early childhood, and I got him in kindergarten. So, we would email about issues with him, to find out what she tried that I hadn't thought of. (Interview 1, October 29, 2009)

Sharon described how the collaboration had increased as other music teachers in the district received the same type of methodological training: "Now the four of us are collaborating. . . . Even though I kind of was the first one, I'm learning from them. . . . So we'll share, and we'll trade, and we're all learning from each other" (Interview 1, November 5, 2009). After observing a difference in the way her son's early childhood music teacher taught, Christine sought the advice from other teachers, and through that communication she felt that her teaching practices were confirmed.

Early Childhood Classroom Teachers

The participants' communication with early childhood classroom teachers and teaching assistants focused on helping individual students. They shared that they did not have opportunities to communicate formally with classroom teachers in conferences or IEP meetings, yet both participants informally spoke with classroom teachers outside of instructional time. For instance:

> I have this much time [*pinches thumb and forefinger to show a small amount*] in order to contact other teachers in the building, so we try to get with each other before school, after school, whenever we can. (Sharon, Interview 2, November 12, 2009)

> I communicate pretty frequently with the classroom teacher, not officially, but when I see her at lunch time. Sometimes she tells me the things that I need to know. (Christine, Interview 2, November 12, 2009)

The communication and collaboration frequently occurred as dialogue passed between the early childhood classroom teacher and the music teachers, and the participants valued these opportunities. As Sharon related:

> We will brainstorm together, because they may have a technique that's working in the room that I need to know about, or maybe there's something that's working in here, that music may be magical for them. . . . So, we're very collaborative, very fortunate. (Interview 1, November 5, 2009)

Teaching Assistants and Physical/Occupational Therapist

The greatest amount of communication and collaboration seemed to occur with the TAs, because they were with the preK students all day, even during music class. As Christine said, "Sometimes they will share information about the kids, right on the spot" (Interview 1, October 29, 2009). Christine and Sharon also knew which TAs could model correct musical responses, and that they could count on the TAs for assistance in dealing with bathroom emergencies and accommodating the special needs of students: "I think I just tend to plan globally, and then when I get in there, I kind of rely on the teaching assistant, because they know their abilities better than I do for movement" (Christine, Interview 1, October 29, 2009).

A physical/occupational therapist (PT/OT) began attending Christine's music class to provide services to a child with cerebral palsy and limited mobility. (Previously, the child had been pulled from music class once a week to work with the PT/OT.) During one observation, Christine had her students take turns bouncing on a small trampoline to the steady beat as she held their hands and sang a song. When it came to be the turn of the child with cerebral palsy, rather than having him use his walker, Christine picked him up under his arms and said, "We're gonna fly here!" As she placed him on the trampoline, she turned to the PT/OT and asked, "Is it okay if I hold him under here?" The PT/OT told her it was fine, and the child enjoyed both the experience of flying and the opportunity to bounce on the trampoline (Field notes, October 28, 2009). Later, Christine described how she viewed the PT/OT "as a resource" to improve her instruction for that particular child.

The participants' relationship with the TAs also had negative aspects. Although they described the TAs as "invaluable" in the classroom, Christine and Sharon held high expectations for the TAs: "I want them to be musical. . . . I want them to interact with children. . . . I want them to be knowledgeable. . . . They're given a lot of responsibility" (Sharon, Interview 1, November 5, 2009). Christine shared that, in the past, the TAs had been "critical" of her teaching: "They would . . . [*as though choosing her words carefully*] pipe up . . . with suggestions and stuff. So that was challenging" (Interview 1, October 29, 2009).

Both participants described having to instruct the TAs about how to participate and assist in an activity. Christine described how the TAs "tend to jump in and discipline the kids," which sometimes overstepped her authority as the teacher (Interview 1, October 29, 2009). Overall, Christine and Sharon perceived their relationship with the TAs as a positive influence on the children's learning experiences, but also felt that addressing issues with the TAs took their focus away from the students.

Parents

The participants expressed that they did not communicate with parents as much as they would like. While they sent home newsletters and had an open-door policy, they did not feel that they communicated enough with that particular group. They both felt that they did not have time or opportunities to communicate with the parents because of their full schedules. Christine described feeling "overwhelmed" by the idea of communicating with her preK students' parents because she taught so many other grades, even though NAEYC (2009) stresses the importance of having relationships with family members. However, the classroom teachers occasionally communicated information from the parents to the music teachers. Here, Christine relates an anecdote communicated by a classroom teacher:

> One time, there was a boy, and . . . at conferences [his parents] said that he had never sung before, but when he started at [*names her school*], he started to sing at home. . . . So, things like that filter down to me, but I really don't have direct contact with parents. (Interview 2, November 12, 2009)

The participants both considered their lack of communication with parents as a weakness in their preK teaching. Despite their negative perceptions concerning the amount of communication with parents and the occasional difficulty working with TAs, the participants believed that communication and collaboration provided them with support and were important factors in the success of their preK teaching.

DISCUSSION AND IMPLICATIONS

Sharon and Christine perceived their preK music teaching to be "unique" or different from their elementary music teaching. Within *teacher roles*, they felt as though they had several parts to play in teaching their early childhood students. They described two kinds of roles related to teaching music and broader roles that related to nurturing their preK students' social skills and vocabulary. Their *teaching influences* ranged from early childhood university professors and workshops to their personal experience as mothers. The theme of *flexibility* emerged as the participants adapted their instruction to accommodate their early childhood students. Finally, the participants exhibited *communication and collaboration* as they interacted with a variety of adults, including other music teachers, early childhood classroom teachers, teaching assistants, and physical and occupational therapists, but felt as though their communication with early childhood parents was lacking.

Because role-identities are determined by how a person *"likes to think of himself being and acting"* (italics in original), the perspectives of these teachers is valuable in understanding their frame of reference in their preK teaching (McCall and Simmons, 1966, p. 67). The participants described both musical and nonmusical roles as important parts of their preK music teaching, similar to the findings of previous research (Bouij, 2004; Brewer, 2009; Frierson-Campbell, 2004). Also, they recognized flexibility as an important skill for working with these classes, which supports the work of Frierson-Campbell (2004).

Sharon did not seem to perceive musical and nonmusical roles as separate from her overall teaching identity, which suggests that she may not have recognized a separate role-identity for teaching early childhood music. However, this may have been the result of her twenty years of teaching experience and the fact that she taught early childhood frequently as part of her teaching load. Conversely, Christine, who taught fewer sections of early childhood music, seemed sensitive to her perceived role as a *primary music maker* in her preK music classes.

In addition to being musical role models and music makers for their preK students, the participants recognized that they needed to be positive role models in other aspects of the children's development, and they constructed the roles of *social model* and *language model* to accommodate their students' special needs. While other research has identified how music teachers possess separate roles as musicians and teachers (Bouij, 2004; Brewer, 2009; Frierson-Campbell, 2004), the *social model* and *language model* roles indicated that Sharon and Christine had more diversity in their roles than previous research has identified. More research is needed to explore the strength and frequency in which other preK music teachers of children with special needs choose to create and express these diverse roles, and how they affect student learning.

Within *teaching influences*, the teachers were influenced primarily by receiving methodological training in early childhood music and in experiences with their own children. Having opportunities to observe both children and teachers in early childhood music classes served to be important for Sharon and Christine, and observing music therapy settings may have helped Sharon to better understand the situational context of her preK teaching, including the developmental differences among young children and the acquisition of effective teaching strategies for special needs children. Having additional opportunities to learn from their MLT professor, whom they both respected, may have provided an early childhood teaching model for them to follow, helping them feel more successful (Isbell, 2008).

The participants described the importance of the communication and collaboration with a variety of professionals who had varying backgrounds of specialization in music, special needs, and early childhood. By working with these individuals, Sharon and Christine received "role-support," or an "implied confirmation" of their identities as early childhood music teachers (McCall and Simmons, 1966, p. 73), which is similar to the support experienced by both student teachers and cooperating teachers in their relationships (Draves, 2010). This complex system of relationships not only supported the participants' role-identities, but the participants also viewed these relationships as necessary factors in the success of their early childhood teaching. However, the relationships with teaching assistants and parents did not prove to be as successful, due to a conflict in the role expectations with the former and a lack of opportunity with the latter. More research is needed to discover how role relationships between professionals affect music teachers and their role identities.

Through the framework of role-identities, this study explored the perceptions and influences of elementary music teachers who teach preK music to students with special needs. While only Christine seemed to express a separate role-identity for teaching preK music, through their dedication to seeking out new knowledge, adapting their teaching skills, and collaborating with others, both Christine and Sharon were able to develop positive perceptions for teaching preK music to students with special needs.

While the findings of this study are unique to Christine and Sharon, early childhood music educators might consider how to help teachers develop positive perceptions of their teaching contexts, develop strategies like flexibility and communication, and recognize that music teachers may need to embody a variety of roles. Fostering these perceptions and attitudes may improve music teachers' ability to musically educate *all* students. Like Christine and Sharon, music teachers need opportunities to learn about early childhood music and students with special needs, as well as how to interact with students with these characteristics. Through coursework and fieldwork, these aspects could be included as part of the undergraduate curriculum. Then, rather than being something that they have to "learn along the way" (Interview 1, Sharon, November 5, 2009), music teachers will have positive role-identities that help them when new challenges arise in their teaching of young children.

REFERENCES

Bernard, R. J. (2004). *Striking a chord: Elementary general music teachers' expressions of their identities as musician-teachers.* Unpublished doctoral dissertation, Harvard University, Cambridge, MA.

Bouij, C. (2004). Two theoretical perspectives on the socialization of music teachers. *Action, Criticism, and Theory for Music Education, 3*(3). Retrieved from http://mas.siue.edu/ACT/v3/Bouij04.pdf.

Brewer, W. (2009). *Conceptions of effective teaching and role-identity development among preservice music educators.* Unpublished doctoral dissertation, Arizona State University, Tempe.

Conkling, S. W. (2004). Music teacher practice and identity in professional development partnerships. *Action, Criticism, and Theory for Music Education, 3*(3). Retrieved from http://mas.siue.edu/ACT/v3/Conkling04.pdf.

Creswell, J. W. (2007). *Qualitative inquiry and research design* (2nd ed.). Thousand Oaks, CA: Sage.

Draves, T. J. (2010). Fostering and sustaining preservice and inservice music teacher identity in the teaching experience. In L. K. Thompson and M. R. Campbell (Eds.), *Issues of identity in music education: Narrative and practices* (pp. 15–35). Charlotte, NC: Information Age.

Emerson, R. M., Fretz, R. I., and Shaw, L. L. (1995). *Writing ethnographic fieldnotes.* Chicago: University of Chicago Press.

Frierson-Campbell, C. (2004). Professional need and the contexts of in-service music teacher identity. *Action, Criticism, and Theory for Music Education, 3*(3). Retrieved from http://act.maydaygroup.org/articles/FriersonCampbell3_3.pdf.

Gordon, E. E. (2003). *A music learning theory for newborn and young children.* Chicago: GIA.

Hourigan, R. M. (2009). Preservice music teachers' perceptions of fieldwork experiences in a special needs classroom. *Journal of Research in Music Education, 57*(2), 152–68.

Isbell, D. S. (2008). Musicians and teachers: The socialization and occupational identity of preservice music teachers. *Journal of Research in Music Education, 56*(2), 162–78.

McCall, G. J., and Simmons, J. L. (1966). *Identities and interactions*. New York: Free Press.

National Association for the Education of Young Children (NAEYC). (2009). *Developmentally appropriate practice in early childhood programs serving children from birth through age 8*. Retrieved from www.naeyc.org/files/naeyc/file/positions/position%20statement%20Web.pdf.

Sideridis, G. D., and Chandler, J. P. (1995). Attitudes and characteristics of general music teachers toward integrating children with developmental disabilities. *Update: Applications of Research in Music Education, 14*(1), 9–15.

Roberts, B. (2006). Music making, making selves, making it right: A counterpoint to Rhoda Bernard. *Action, Criticism, and Theory for Music Education, 6*(2). Retrieved from http://act.maydaygroup.org/articles/Roberts6_2.pdf.

Stake, R. E. (1995). *The art of case study research*. Thousand Oaks, CA: Sage.

Wilson, B., and McCrary, J. (1996). The effect of instruction on music educators' attitudes toward students with disabilities. *Journal of Research in Music Education, 44*(1), 26–33.

Chapter Eight

Preschool Children's Uses of a Music Listening Center during Free-Choice Time

Wendy L. Sims, Lecia Cecconi-Roberts, and Dan Keast

The purpose of this study was to observe preschool-age children's use of a music listening center made available during their regular free-choice activity time. The activities in which nine children engaged each day for four consecutive days of free-choice time were timed and recorded when the children were four years old and again one year later when they were five (approximately 6.45 hours per child). Time spent per visit at the music center averaged 9.72 minutes at age four and 9.52 minutes at age five. On average, at age four the focus children spent 29.9 percent of their daily free-choice time at the listening center, and at age five, the average was 19.7 percent. A significant correlation found between responses of the focus children at the interval of one year was consistent with individual listening patterns described in the literature. We also documented the use of the listening center by all children in the classes being observed (N = 37). Visits ranged from 2.03 to 40.9 minutes, with an average of 12.15, and twenty instances of children spending greater than twenty minutes in one sitting. Many of the children spent time at the center comparable to, or greater than, time spent in the competing activities.

Listening to recorded music can be a source of pleasure, enrichment, and learning throughout life. To confirm this, one only needs to observe the number of MP3 players "attached" to people as they go about the day, the inclusion of high-quality stereo equipment as a standard component of new automobiles, the wealth associated with the recording industry and it's concerns about copyright and music piracy, the proliferation of "Mozart for Baby"–type commercial recordings, and so on.

Roulston (2006), who found that the children she studied listened to music via an array of technologies, noted that "private space for listening offered by new technologies in which individuals are able to express individual choice may well change the way children listen to and respond to music" (p. 18). Given all this, we continue to find it a source of puzzlement and even dismay that very few classrooms for preschool-age children provide the opportunity for children to listen to music individually as one of their free-choice activities (Sims and Cecconi-Roberts, 2005). When individual playback equipment and headphones are found in preschools,[1] the recordings provided are typically books-on-tape, which may include background music but primarily serve the purposes of the literacy curriculum.

The inaccessibility of music for individual listening may be related to teachers' underestimation of children's ability to listen to music for extended periods of time (Sims and Nolker, 2002). Traditional wisdom has been that children have short attention spans for music listening, yet it has repeatedly been found that this is not the case (Merrion, 1989; Sims, 1986, 2001, 2005; Sims and Cassidy, 1997; Sims and Nolker, 2002). Sims (2005) found, for example, that seven preschool-age children spent between twelve and twenty minutes in one sitting listening to recordings during their free-choice time, and three children listened for twenty-two to thirty minutes, all while fully aware that they could choose to stop the music and go on to another activity at any time.

Early childhood educators, whether they are music or nonmusic specialists, have little research-based knowledge available about children's music listening interests, skills, and potential. What is known comes primarily from music preference literature, which has concluded that young children's attitudes toward most kinds of music are generally quite positive and highly idiosyncratic (Sims and Cassidy, 1997).

The attitudes of four- and five-year-old children from Australia and Hong Kong toward singing, listening, playing musical instruments, and dancing/ moving as activities in their child care centers have been investigated using questionnaires and interviews (Yim and Ebbeck, 2009). Results related to listening indicated that "children in both cultural contexts enjoy the fun, aesthetic satisfaction and family support through music listening" (p. 105). The researchers also found that the children from Hong Kong "seemed to have more recurrent and predictable opportunities to listen to music as part of their daily routine in child care centres" (p. 105), occurring primarily during meals and naptimes. The results of this study support the supposition made by Sims and Cecconi-Roberts (2005) that opportunities for young children to participate in music listening experiences would be related to the development of positive attitudes toward music listening.

Young children demonstrate uncanny consistency as far as time spent listening, when listening to several pieces representing the same style and genre for as long or as short as they choose—a phenomenon Sims labeled *listening patterns* (Sims, 1986, 2001, 2005; Sims and Cassidy, 1997; Sims and Nolker,

2002). Preschoolers' listening patterns were found to remain reasonably stable across time (replications at twelve and eighteen months) and setting (alone with the researcher or as an in-classroom free-choice activity). Use of a listening-stimulated worksheet activity, however, resulted in shorter listening times than listening without the activity (Sims, 2005).

RESEARCH PURPOSE AND QUESTIONS

No previous research gathered behavioral data regarding how preschool children would use a listening center if it were provided during free-choice time in their classroom, in the same manner as the other activities. The purpose of this study was to begin to gather such data. Many questions were of interest: Would children choose to listen to music when that choice was competing with all the other possible activities? If yes, for how long? Would this interest be sustained over several days? How would children's participation in this activity be similar or different after one year? How would children's use of the listening center compare to their use of the other centers and play areas available simultaneously?

As implied above, the music education literature offers little guidance. A thorough literature search turns up numerous recommendations about, and descriptions of, music centers as free-choice activities. These typically refer to centers that include instrument play, sound exploration, or music and movement. As of yet, research or curriculum articles that address individual music listening as a free-choice activity do not appear to exist.

There is a small body of research concerning children's selection of activities during free-choice time. Although not always addressing music, some of these studies report on relevant aspects of children's free-choice behaviors. In the early days of microcomputer use in classrooms, Lipinski, Nida, Shade, and Watson (1986) were interested in the effects of a new computer on free-play choices of four- and five-year-old children. One of their primary concerns was examining what they identified as a fear that computer use would "inhibit other more social/learning activities" (p. 163). Their results indicated that this did not happen and that "interacting with the micro-computer was attractive but not engrossing" (p. 164). When the computer was first introduced, the children's use of the other free-play choices declined, which the authors called a *novelty effect* since by the third week they had generally returned to the precomputer levels. Music was not one of the activities available to the children in this study.

The authors of an observational study designed to examine ways to influence young children's selection of free-choice activities to increase participation in one-on-one direct instruction, library (literacy), and science noted that some children may play too long with one type of activity and thus not benefit from developing skills in other areas, while children on the opposite end of the spectrum may interact only briefly with many activities and thus not develop depth of skills with any activity (Hanley, Tiger, Ingvarsson, and Cammilleri, 2009). Their preschool-age participants were given nine choices of activities, including art, but not music.

A large investigation of children's use of free-play space did include music activities—one of the categories of activities observed by Harper and Huie (1998) that was labeled *music/gross motor*. They provided no further explanation of what that entailed, but we assumed that it means movement to music and/or playing instruments. The music/gross motor area was one of the seven most popular of the indoor play areas observed, receiving a *substantial* amount of use. After reviewing literature dating back to the 1920s, and their own results, the authors concluded that "a wide variety of factors have been shown to affect preschooler's immediate responses to their environments" (p. 425). These included the range of activities available, layout, amount of space for the activities, adult expectations, characteristics of the children including socioeconomic background, age, gender, culture/nationality, response to crowding, and the particular make-up of a play group.

METHOD

The purpose of this study was to observe preschool-age children's use of a music listening center made available during their free-choice activity time. Children from middle-income families enrolled in two classrooms in a small-city childcare center were observed. The first year, all children in the four-year-old classroom in attendance on the days of the study served as participants (N = 17), as did all children in the five-year-old classroom (N = 20) the second year. There were nine children, six girls and three boys, who were in attendance both years, so they served as the focus children for many of the comparisons. The center typically offered free-choice time after breakfast for about forty to sixty minutes, with activities including arts and crafts, computers, dramatic play, puzzles, and other manipulatives.

Each day, for four consecutive days, when free-choice time was available (field trips precluded free-choice time once during each week) during mid-June each year, we set up a listening center at one of the activity tables in the classroom. There were three cassette tape players with child-sized stereo headphones and multiple copies of two different cassettes, *The Carnival of the Animals*, by Camille Saints-Saëns (from *Classics for Children*, RCA Victor/BMG Music, 1988), and *A Child's Gift of Lullabies* (J. Aaron Brown,

JABA Records, 1987). These were selected because pieces from them had been used in several of the listening time studies cited above.

In these classrooms, it was normal practice to have adult supervision or assistance at some of the centers, particularly arts and crafts. One of the researchers, familiar to the children because she was a mother of one of them (her child was eliminated from consideration as a participant), assisted the children with the equipment, rewound the tapes, and so forth during the activity. Children were free to choose the listening activity whenever a space was available, and to come and go at will. Because on some days more children wanted turns than could be accommodated, a "waiting list" was compiled and waiting children had a chance to be first the next day if necessary.

In order to place the children's use of the music activity in context, we recorded all of the children's activity choices, necessitating that we videotape all of the classroom areas for subsequent viewing. Because of the limitations of the VHS video recorders' lens angles, this required filming with two cameras from different corners of the room simultaneously. We were able to use the same models of equipment for recording and for playback, so running speeds were almost identical and the two tapes per day could be viewed at the same time on VCRs and monitors set up next to each other. An enormous amount of data was generated; each of the nine focus children was observed one at a time for each day of attendance, so it took approximately six hours and forty-five minutes to record data for one focus child through all eight sessions. Additionally, data were compiled on all visits to the music table by *all* children each day.

Observation of the video data was straightforward. Each child's location was tracked continuously during each day of the study. Using observation software (*SCRIBE*) (Duke and Farrer, 2000), an on-screen template was generated with each activity area represented by its own "button." Each video was calibrated to begin at the same spot each time for each viewing. Clicking the mouse on the appropriate activity's button initiated a timer that recorded duration in minutes and seconds until a different activity button was clicked. There were four areas in addition to the music table available each day, plus two more possible categorizations: (a) *other*, used when a child was doing something besides an activity, such as getting a drink of water, and (b) *moving*, to record when a child was in transition between activities.

DATA ANALYSIS AND RESULTS

Data were analyzed in a variety of ways for the nine focus children. Identification and descriptions of patterns in how they used the music center were of primary interest. Each child made between zero and three visits per day, for a total of forty-seven visits across the eight days of the study (four days per year). At age four, time spent per visit at the music center ranged from a minimum of 1.1 minutes to a maximum of 26.6, with a mean of 9.72 (SD = 7.83). At age five, time spent per visit ranged from 2.23 to 22.92 minutes (M = 9.52, SD = 7.14). Individual's means ranged from 2.93 (SD = 2.31) to 15.80 (SD = 9.02) minutes at age four, and from 0.00 to 21.49 (SD = 2.03) at age five. The correlation between children's mean listening times at age four and age five was positive and significant (r = .637, p < .05).

Another way to analyze the data was to compare listening center use with use of the other areas. Time spent at each location was converted to percentages for these comparisons. On average, at age four the focus children spent 29.9 percent (SD = 18.38) of their daily free-choice time at the listening center, with individual daily mean percentages ranging from 10.9 percent to 45.2 percent (SD = 0.0 and 16.76 respectively). At age five, the average was 19.7 percent (SD = 15.07), with a range of 0.0 to 32.5 percent (SD's both = 0.0). There was a positive, but not significant, correlation between percentages at age four and age five (r = .44, p > .05).

Careful inspection of the data revealed that children tended to spend time at a few centers each day, neither staying at one for the whole time nor spending time at every one. The music center received the greatest percentage of time on one or more of the eight days for eight of the nine focus children; once for four children, twice for two children, three times for one child, and four times for one child. The percentage of time spent at the two sites that accounted for the largest amount of time on any given day for each child exceeded 51 percent for every target child, with an average of 71.3 percent (SD = 5.81) at four years and 83.5 percent (SD = 8.46) at age five. Each child's highest three sites accounted for an average of 84.9 percent (SD = 3.99) of the four-year-olds' time and 92.4 percent (SD = 3.90) of the five-year-olds', with a minimum of 68.8 percent and maximum of 100 percent.

In addition to assessing the use of the music listening center by the focus children, we kept track of all listening center visits by all thirty-seven children who were in the classroom during the eight days of the study. This ranged from ten to seventeen visits per day by eight to fourteen children each, some of whom visited the center two or three times in one day, for a total of one hundred visits over the course of the study. The average time spent per visit was 12.15 minutes (SD = 8.93). The relatively large standard deviation indicates the wide range of individual differences represented; visits ranged from 2.03 to 40.9 minutes. Of all children, only two of the four-year-olds did not spend any time at the music center, and there were twenty instances of children spending greater than twenty minutes in one sitting.

DISCUSSION

The most striking finding emerging from these data is the extent to which the children used the music listening center. Many of the children visited often and spent time at the center comparable to, or greater than, time spent in the competing activities. Children lined up to take turns at the center, and interest was sustained across the four-day periods. A logical follow-up study would be to investigate children's use of a music listening center available to them over a longer period of time, to see if there was a *novelty effect* that might wear off or level out, as noted for the computer (Lipinski et al. 1986). Harper and Huie (1998) reported that the music/gross motor site was one of their participants' top seven choices, and, with a similar type of long-term study, a music listening center's use and comparative ranking could be ascertained. A larger study would allow for examination of influences on the music listening activity with respect to the various factors identified by previous researchers (Harper and Huie, 1998; Yim and Ebbeck, 2009).

In prior studies, listening time was limited by the musical examples or by the lengths of the tapes, based on expectations of the limits of children's ability or interest for listening to recorded music (Sims, 1986, 2001, 2005; Sims and Cassidy, 1997; Sims and Nolker, 2002). In this study, when children were allowed to listen freely and were limited only by their own interest (and occasionally because the free-choice period was over), many listened for longer durations than have been documented previously. Although this activity was much less structured than those in the previous studies, the significant correlation found here between responses of children at the interval of one year are consistent with the individual listening patterns described in the literature. There also was a wide range of time children spent at visits to the listening center. Because each child approached music listening so differently, it only seems reasonable that opportunities for individual listening experiences be provided to accommodate children's different styles and needs.

When we examine the evidence from this study and earlier studies of children's listening behaviors, it seems clear that children find value and meaning in individual music listening. Certainly, music educators believe that listening to music is a valuable endeavor. Why, then, is individual music listening not a normal part of the preschool experience? Perhaps this is because it does not fit easily into any of the typical categories. It is not really play, does not develop social skills, and is not manipulative in the usual sense. But maybe it equates in some way to providing books for children who cannot yet read to peruse on their own—if immersion in print leads to valuing books and eventually to language literacy, perhaps immersion in music leads to emerging aesthetic responses and eventual musical literacy. Individual listening is an "authentic" way people experience music, the data appear to indicate that children are capable and interested, and the technology is accessible, relatively inexpensive, and easy for young children to operate (Roulston, 2006).

As Roulston noted, research exploring "how new technologies have impacted children's music preferences and their participation in school music programs . . . is needed if we are to develop a more complete understanding of children's musical preferences and listening habits, and by extension, how children develop as composers, singers, and performers" (p. 19).

There seem to be benefits to accrue by introducing and providing for individual listening experiences in the early childhood years, and this would be a valuable topic for future research. Research to investigate effective ways for encouraging teachers and caregivers to include music listening centers in their preschool classrooms would seem to be a worthy undertaking. Providing children with regular opportunities to choose to listen to music and to control their own music listening experiences has the potential to enhance children's immediate musical environment and ultimately to expand children's musical development and learning.

REFERENCES

Duke, R. A., and Farrer, A. (2000). *SCRIBE: Simple Computer Recording Interface for Behavioral Evaluation.* Austin, TX: Teaching and Learning Associates.

Harper, L. V., and Huie, K. S. (1998). Free play use of space by preschoolers from diverse backgrounds: Factors influencing activity choices. *Merrill-Palmer Quarterly, 44*, 423–46.

Hanley, G., Tiger, J., Ingvarsson, E., and Cammilleri, A. (2009). Influencing preschoolers' free-play activity preferences: An evaluation of satiation and embedded reinforcement. *Journal of Applied Behavior Analysis, 42*, 33–41.

Lipinski, J. M., Nida, R. E., Shade, D. D., and Watson, J. A. (1986). The effects of microcomputers on young children: An examination of free-play choices, sex differences, and social interactions. *Educational Computing Research, 2*, 147–68.

Merrion. M. (Ed). (1989). *What works: Instructional strategies for music education.* Reston, VA: MENC.

Roulston, K. (2006). Qualitative investigation of young children's music preferences. *International Journal of Education and the Arts, 7*(9), 1–23.

Sims, W. L. (1986). The effect of high versus low teacher affect and passive versus active student activity during music listening on preschool children's attention, piece preference, time spent listening, and piece recognition. *Journal of Research in Music Education, 34*, 73–191.

Sims, W. L. (2001). Characteristics of preschool children's individual music listening during free choice time. *Bulletin of the Council for Research in Music Education, 149*, 53–63.

Sims, W. L. (2005). Effects of free versus directed listening on duration of individual music listening by prekindergarten children. *Journal of Research in Music Education, 53*, 78–86.

Sims, W. L., and Cassidy, J. W. (1997). Verbal and operant responses of young children to vocal versus instrumental song performances. *Journal of Research in Music Education, 45*, 234–44.

Sims, W., and Cecconi-Roberts, L. C. (2005). Availability of recorded music in selected prekindergarten classrooms. *Missouri Journal of Research in Music Education, 52*, 58–76.

Sims, W. L., and Nolker, B. (2002). Individual differences in music listening responses of young children. *Journal of Research in Music Education, 50*, 292–300.

Yim, Y. H., and Ebbeck, M. (2009). Children's preferences for group musical activities in child care centres: A cross-cultural study. *Early Childhood Education, 37*, 103–11.

NOTE

1. The term "preschool" in this chapter will be used generically to refer to group settings for children prior to their enrollment in the formal school system.

Chapter Nine

Tonal Patterns: Providing the Vocabulary for Comprehensive Vocal Improvisation

Krista N. Velez

In this research, the effect of tonal pattern instruction on the vocal improvisations and developmental tonal music aptitudes of first- and second-grade students was examined. Participants were eighty-two first-grade students from four intact classes and one hundred second-grade students from four intact classes. Two classes of first-grade students and two classes of second-grade students were selected as treatment groups. The same music learning theory-based activities were taught within each grade over a full school year of instruction. In addition, the treatment groups received tonal pattern instruction consisting of major and minor patterns. Intermediate Measures of Music Audiation was administered as a pretest, midtest, and posttest to measure students' developmental tonal music aptitudes. After instruction, students improvised endings to unfamiliar songs in major/ duple, minor/triple, major/triple, and minor/duple and each student created a song without words. The improvisations were rated to measure the students' ability to maintain the dimensions of keyality, tonality, and harmonic function. For the vocal improvisation tasks, the treatment groups scored significantly higher than the control groups. The treatment and control groups in both grades experienced statistically significant gains in developmental tonal music aptitudes, and no strong relationships were found to exist between developmental tonal music aptitude and the tonal cohesiveness of vocal improvisations. Results of this study show that tonal pattern instruction in a music curriculum positively influences students' ability to improvise with tonal cohesion. Also, a music learning theory-based curriculum with repeated opportunities for vocal improvisation may increase students' developmental tonal music aptitudes.

Improvisation, the spontaneous creation of music, is an essential musical skill for students of all ages (Consortium of National Arts Education Associations [CNAEA], 1994). Improvising, which is a type of musical creativity, serves as an avenue for expressing musical ideas that are unique to each individual. With developmentally appropriate guidance, all students can learn to improvise, thus developing their abilities to express themselves through music and fostering their creative musical thought.

Improvisation can be defined as spontaneous audiation exhibited through performance using tonal, rhythm, and harmonic patterns within musical guidelines, such as within the context of a tonality, meter, or harmonic structure (Azzara, 1991; Gordon, 2007). Embedded in this definition is the idea that a musical vocabulary is needed to improvise successfully. Learning a music vocabulary in order to improvise musically is similar to learning a language vocabulary that one needs in order to converse with language. To engage in the improvisatory act of language conversation, one must know and be able to use a vocabulary of words. To engage in improvisation, one must know and be able to use a vocabulary of tonal, rhythmic, and harmonic patterns (Azzara, 1993; Gordon, 2007).

Researchers agree about the value of improvisation for a student's complete musical development (Azzara, 1999; Gordon, 2003; Guilbault, 2004; Kiehn, 2003). The need for and importance of creativity and improvisation in the music classroom is addressed by MENC in the *National Standards for Arts Education* (CNAEA, 1994). Although music educators recognize the importance of improvisation, few music educators place developing the skills needed to improvise with tonal, rhythmic, and harmonic cohesiveness as a primary curricular goal (Azzara, 1999; Gordon, 2003; Guilbault, 2004). Additionally, music educators who lack improvisational skills are unlikely to include developmentally appropriate classroom activities to aid their students' improvisational development (Azzara, 1999). Because of the lack of improvisation included in music classrooms and the absence of improvisational skills of many music educators, there is a great need both for teacher education concerning improvisation and for research to guide the development of an appropriate and comprehensive method of teaching improvisation to students of all ages.

Research on music creativity has focused on how the traits of the musically creative person and the musical environment affect the creative processes and products of both composition and improvisation. Composition, like improvisation, is a musically creative process that relies on the use of a musical vocabulary to express and refine musical ideas. However, whereas improvisation is the spontaneous creation of music, composition allows time for reflection and modification of the musical product (Kratus, 1989).

Studies have demonstrated that traits of the musically creative person can affect the person's musically creative processes and products (Auh, 1997; Baltzer, 1988; Burton, 1998; Kiehn, 2003; Kratus, 1989; Vaughan and Myers, 1971). There does not seem to be a relationship between the musically creative person and academic achievement, personality traits, mental ability (IQ), gender, or age (Baltzer, 1988; Burton, 1998; Kiehn, 2003). However, there may be a relationship between age and compositional processes. Examining the compositional processes and products of seven-, nine-, and eleven-year-old students, Kratus (1989) found that the nine- and eleven-year-old children were able to compose meaningful products using development and repetition in the compositional process. The seven-year-old children's extensive use of exploration in the compositional process suggests that students at this age may be less successful with improvisation.

Gordon (2007) believed that audiation is necessary for a person to create music; however, there are mixed results regarding the relationships between musical creativity, the process of composition, music aptitude, and the ability to audiate. Auh (1997) found that tonal music aptitude is a significant predictor of compositional creativity, and Kratus (1991) found a meaningful positive relationship between the ability to audiate and the use of time to develop instead of explore during the compositional process. Henry (2002) concluded that music aptitude did not directly affect the composing process, and Vaughan and Myers (1971) found that a person's level of music aptitude was not related to musical creativity.

Immersion in an environment rich with musical experiences, either formal or informal, may have a positive effect on musical creativity, and, for this reason, the music classroom is an extremely important place for development of musical creativity. When engaged in a creative process, students should feel comfortable and accepted rather than judged by their teacher and classmates (Kaschub, 1997). A well-qualified, musically trained teacher with a creative personality may provide the best musical opportunities and situations for fostering creativity from the students (Kalmar and Balasko, 1987). Scholars agree that the quality of music instruction influences a student's development of musical creativity (Henry, 2002; Kalmar and Balasko, 1987; Laczo, 1981; Vaughan and Myers, 1971). The quality and amount of musical experiences a student has will foster or hinder the development of that student's music creativity. When a student is given repeated opportunities to create in the music classroom, through improvisation or composition, the student's development of musically creative skills is facilitated (Henry, 2002; Kalmar and Balasko, 1987; Laczo, 1981; Vaughan and Myers, 1971). Also, combining pattern instruction with repeated compositional activities was shown to be an effective instructional method for teaching composition (Henry, 2002). Informal music experiences, such as watching music television, listening to music on CDs or radio, and attending concerts, may be strong indicators of compositional creativity (Auh, 1997).

Research suggests that improvisation is developmental. Kratus (1996) developed seven levels for music educators to use as a guideline for teaching improvisations. Exploration is the first level, during which students do not have the ability to audiate, and is most concerned with experimenting with different types and combinations of musical sounds using their voice or an instrument. The student then moves through process-oriented improvisation, during which the student is concerned more with the process of improvising than with the end result, to product-oriented improvisation, during which the student's improvisations begin to reflect tonality, meter, phrasing, and structure. When engaged in the fourth level, fluid improvisation, the student becomes more comfortable with the medium of performance. In the fifth level, structural improvisation, the student uses his or her developing musicianship to employ musical strategies such as tension and release. The student is able to perform in different styles and pushes the boundaries of existing styles at the last two levels: stylistic improvisation and personal improvisation.

The research of Flohr (1985) and Brophy (1999, 2005) supports the seven levels of improvisational development by articulating the ages at which these levels may often occur for instrumental improvisation (specifically, xylophones). Flohr (1985) studied the instrumental improvisations of children ages two and eight and found that the formal properties of music, including the emergence of tonality and a sense of formal structure (characteristics of product-oriented improvisations) surface between these years. Before this, students need the opportunity to explore the instrument, experiment with musical sounds, and practice improvising. Brophy (1999) examined the instrumental improvisations of children between the ages of six and twelve and found that a dynamic stage of development may exist between ages six and nine, with the most significant change between the ages of eight and nine, during which children move from process-oriented to product-oriented improvisations. After children reach age nine, Brophy suggests that there is a developmental plateau. To study this dynamic stage of improvisation development, Brophy (2005) conducted a longitudinal study over a three-year period. The participants began the study at age seven and ended at age nine. In this study, the most musically characteristic changes occurred between the ages of seven and eight. The studies of Flohr (1985) and Brophy (1999, 2005), both focusing on instrumental improvisation, suggest that, between the ages of two and seven, students move from exploration to process-oriented improvisation, and from ages seven to nine, students move from process to product-oriented improvisation.

Petzold (1969) studied the vocal improvisations of children between the ages of six and twelve and found that the greatest gains in improvements in vocal improvisations were between grades 1 and 2 (approximately ages six to eight). The nonmelodic improvisations by the first-grade students mostly were eliminated by second grade, due to a gain in auditory perception and vocal control. These findings parallel the shift from process- to product-oriented improvisations between similar ages with instrumental improvisation found by Flohr (1985) and Brophy (1999, 2005).

Specific factors, such as the amount of music education and the quality of music education, directly affect students' vocal improvisations. Laczo (1981) found that, the more exposure students have to a musical environment, the more tonal, rhythmic, and musically structured their improvisations. Kalmar and Balasko (1987) concluded that a creative, musical, and enthusiastic teacher fosters musical creativity. Both studies demonstrate the importance of a musically creative and rich environment.

Guilbault (2004, 2009) studied the effect of root melody instruction on the vocal improvisations of students' in kindergarten through sixth grade. She concluded that students who received root melody accompaniment with song instruction were able to improvise better with implied harmonic changes and harmonic rhythm in all grades than those who did not have root melody instruction. Oddly, there were no differences in improvisations according to age. These results suggest that musical age is the determining factor in improvisation skills rather than chronological age, since none of the students in her study had previous experiences with the type of musical instruction given. Guilbault's conclusions are different from those of Flohr (1985) and Brophy (1999, 2005), who found differences between the ages; however, Guilbault's work is supported by the work of Kalmar and Balasko (1987) and Laczo (1981), who concluded that exposure to musical experiences and musically rich and creative environments aid in students improvising with musical meaning, regardless of age level.

Based on this review of literature, the research on children's vocal improvisations, including developmentally appropriate instructional methods, is still in its infancy. Given that musical creativity is developmental in children, requires musically rich environments and opportunities, and is avoided in many classrooms, it is important to determine the best pedagogical approach to support the development of music improvisational skill in children. Therefore, the purpose of this study was to examine the effect of tonal pattern instruction on the tonal cohesiveness of vocal improvisations and developmental music aptitude of early elementary-age children. Specific research questions addressed are as follows: (a) Are the vocal improvisations of first- and second-grade students who had tonal pattern instruction in major and minor harmonic more tonally cohesive than the vocal improvisations of first- and second-grade students who did not have such instruction? (b) Does the inclusion of tonal pattern instruction in major and minor harmonic have an effect on developmental tonal music aptitude as measured by *Intermediate Measures of Music Audiation* (IMMA) (Gordon, 1986)? (c) Is there a relationship between developmental tonal music aptitude and the tonal cohesiveness of students' vocal improvisations?

METHOD

Site and Participants

The study was conducted at a midsize elementary school in Delaware. The participants were eighty-two first-grade students from four intact classes and one hundred second-grade students from four intact classes. Two classes of first-grade students (N = 45) and two classes of second-grade students (N = 50) were selected randomly to be the treatment groups. The remaining two first-grade classes (N = 37) and second-grade classes (N = 50) served as the control groups. The teacher-researcher was a second-year graduate student at the University of Delaware with classroom experience teaching music through practicum-based college courses, student teaching, private flute and piano lessons, and early childhood classes. Prior to conducting the study, the teacher-researcher earned certificates from the Gordon Institute of Music Learning for Elementary General Music Level 1 and Early Childhood Level 1.

Procedure

The study was conducted over the entire 2006–2007 school year (see table 9.1) and included the following criterion measures: (a) *Intermediate Measures of Music Audiation* (IMMA) (Gordon, 1986) and (b) a set of five vocal improvisation tasks. IMMA was administered as a pretest, midtest, and posttest to determine whether the inclusion of tonal pattern instruction affects developmental tonal music aptitude. IMMA is a standardized test that measures developmental music aptitude of children in grades 1–4. IMMA was used rather than the *Primary Measures of Music Audiation* (PMMA) (Gordon, 1986) because it contains more challenging tonal patterns. This helps to differentiate the audiation abilities of the students more than PMMA, resulting in a larger range of scores and providing more information on an individual's capability to audiate. While it includes subtests for both tonal aptitude and rhythm aptitude, only the tonal subtest was used for this study. The reliability of this test for first grade is .76 and second grade is .78 according to the test manual (Gordon, 1986). The vocal improvisation tasks were given as a posttest to determine whether the inclusion of tonal pattern instruction affects the tonal cohesiveness of vocal improvisations. Students were asked to improvise endings to four unfamiliar songs composed by the researcher, as well as to create a song.

Table 9.1. Procedural Outline

Week	Task
1	Introductory Musical Activities
2	Pretest IMMA
3–16	Formal Instruction
17	Midtest IMMA
18–36	Formal Instruction
37–38	Vocal Improvisation Tasks
39	Posttest IMMA
40–41	Make-ups and Musical Activities

The first week of class was devoted to introductory musical activities, learning the students' names, and reviewing the procedures of the music classroom. To test for developmental tonal music aptitude, the students were administered the tonal subtest of IMMA as a pretest during the second week.

The subsequent weeks were devoted to formal instruction, which is defined as a curriculum in which content and the development of music skills are structured and sequenced (Gordon, 2007). The first-grade students received twenty-two lessons, and the second-grade students received twenty-four lessons over this period. The first- and second-grade classes received the same instruction for the first six lessons; however, because the second-grade students received a year of developmentally appropriate instruction prior to this study and the first grade did not, the researcher decided to create separate lessons for the grades in order to musically challenge the students appropriately.

All students received instruction based on Edwin Gordon's music learning theory, which describes how music is learned in a sequential and developmental manner and bases its activities on this information (Gordon, 1971). The curriculum focused on the audiation of tonalities and meters in order to aid in the understanding of music. Students listened to and performed songs in a variety of tonalities and meters, first with neutral syllables and then with moveable do tonal syllables. Students also listened to and performed chants in various meters, first with neutral syllables and then with rhythm syllables. The rhythm syllables for macrobeats (the fundamental beat) were "du" and microbeats (equal division) for duple meter were "du de" and triple meter were "du da di" (Gordon, 2007). Music was learned through singing, chanting, and moving. Students sang in solo and as a group in a variety of tonalities and meters. Students performed rhythmic chanting in solo and as a group in a variety of meters. Movement included body awareness, microbeat and macrobeat movement, informal circle dances, and formal folk dances. The skills learned through singing, chanting, and moving were then applied to nonpitched and pitched percussion instruments.

During formal instruction, all students received multiple opportunities for improvisation during music class. The activities were developed to allow the students to audiate spontaneously and perform within tonal and rhythmic parameters of major and minor tonalities and duple and triple meters. The students improvised endings to unfamiliar songs, sang on a neutral syllable, and held musical conversations with the teacher-researcher, taking turns singing or chanting four-macrobeat phrases in a given tonality and/or meter.

During the weeks of formal instruction, the treatment group received tonal pattern instruction based on major and minor tonic and dominant chords, as sequenced by the *Jump Right In: Tonal Register Book 1* (Gordon and Woods, 1990). Each unit of the register book focuses on a skill within a tonality, such as singing the resting tone after a pattern, repeating a pattern, or labeling pattern function, such as tonic and dominant in major and minor. Each activity provides an easy, medium, and difficult pattern so that each student can be challenged according to his tonal music aptitude as measured by IMMA. Students sang individual tonal patterns in solo and class patterns as a group. Pattern instruction for the treatment groups was given every lesson for seven to ten minutes. The control group did not receive formal tonal pattern instruction. Instead, the teacher-researcher was able to extend each activity (including the hello and goodbye songs) by a minute or two.

After the formal instruction period, during the thirty-seventh and thirty-eighth week of school, each student was audio-recorded individually completing five vocal improvisation tasks. Each student improvised endings to unfamiliar songs in (a) major tonality and duple meter (major/duple), (b) minor tonality and triple meter (minor/triple), (c) major tonality and triple meter (major/triple), and (d) minor tonality and duple meter (minor/duple). The unfamiliar songs, composed by the teacher-researcher, purposefully implied tonic and dominant harmonies, were equal in length, and ended on an implied dominant to provide the students an opportunity to resolve to the tonic at the end of the song. Each student also created a song with a researcher-supplied keyality of D. To allow the student to choose his own tonality and meter, the researcher sang the fifth (A) and tonic (D) to provide a comfortable singing range on a neutral syllable without meter. The improvisations were judged independently by two judges using continuous rating scales to measure the tonal cohesiveness of the endings of the criterion songs and the students' created songs. The rating scales measured the students' abilities to maintain tonality, keyality, and the implication of harmonic function within the improvisations. After the vocal improvisation tasks were complete, the students took the tonal subtest of IMMA a third time to determine whether major and minor harmonic tonal pattern instruction had an effect on developmental tonal music aptitude of the children and whether a relationship exists between developmental tonal music aptitude and the ability to vocally improvise with tonal cohesion.

RESULTS

Data were gathered and evaluated to examine the specific questions: (a) Are the vocal improvisations of first- and second-grade students who had pattern instruction with major and minor harmonic tonal patterns more tonally cohesive than the vocal improvisations of first- and second-grade students who did not have such instruction? (b) Does pattern instruction with major and minor harmonic tonal patterns have an effect on developmental tonal music aptitude as measured by IMMA? (c) Is there a relationship between developmental tonal music aptitude and the tonal cohesiveness of students' vocal improvisations and songs?

Vocal Improvisation Tasks

The participants in the study completed five vocal improvisation tasks. Each task was rated on a continuous rating scale for the students' ability to maintain dimensions of (a) keyality, (b) tonality, and (c) harmonic function. Interjudge reliability for the continuous rating scales ranged from .398 to .689 for first grade (see table 9.2) and from .266 to .341 for second grade (see table 9.3). While the interjudge reliabilities were moderately low, they were satisfactory for combining the judges' scores for statistical analyses.

To determine whether the vocal improvisations of the students who had pattern instruction with major and minor tonal patterns were more tonally cohesive than the students who did not have such instruction, two-tailed t-tests assuming equal variance were performed to compare each dimension and the composite scores of the vocal improvisation tasks. Results for the analysis of the first-grade scores revealed statistically significant differences ($p < .05$) according to treatment, with participants in the treatment group creating more tonally cohesive improvisations when improvising the ending of unfamiliar songs in major and minor tonalities and duple and triple meters (see table 9.4). While the means for the treatment group are higher for song creation, the

Table 9.2. First Grade Interjudge Reliabilities

Task	r Keyality	r Tonality	r Harmonic Function	r Composite
Maj/Dup	.677	.630	.639	.689
Min/Tri	.634	.647	.626	.664
Maj/Tri	.583	.608	.582	.634
Min/Dup	.640	.599	.560	.635
Song Creation	.436	.428	.398	.448

Table 9.3. Second Grade Interjudge Reliabilities

Task	r Keyality	r Tonality	r Harmonic Function	r Composite
Maj/Dup	.549	.485	.443	.523
Min/Tri	.584	.593	.584	.615
Maj/Tri	.596	.606	.601	.640
Min/Dup	.459	.442	.409	.479
Song Creation	.341	.309	266	.333

results are not significant, perhaps because the reliabilities for these ratings were particularly low.

Results for the analysis of second-grade vocal improvisation task scores revealed statistically significant differences ($p < .05$) between treatment groups, with participants in the treatment group creating more tonally cohesive improvisations when improvising the ending of unfamiliar songs in major tonality and duple meter (see table 9.5). The treatment group also maintained keyality for the minor/duple improvisation and creating a song better than the

Table 9.4. First Grade Means and Standard Deviations for Vocal Improvisation Task Dimensions

Task	Dimension	Treatment		Control			
		M	SD	M	SD	t	P
Maj/Dup	Keyality	2.68	1.06	2.25	1.05	2.547	.012*
	Tonality	2.91	1.07	2.50	1.06	2.703	.008*
	Harmonic	2.96	1.08	2.47	1.08	2.853	.005*
	Composite	8.54	3.11	7.19	3.12	2.771	.006*
Min/Tri	Keyality	2.64	1.07	2.28	1.20	2.030	.044*
	Tonality	2.83	1.08	2.50	1.14	2.150	.033*
	Harmonic	2.87	1.12	2.46	1.14	2.297	.023*
	Composite	8.34	3.20	7.20	3.43	2.202	.029*
Maj/Tri	Keyality	2.80	1.09	2.50	1.14	1.717	.088
	Tonality	3.03	1.08	2.70	1.07	1.964	.051*
	Harmonic	3.03	1.05	2.70	1.08	1.975	.050*
	Composite	8.87	3.12	7.91	3.21	1.938	.054*
Min/Dup	Keyality	2.78	0.70	2.47	1.04	1.942	.054*
	Tonality	2.96	0.96	2.66	1.04	1.879	.062
	Harmonic	3.00	1.01	2.66	1.04	2.111	.036*
	Composite	8.73	2.85	7.80	3.05	2.028	.044*
SCreation	Keyality	2.60	1.05	2.35	1.03	1.527	.129
	Tonality	2.80	0.99	2.58	1.03	1.385	.168
	Harmonic	2.78	0.98	2.58	1.03	1.247	.214
	Composite	8.18	2.94	7.51	3.00	1.428	.155

students in the control group. The remaining results were not statistically significant, although the scores for the treatment group consistently were higher for all tasks than those of the control group.

Intermediate Measures of Music Audiation

IMMA pretest, midtest, and posttest split-halves reliabilities were computed and corrected using the Spearman-Brown Prophecy Formula. Reliability for the first-grade pretest was .75, midtest was .78, and posttest was .83. Reliability for second-grade pretest was .76, midtest was .75, and posttest was .82. These reliabilities are moderately high and are comparable to those reported in the manual.

Data were analyzed using a repeated measures analysis of variance (ANOVA). Developmental music aptitude was measured as a pretest before treatment, a midtest seventeen weeks into treatment, and a posttest directly following treatment. IMMA results for the first-grade students demonstrated

Table 9.5. Second Grade Means and Standard Deviations for Vocal Improvisation Task Dimensions

| Task | Dimension | Treatment | | Control | | | |
		M	SD	M	SD	t	P
Maj/Dup	Keyality	3.03	1.04	2.66	1.02	2.544	.012*
	Tonality	3.21	1.00	2.83	1.01	2.682	.008*
	Harmonic	3.25	0.98	2.88	1.02	2.621	.010*
	Composite	9.49	2.93	8.37	2.94	2.699	.008*
Min/Tri	Keyality	3.01	1.06	2.73	0.95	1.967	.051*
	Tonality	3.11	1.03	2.89	0.92	1.590	.114
	Harmonic	3.14	1.06	2.90	0.94	1.693	.092
	Composite	9.26	3.10	8.52	2.74	1.791	.075
Maj/Tri	Keyality	3.03	1.05	2.81	1.00	1.517	.131
	Tonality	3.17	1.00	3.12	0.91	0.370	.712
	Harmonic	3.21	1.01	3.13	0.92	0.587	.558
	Composite	9.41	2.98	9.06	2.73	0.867	.387
Min/Dup	Keyality	2.93	1.01	2.78	0.95	1.084	.280
	Tonality	3.15	.94	3.04	0.92	0.838	.403
	Harmonic	3.21	.98	3.03	0.93	1.337	.183
	Composite	9.29	2.8	8.85	2.72	1.128	.261
SCreation	Keyality	2.73	.98	2.45	0.89	2.109	.036*
	Tonality	2.95	.06	2.76	0.92	1.429	.155
	Harmonic	2.97	.95	2.75	0.96	1.633	.104
	Composite	8.65	2.8	7.96	2.66	1.785	.076

significance for time ($F = 30.888$, $df[2]$, $p = .0001$), but neither the main effect for group nor the group-by-time interaction was significant (respectively, $F = 1.610$, $df[1]$, $p = .2082$; $F = .83$, $df[2]$, $p = .4353$). The main effect for time for the second-grade students was significant ($F = 14.022$, $df[2]$, $p = .0001$), but neither the main effect for group nor the group-by-time interaction was significant (respectively, $F = .001$, $df[1]$, $p = .9783$; $F = .965$, $df[2]$, $p = .3829$).

Intermediate Measures of Music Audiation and Vocal Improvisation Tasks

Pearson-product moment correlations were performed to determine whether relationships existed between developmental tonal music aptitude as measured by the IMMA posttest and the students' scores on the vocal improvisation tasks. The relationships between developmental tonal music aptitude and the vocal improvisations tasks were found to be weak for both first and second grade (see table 9.6). The first-grade results showed a stronger relationship between IMMA and task scores for the first four tasks; however, the

Table 9.6. Vocal Improvisation Task Scores and Posttest IMMA Correlations

Task	Dimension	First Grade		Second Grade	
		Treatment r	*Control r*	*Treatment r*	*Control r*
Maj/Dup	Keyality	.328	.094	.133	.121
	Tonality	.311	.136	.153	.013
	Harmonic	.290	.144	.148	.002
	Composite	.315	.126	.147	.048
Min/Tri	Keyality	.306	.086	.050	.143
	Tonality	.274	.040	.081	.153
	Harmonic	.253	.040	.079	.108
	Composite	.281	.056	.071	.137
Maj/Tri	Keyality	.277	.176	.128	.060
	Tonality	.242	.103	.138	.052
	Harmonic	.267	.085	.140	.094
	Composite	.266	.124	.137	.070
Min/Dup	Keyality	.070	-.066	.142	.042
	Tonality	.115	-.084	.143	.034
	Harmonic	.060	-.084	.126	.029
	Composite	.083	-.079	.141	.036
SCreation	Keyality	-.003	-.003	.011	.084
	Tonality	-.030	-.029	.088	.074
	Harmonic	-.023	-.029	.088	.064
	Composite	-.018	-.021	.063	.077

song creation scores indicated virtually no relationship. Again, this possibly may be attributed to the poor interjudge reliabilities for those ratings. The second-grade results showed slightly stronger relationships in the treatment group for the major/duple, major/triple and minor/duple tasks and in the control group for the minor/triple task. Both groups in second grade showed weak relationships for the song creation task.

Summary

The results of this study indicate significant differences between the treatment and control groups among both the first- and second-grade students. Given the number of significant differences found on the vocal improvisation tasks, tonal pattern instruction appeared to have a positive effect on the students' ability to vocally improvise within a given keyality, tonality, and with implied harmonic function. Tonal pattern instruction did not seem to have an effect on developmental tonal music aptitude, since both treatment and control groups in first and second grade achieved significantly higher IMMA scores by the end of instruction. For both first and second grade, there does not seem to be a meaningful relationship between the ability to vocally improvise and developmental tonal music aptitude.

DISCUSSION, CONCLUSIONS, AND IMPLICATIONS

Based on the results of this study, tonal pattern instruction improves first- and second-grade students' abilities to improvise vocally within a given keyality, tonality, and with harmonic implications. This may be due to the students' learning of a tonal vocabulary. During pattern instruction, students internalize a vocabulary of primary chord functions. This vocabulary of tonic and dominant patterns provides the means with which to improvise vocally within musical guidelines, such as within a keyality, tonality, and harmonic progression.

For the first-grade students, this effect was primarily found on all tasks that involved improvising an ending to an unfamiliar song. For the second-grade students, the students who had tonal pattern instruction improvised an ending better to an unfamiliar major duple song, and maintained keyality better when improvising an ending in major tonality and triple meter and when creating a song. There were no significant differences according to treatment for the remainder of the second-grade scores, although the students who had tonal pattern instruction scored higher on every dimension of each task, and many of these differences approached significance. The moderately low interjudge reliability scores may have been a factor for the lack of statistically significant differences.

Repeated opportunities to improvise with musical parameters may help students to create tonally cohesive products when improvising. When creating a song, significant differences were markedly less according to treatment. This may have been due to the students' lack of experience creating a song without guidelines for keyality, tonality, and harmonic progression or to the low interjudge reliabilities for that task. Over the course of the school year, students had opportunities to improvise endings to unfamiliar songs in major tonality, minor tonality, duple meter, and triple meter. They also experienced musical conversations (creating antecedent/consequent phrases) in which rhythmic or melodic phrases were used. However, the students had never experienced creating an entire song without tonal and rhythmic restrictions in music class. The lack of experience and understanding the students had with this task may have led to song creations that were less tonally cohesive than the improvised endings.

Providing keyality, tonality, meter, length, and structure restrictions benefits a young student's ability to improvise vocally with tonal cohesiveness. The first four tasks were designed to allow the student to hear the keyality, tonality, harmonic progressions, and structure of the unfamiliar song before the students had to create an ending. In addition, the endings were also relatively short, since the students improvised an ending after two-measure phrases, implying that the improvisations should be two measures in length to provide balance between the phrases, which many students were able to do because it was practiced during formal instruction. On the other hand, the restrictions for the song creation were different and minimal. The researcher suggested a keyality (which did not have to be used), but did not suggest a tonality, meter, or length for the improvisation. The lack of restrictions for this task may have made it difficult for the students to understand, leading to vocal improvisations that lacked tonal cohesion. This also may have affected the judges' abilities to pinpoint each student's keyality, tonality, and underlying harmonic progression, thereby causing lower interjudge reliabilities.

Tonal pattern instruction did not have an effect on students' developmental tonal music aptitudes. In both first and second grade, the students experienced significant growth in developmental tonal music aptitude over time, but not according to treatment or treatment-by-time. Since there were no significant differences between groups, the gains in developmental tonal music aptitude cannot be attributed to tonal pattern instruction. The gains for all groups in both grades may be due to the music learning theory-based instruction that all participants received, because the ability to audiate is fundamental to developing music aptitude (Gordon, 2007). This result in both first and second grade demonstrates that certain types of instruction may help to develop students' ability to audiate. The gains also may be due to maturation.

The skills demonstrated during tonal pattern instruction may be independent of developmental tonal music aptitude. During tonal pattern instruction, students repeated, audiated, and sang both tonic and dominant tonal patterns individually and as a group. On the other hand, to determine developmental tonal music aptitude, students listened to two tonal patterns and labeled them same or different. Tonal pattern discrimination may be a different skill than tonal performance. This is supported by Feierabend and Saunders' (1998) research examining the relationship between the ability to discriminate aurally between tonal patterns and the ability to perform orally the same tonal patterns. They found a weak relationship when correlating students' scores on an aural discrimination test and their abilities to orally reproduce patterns. Feierabend and Saunders (1998) concluded that aural discrimination and oral performance may be independent abilities.

The ability to improvise vocally with tonal cohesiveness is not related to developmental tonal music aptitude as measured by IMMA. Correlations indicated almost no relationship between developmental tonal music aptitude and the tonal cohesiveness of vocal improvisations when examined as a whole. It may be that music achievement and developmental music aptitude, as measured by discrimination tests, are unrelated.

Implications for Early Childhood Music Educators

Based on the results of this study, the inclusion of tonal pattern instruction positively affects a students' ability to improvise with tonal cohesion, which is a reflection of a students' musical understanding. By including tonal patterns based on major and minor tonic and dominant chords, and by challenging students individually according to their musical ability, students develop a tonal vocabulary that helps them in their audiation of keyality, tonality, and harmonic function, which can be demonstrated through improvisation. Music educators should include tonal pattern instruction on a consistent basis to help students achieve musical comprehension.

Although this study used a formal method to teach tonal patterns to first- and second-grade students, tonal patterns can be included in any curriculum, regardless of a child's age. Pattern instruction from *Jump Right In: Tonal Register Book* (Gordon and Woods, 1990) can be used with students who are ready for formal instruction and are able to follow directions in order to sing patterns together and individually.

Music educators should implement a curriculum that focuses on the development of audiation with repeated opportunities for vocal improvisation.

Such a curriculum may have a positive effect on developmental tonal music aptitude and can be started appropriately at any age. A teacher who implements a curriculum with activities to develop audiation, focusing on elements such as beat competency, audiation of resting tone, and formal and stylistic movement, may have a positive influence on the students' musical achievement and developmental music aptitudes.

Music educators should provide musically contextual restrictions for tonality, keyality, and meter when teaching improvisation to young students. Activities such as improvising endings to songs and holding tonal or rhythm conversations within a tonality and meter provide students with a musical structure in which to create. This may serve as readiness for creating songs. Students in first and second grade may not have the musical skills and knowledge to spontaneously create a song without restrictions provided by a music teacher. Yet improvisation preparation and activities can be an integral part of any music curriculum. While students may not be ready to improvise with a sense of tonality, form, and musical structure before first grade, they can begin to acquire a vocabulary of patterns to use in their improvisations, as well as to participate in activities to experiment and explore with musical sounds (Flohr, 1985; Kratus 1989, 1996).

The development of creativity and improvisational skills should play a vital role in every music classroom. Improvisation provides students with opportunities for individual musical expression and teachers with opportunities to assess their students' musical understanding. This study demonstrates that the inclusion of pattern instruction positively affects students' abilities to improvise, making it an appropriate means of developing improvisational skills. More research needs to be conducted concerning how students learn to improvise with tonal cohesiveness. With a deeper understanding of how children develop music comprehension through improvisation and musical creativity, music educators will be able to develop and implement an appropriate, sequential, and comprehensive method of teaching improvisation to children of all ages.

REFERENCES

Auh, M. (1997). Prediction of musical creativity in composition among selected variables for upper elementary students. *Bulletin for the Council for Research in Music Education, 133*, 1–9.

Azzara, C. D. (1991). Audiation, improvisation, and music learning theory. *Journal of Music Teaching and Learning, 2*(1–2), 106–9.

Azzara, C. D. (1993). Audiation-based improvisation techniques and elementary instrumental students' music achievement. *Journal of Research in Music Education, 41*(4), 328–42.

Azzara, C. D. (1999). An aural approach to improvisation. *Music Educators Journal, 86*(3), 21–25.

Baltzer, S. (1988). A validation study of a measure of musical creativity. *Journal of Research in Music Education, 36*(4), 232–49.

Brophy, T. S. (1999). The melodic improvisations of children ages six through twelve: A developmental perspective. *Dissertation Abstracts International, 59*(9), 3386A.

Brophy, T. S. (2005). A longitudinal study of selected characteristics of children's melodic improvisations. *Journal of Research in Music Education, 53*(2), 120–33.

Burton, S. L. (1998). An investigation between musical creativity and personality traits. *Masters Abstracts International, 36*(1), 28.

Consortium of National Arts Education Associations (CNAEA). (1994). *National standards for arts education.* Reston, VA: MENC.

Feierabend, J., and Saunders, C. (1998). The relationship between aural and oral musical abilities in first, second, and third grade students. *Early Childhood Connections, 4*(3), 10–18.

Flohr, J. (1985). Young children's improvisations: Emerging creative thought. *Creative Child and Adult Quarterly, 10*(2), 79–85.

Gordon, E. E. (1971). *The psychology of music teaching.* Englewood Cliffs, NJ: Prentice-Hall.

Gordon, E. E. (1986). *Primary measures of music audiation and intermediate measures of music audiation: Manual.* Chicago: GIA.

Gordon, E. E. (2003). *Improvisation in the music classroom.* Chicago: GIA.

Gordon, E. E. (2007). *Learning sequences in music: A contemporary music learning theory.* Chicago: GIA.

Gordon, E. E., and Woods, D. G. (1990). *Jump right in: Tonal register book one.* Chicago: GIA.

Guilbault, D. M. (2004). The effect of harmonic accompaniment on the tonal achievement and tonal improvisations of children in kindergarten and first grade. *Journal of Research in Music Education, 52*(1), 64–76.

Guilbault, D. M. (2009). The effects of harmonic accompaniment on the tonal improvisations of students in first through sixth grade. *Journal of Research in Music Education, 57*(2), 81–91.

Henry, W. (2002). The effects of pattern instruction, repeated composing opportunities, and musical aptitude on the compositional process and product of fourth-grade students. *Contributions to Music Education, 29*(1), 9–28.

Kalmar, M., and Balasko, G. (1987). Musical mother tongue and creativity in preschool children's melody improvisations. *Bulletin of the Council for Research in Music Education, 91*, 77–86.

Kaschub, M. (1997). Exercising the musical imagination. *Music Educators Journal, 84*(3), 26–32.

Kiehn, M. T. (2003). Development of music creativity among elementary school students. *Journal of Research in Music Education, 51*(4), 278–88.

Kratus, J. (1989). A time analysis of the compositional processes used by children ages 7–11. *Journal of Research in Music Education, 37*(1), 5–20.

Kratus, J. (1991). Relationships among children's music audiation and their compositional processes and products. *Journal of Research in Music Education, 42*(2), 115–30.

Kratus, J. (1996). A developmental approach to teaching music improvisation. *International Journal of Music Education, 26,* 27–38.

Laczo, Z. (1981). A psychological investigation of improvisation abilities in the lower and higher classes of the elementary school. *Bulletin of the Council for Research in Music Education, 66–67,* 39–45.

Petzold, R. G. (1969). Auditory perception by children. *Journal of Research in Music Education, 17*(1), 21–43.

Vaughan, M., and Meyers, R. (1971). An examination of musical process as related to creative thinking. *Journal of Research in Music Education, 19*(3), 337–41.

Part III

MUSICAL PARENTING

Chapter Ten

Parents' Documentation of Their Children's Music-Related Behaviors

Wendy H. Valerio, Alison M. Reynolds, John Grego, Ching Ching Yap, and Anne McNair

The purpose of this research was to investigate parents/guardians' documentation of children's music-related behaviors. Research questions were as follows: (a) How reliably can parents/guardians (parents) document their children's music behaviors using the Child Music-Related Behavior Questionnaire *(CMRBQ), a researcher-developed instrument? (b) Are there differences in the frequencies of children's music-related behaviors based on age, and the music activities parents perform with them? The CMRBQ comprises demographics, part 1 (types of children's music behaviors) and part 2 (parent's music activities with children). With a 32.5 percent return rate (N =249), subscale reliabilities ranged from α = .77 to α = .95. Researchers conducted a 5 $\times$ 3 (age category $\times$ parent level) MANOVA with seven dependent variables and detected a significant interaction effect with Pillai's trace = .329, F (56, 1554) = 1.37, p = .0377; Wilks's Lambda = .707, F (56, 1168.5) = 1.39, p =.0331, and Hotelling's T-squared = .366, F (56, 763.23), p = .0314. Researchers identified canonical variables for the age category main effect, parent level main effect, and the (age category $\times$ parent level) interaction effect. Parents who performed the most music activities with their children reported their children performing the most music-related behaviors. In general parents reported that music-related behaviors increased as a function of age category, though the amount of increase became steadily smaller as children aged. Researchers may use the CMRBQ to gain information reliably from parents about the music-related behaviors that they observe their children perform and the music activities that they perform with their children.*

Since approximately 1980, researchers and practitioners have increased their emphasis on early childhood music education in the United States, and more recently, their efforts to document rapid changes within the field (Custodero, 2008; Custodero and Chen-Hafteck, 2008; Nardo, Custodero, Persellin, and Fox, 2006; Overland and Reynolds, in press; Persellin, 2007). Persellin (2007) has called for improved dialogue among early childhood researchers and practitioners to further increase "access to the highest-quality musical experiences" for the approximately 57 percent of children in the United States who attend childcare programs. Furthermore, the National Association for the Education of Young Children (Bredekamp and Copple, 2009) recommends researchers and practitioners actively involve parents in the education of their young children. Collaboratively, researchers and practitioners must consider parents' contributions—to improve our understandings of children's musical needs and to enrich conversations among researchers, practitioners, and policymakers about meeting those needs in educational settings.

Numerous early childhood music education researchers have identified and described children's music behaviors, primarily conducting their observations of children in laboratory, early childhood education, or early childhood music settings; and occasionally in children's home settings. They have observed parent-child music interactions at home and in early childhood education settings, or have collected parents' descriptions of their motivations for supporting their child's music experiences or musical expectations parents have for their children (Dai and Schader, 2001). In most cases, the limited amount of time available for researchers to conduct such observations suggests that the frequency and types of children's music behaviors may be underreported. Because parents are recognized as a child's first ideal music teacher (Trehub, 1999), and parent-child, social-music interactions have been described as natural (Bergeson and Trehub, 1999; Papousek, 1996; Trehub, 1999) and integral to the overall parent-child relationship (Berger and Cooper, 2003; Bergeson and Trehub, 1999; Custodero, Britto, and Brooks-Gunn, 2003; Custodero, Britto, and Xin, 2002; Custodero and Johnson-Green, 2003, 2008; Gratier, 1999; Griffith and Valerio, 2008; Papousek, 1996; Preston, 2007; Robb, 1999; Rudzinski, 2009; Trehub, 1999; Trehub et al., 1997), parents may be in an ideal position to offer insights from their interactions with their children and observations of their children's music development.

RESEARCH PURPOSE AND QUESTIONS

Researchers have found that parents document their children's cognitive, physical, social, or emotional competence with sufficient reliability (Glascoe, 1998; Henderson and Meisels, 1994; Ireton, 1996; Ireton and Glascoe, 1995; Squires, Bricker, Heo, and Twombly, 2001; Squires, Bricker, and Twombly, 2002). Early childhood music researchers less frequently have sought parents' descriptions and observations of their children as a way to further understand music behaviors and how they develop in early childhood (Custodero and Johnson-Green, 2008; Preston, 2007; Rudzinski, 2009; Trehub, 1999). With the intent to further understand early childhood music development and reliably identify musical awareness and sensitivity within young children, the purpose of this research was to investigate parents/guardians' documentation of children's music-related behaviors. The questions of this study were as follows: (a) How reliably can parents/guardians (parents) document their children's music behaviors using the *Child Music-Related Behavior Questionnaire*, a researcher-developed instrument? (b) Are there differences in the frequencies of children's music-related behaviors based on age and the music activities parents perform with them?

METHOD

Questionnaire Development

Because researchers have established questionnaires as reliable instruments for collecting data regarding parents' observations of children's cognitive and social development (Glascoe, 1998; Ireton, 1996; Ireton and Glascoe, 1995; Squires et al., 2001; Squires et al., 2002), the researchers of this study developed a questionnaire to collect data from parents. The researchers consulted research, theory, and practice to identify young children's music behaviors and descriptions of interactive music behaviors between parents or early childhood caregivers and children (see bibliography). They created and categorized questionnaire items to develop an initial questionnaire instrument. A focus group of fifteen parents provided feedback regarding the initial instrument, which the researchers and two measurement specialists used to construct the instrument for this study: the *Children's Music-Related Behavior Questionnaire* (CMRBQ). The researchers used Flesch-Kincaid readability scores generated by Microsoft Word 12.2.3 (Flesch Reading Ease [66.3], Flesch-Kincaid Grade Level of 7.1.) to determine that persons with an education level seventh grade or higher should be able to read and understand the questionnaire.

The final questionnaire format comprised demographics—part 1, *types of children's music behaviors*, and part 2, *parent's music activities with children*. Part 1 was divided into eight sections: (a) attention and emotion (ten items), (b) vocalizations (ten items), (c) moving (ten items), (d) daily routines (ten items), (e) requests (twelve items), (f) taking turns, initiating, sharing (eleven items), (g) creativity (eight items), and (h) other music behaviors. Part 1 items in sections A, B, C, D, E, F, and G offered a four-point Likert-type response scale with an *I don't know* option. Section H offered an open-ended opportunity for respondents to list other music-related behaviors that they had seen or heard their child do. Part 2 included twenty-nine four-point Likert-type response options and one *yes/no* item. The four-point Likert-type responses for part 1 and part 2 were *never, rarely, sometimes, frequently*. Sample questionnaire items for part 1 and part 2 are presented in figure 10.1 and figure 10.2, respectively.

Questionnaire Distribution

Researchers distributed 763 questionnaires to ten early childhood centers in the Southeastern United States. Parents whose children were enrolled at the centers were asked to complete one questionnaire about each child who was five years or younger, or one about their youngest child. As incentive for participation, each center that achieved a return rate of 50 percent or greater received the opportunity for a free music workshop, provided by the researchers, for parents, teachers, and children. Three centers earned that opportunity.

MY CHILD	Never	Rarely	Sometimes	Frequently	I don't know
Is calmed when I sing or chant rhythms/rhymes to him/her if he/she is anxious or upset	☐	☐	☐	☐	o
Vocally babbles **after** I sing songs or chant rhythms/rhymes to him/her	☐	☐	☐	☐	o
Performs recognizable songs/rhythms/rhymes **alone, but not quite accurately**	☐	☐	☐	☐	o
Changes speed of moving/dancing to match the speed/tempo of music	☐	☐	☐	☐	o
Listens to **recorded music** while riding in the car	☐	☐	☐	☐	o
Asks for favorite songs or rhythms/rhymes to be performed	☐	☐	☐	☐	o
Takes turns with me by **patting/beating rhythms**	☐	☐	☐	☐	o
Sings or performs original or different words to familiar songs or rhythms/rhymes	☐	☐	☐	☐	o

Figure 10.1.   Sample Questionnaire Items from Part 1: Types of Children's Music Behaviors

I	Never	Rarely	Sometimes	Frequently
Sing songs or perform rhythms/rhymes **for** my child	☐	☐	☐	☐
Sing songs or perform rhythms/rhymes and **leave out a note or phrase** to see what my child does	☐	☐	☐	☐
Encourage my child **to make up** his/her own songs or rhythms/rhymes	☐	☐	☐	☐
Play recorded music **for** my child in the house or car when he/she is **awake**	☐	☐	☐	☐
Dance around **with** my child **while I** sing songs or perform rhythms/rhymes **for** my child	☐	☐	☐	☐
Attend **early childhood music classes** with my child	☐	☐	☐	☐

Figure 10.2.   Sample Questionnaire Items from Part 2: Parent's Music Activities with Children

ANALYSIS, RESULTS, AND INTERPRETATIONS

The overall return rate was 32.5 percent with 249 questionnaires returned. All responses were entered by hand on an Excel spreadsheet, and Likert-type responses were recoded from *never, rarely, sometimes, frequently* to *1, 2, 3, 4,* respectively. Two items were appropriately reverse-coded. *I don't know* responses were coded as missing data. The open-end item from part 1 and the *yes/no* item in part 2 were excluded from analysis due to limited response.

With regard to respondents' demographic information, the majority of respondents were mothers (88.3 percent). Most respondents had earned a bachelor's degree (31 percent) or master's degree (54 percent). Most reported earning (a) less than $50,000 (14 percent), (b) between $50,000 and $85,999 (22 percent), or (c) $86,000 or more (60 percent) during 2008. Most respondents were white (83 percent), and a few were African American (10 percent) or Asian (4 percent). Many respondents reported living in a household with two adults (88 percent). Respondents reported living with one child (44 percent), two children (42 percent), or more than two children (12 percent). Most respondents reported music behaviors for their first-born child (63 percent) or second-born (29 percent) child.

Researchers computed Cronbach's alpha (Cronbach, 1951) to investigate the research question regarding the reliability with which parents documented their children's music-related behaviors using CMRBQ. Cronbach's alpha was computed using only questionnaires with complete data for each subscale. Subscale reliabilities ranged from .64 to .95. The low reliability for section A (α = .64) was due, in part, to lack of variability (α = .35) among the responses. Moreover, three items each had a low, positive relationship to the subscale, α = .28; α = .27; α = .10, respectively. Researchers determined that the wording of those items was confusing. When those three items were removed from the scale, reliability for section A increased (α = .77). Reliability for the twenty-nine items in part 2 was .92. Specific reliability indices for part 1, its individual sections, and part 2 are presented in table 10.1.

To investigate if the frequency of children's music behaviors differed with regard to children's ages and parents' music activities with their children, researchers conducted a 5 × 3 (age category × parent level) MANOVA with seven dependent variables. Researchers excluded twelve questionnaires from analysis because those questionnaires had at least one subscale with every item unanswered (N = 237). The dependent variables—the section subscales from part 1—were standardized prior to analysis to adjust for varying numbers of subscale items. Researchers divided children's ages into five categories:

- age category 1, 0–12 months (N = 28);
- age category 2, 13–24 months (N = 50);
- age category 3, 25–36 months (N = 49);
- age category 4, 37–48 months (N = 61); and
- age category 5, >49 months (N = 49).

Table 10.1. Cronbach's Alpha Reliability Indices for Questionnaire

		α	n
Section A	Attention and Emotion (ten items—three items removed)	.64/.77	191/206
Section B	Vocalizations (ten items)	.86	202
Section C	Moving (ten items)	.91	218
Section D	Daily Routines (ten items)	.80	220
Section E	Requests (twelve items)	.95	223
Section F	Taking Turns, Initiating, and Sharing (eleven items)	.91	204
Section G	Creativity (eight items)	.90	230
Part 2	Parents/Guardians' Music Activities with Children (twenty-nine items)	.92	82

Researchers divided parent music activity into three levels:

- parent level 1 = low music activity, frequency < 68 (N = 82);
- parent level 2 = moderate music activity, frequency = 68–79 (N = 78); and
- parent level 3 = high music activity, frequency > 79 (N = 77).

Each level represented approximately 33 percent of the sample size. Researchers detected a significant interaction effect with Pillai's trace = .329, F (56, 1554) = 1.37, p = .0377; Wilks's Lambda = .707, F (56, 1168.5) = 1.39, p =.0331, and Hotelling's T-squared = .366, F (56, 763.23), p =.0314. Children's age categories and parent music activity levels both contributed to differences in documented frequencies of children's music-related behaviors.

To gain insight regarding the relationships between the unstandardized subscale mean responses, line graphs were created delineating the mean frequency changes for the seven sections of part 1, based on children's age category and parents' music activity level (see figure 10.3). In general, parents reported that older children demonstrated more music behaviors than younger children in all questionnaire sections except section A (attention and emotion). In most of the questionnaire sections, parents who reported performing the most music activities with their children also documented the most music-related behaviors performed by their children with the exception of section F (taking turns, initiating, and sharing); however, to the extent it is present, the interaction can be seen primarily in the magnitude of parent level effects for age category 1 and age category 2. For age category 1, the mean for parent level 2 is close to the mean for parent level 1 for sections B (vocalizations), C (moving), D (daily routines), E (requests), and G (creativity), while the mean for parent level 2 is close to the mean for parent level 3 for section F (taking turns, initiating, and sharing). For age category 2, the mean for parent level 2 is close to the mean for parent level 1 for section E (requests), while the mean for parent level 2 is similar to the mean for parent level 3 for section C (moving). Some of those same patterns are apparent when taking a more formal approach to analyzing the interactions.

Rather than simply studying significant MANOVA effects by analyzing subscales separately, researchers explored the canonical structure for the multivariate hypotheses for each effect. That approach is similar to the use of linear discriminant functions for two-way factorial discriminant analysis (Rencher, 1998). By identifying linear combinations of the response variables that, in a general sense, maximize the separation between effect means, researchers gain insight into the way in which variables affect the multivariate scale (Johnson, 1998).

Legend:

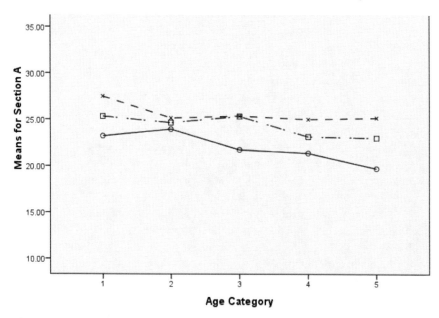

Parent Level 3 =
High Music Activity

Parent Level 2 =
Moderate Music Activity

Parent Level 1 =
Low Music Activity

Figure 10.3. Line Graphs for Means for Individual Sections by Age Categories and Parent Levels

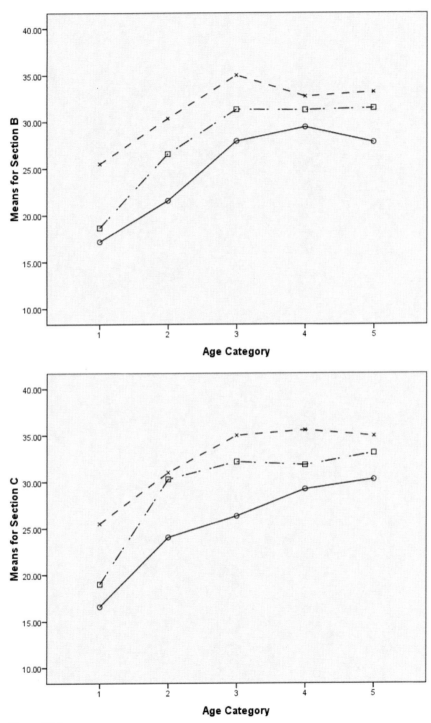

Figure 10.3.

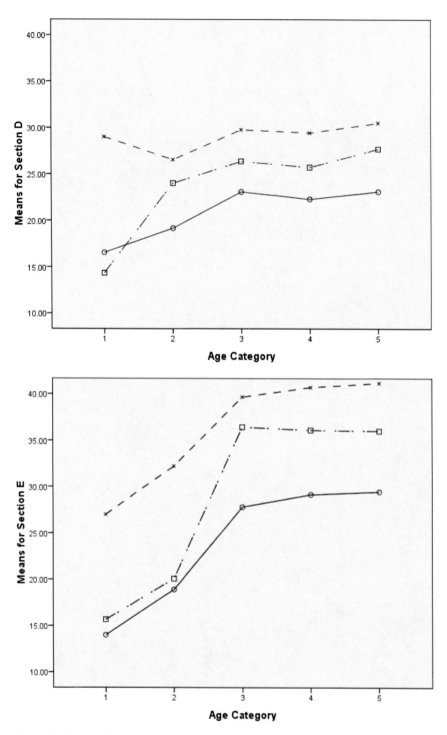

Figure 10.3. (*continued*)

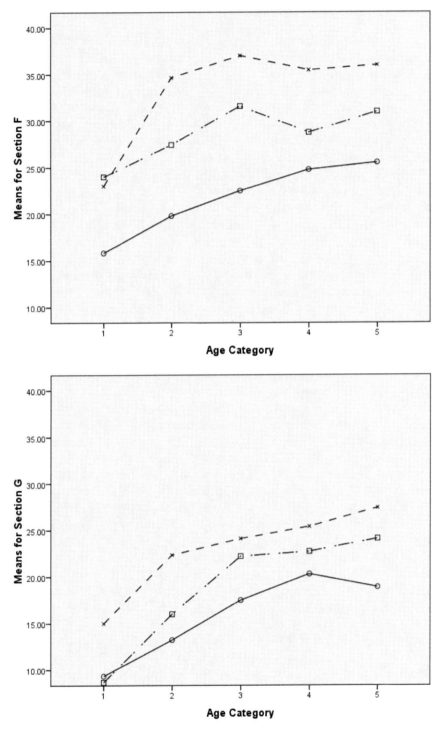

Figure 10.3.

Researchers first identified canonical variables—a set of variables formed from linear combinations of the dependent variables—for each of the effects: age category main effect, parent level main effect, and the (age category × parent level) interaction effect. For a given effect, the first canonical variable is a linear combination of the dependent variables chosen to maximize the ratio of between group sums of squares to within group sums of squares. The second canonical variable, among all linear combinations of the dependent variable orthogonal to the first canonical variable, again maximizes the ratio of between group sums of squares to within group sums of squares, and so on for each canonical variable. An effect with k levels has $k - 1$ canonical variables, unless $k - 1$ is greater than the number of dependent variables. Tests of canonical correlations can be used to determine the number of canonical variables to study for each effect (Johnson, 1998).

In this study, the main effect age category had four canonical variables, the main effect parent level had two canonical variables, and the interaction had seven canonical variables. Tests of canonical correlations showed that the main effect, age category, had (at most) two significant canonical correlations ($p = .2696$ for the test that all other canonical correlations are 0). The associated canonical variables explain 96.11 percent of the variation observed in age category means. The main effect, parent level, had (at most) one significant canonical correlation ($p = .0736$ for the test that all other canonical correlations are 0). The first canonical variable explains 93.26 percent of the variation observed in parent level group means, which suggests the parent level means have a straightforward multivariate structure that can be interpreted by studying a single variable (i.e., the first canonical variable). The interaction effect, age category × parent level, had, at most, one significant canonical correlation ($p = .4941$ for the test that all other canonical correlations are 0). The associated canonical variable explains 45.92 percent of variation observed in the age category x parent level group means. Standardized canonical coefficients for the significant canonical variables and their correlations (loadings) for each dependent variable are presented in table 10.2.

By convention, standardized canonical variable correlations above .30 are considered strong. The canonical variable for the (age category × parent level) interaction correlated with (or loaded on) sections E (requests) and C (moving subscales). Univariate analysis of the (age category × parent level) interaction effect for the interaction canonical variable was strongly significant: $F (8,222) = 4.54$, $p < .0001$. An interaction plot of the canonical variable (see figure 10.4) suggested that parent level 2 had a lower than anticipated canonical variable mean for both age category 1 and age category 2; other modest interaction effects can be seen as well. The interaction may reflect the low means for parent level 2 observed for both age category 1 and

Table 10.2.   Canonical Analysis

	Age Group		Parent Level	Age Group × Parent Level
	Canonical Variable 1 Coefficient (Correlation)	Canonical Variable 2 Coefficient (Correlation)	Canonical Variable 1 Coefficient (Correlation)	Canonical Variable 1 Coefficient (Correlation)
Section A: Attention and Emotion	−.4532 (−.1944)	−.1471 (−.0911)	.1967 (.4363)	.3473 (.2587)
Section B: Vocalizations	.3211 (.4359)	−.0292 (.0847)	−.0603 (.4495)	−.3255 (−.0880)
Section C: Moving	.1547 (.4802)	1.2560 (.6287)	.2134 (.5947)	−.9561 (−.3176)
Section D: Daily Routines	.0808 (.3658)	.0631 (.1239)	.5834 (.6791)	−.3753 (−.0641)
Section E: Requests	1.3054 (.7745)	−1.5762 (−.2706)	.4680 (.7193)	(.4374)
Section F: Taking Turns, Initiating, and Sharing	−.5239 (.2984)	.5502 (.3606)	.6264 (.7840)	−.9013 (−.1770)
Section G: Creativity	.7364 (.6102)	.4207 (.4223)	.1820 (.6017)	.9855 (.2934)

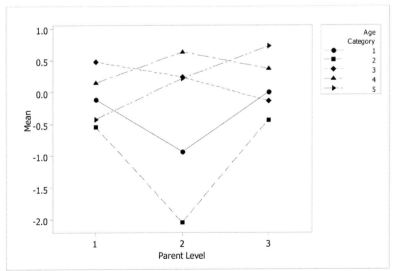

Figure 10.4.   Plot for Age Group × Parent Level Interaction Canonical Variable

age category 2 for section E (requests) versus the high mean for parent level 2 for age category 2 for section C (moving). That effect was similar to an effect noted earlier in the discussion of figure 10.3. Compared with parents who reported performing the most music activities with their children, parents who reported performing a low or moderate number of music activities with their children reported that their children requested fewer music activities during ages one and two, yet they reported their children performing nearly the same number of music related movements during age two.

Researchers also tested canonical variables for the main effects, even in the presence of interaction, because main effects for both variables were reasonably consistent across scales. The first canonical variable for the main effect age category, loaded primarily on sections E (requests), G (creativity), C (moving), B (vocalizations), D (daily routines), and F (taking turns, initiating, and sharing), increased as a function of age category (see figure 10.5), though the amount of increase became steadily smaller as children age. Given the relative size of the canonical coefficients, sections E (requests) and G (creativity) showed the most marked increasing trend as age category increases. The second canonical variable for the main effect age category loaded on sections C (moving), G (creativity), and F (taking turns, initiating, and sharing) and highlighted a threshold effect between age category 1 and all other age categories (see figure 10.6).

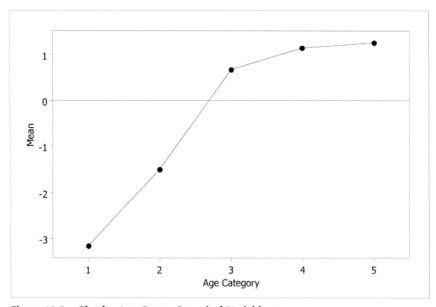

Figure 10.5.   Plot for Age Group Canonical Variable 1

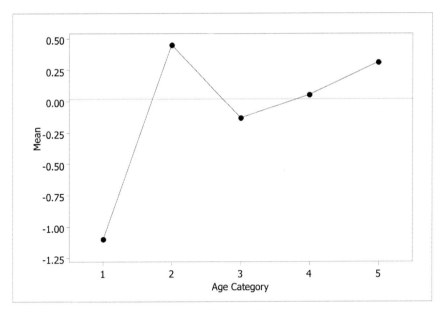

Figure 10.6.   Plot for Age Group Canonical Variable 2

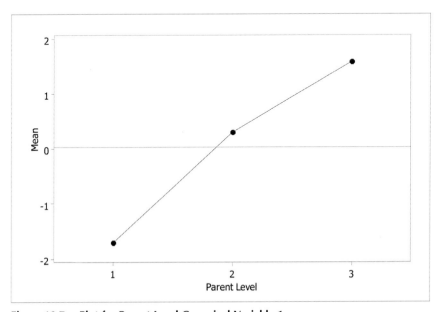

Figure 10.7.   Plot for Parent Level Canonical Variable 1

The canonical variable for the main effect, parent level, loaded on all seven variables; with the exception of section B (vocalizations), all the coefficients were positive and similar in size. As parent involvement increased, parents reported that children performed a linearly increasing (see figure 10.7) number of music behaviors (with the exception of section B).

CONCLUSION

Researchers may use the *Child Music-Related Behaviors Questionnaire* (CMRBQ) to gain information reliably from parents about the music-related behaviors that they observe their children perform and the music activities that they perform with their children with sample populations similar to the one in this study. Because of the age group differences found in this study, the CMRBQ may be best suited for examining music development during the first three years of life. To determine music-related behavior differences among children between the ages of three and five, researchers may need to revise the questionnaire. When using the CMRBQ, parent music activity level seems to be an important factor for gaining the most information from parents about their children's music-related behaviors.

Because, in general, parents in this study who performed the most music activities with their children also documented the most music-related behaviors performed by their children, early childhood music researchers and educators should continue to provide parents with ways to interact musically with their children and encourage parents to interact musically with their children. As recognized by Custodero and Johnson-Green (2003, 2008) and reinforced in this study, music behaviors are identifiable, especially by parents who share music experiences with their young children. With more musically educated parents, early childhood music educators can continue to learn from them about their children, their children's music behaviors, and the relationship of those behaviors to other dimensions of child development. Moreover, by including parents' voices, music educators may increase their understandings of children's musical needs as they continue conversations among researchers, practitioners, and policymakers about meeting those needs in educational settings.

Prior to a mass distribution of the questionnaire for its practical application, researchers should further investigate the reliability of the CMRBQ and effects of age groups and parent music activity levels on parents' documentation of children's music-related behaviors. For example, this study should be repeated with a larger and more diverse sample. Such an investigation will allow researchers to begin to determine the validity of the CMRBQ and generalizability of results gained from its administration.

REFERENCES

Berger, A. A., and Cooper, S. (2003). Musical play: A case study of preschool children and parents. *Journal of Research in Music Education, 51*, 151–65.

Bergeson, T. R., and Trehub, S. E. (1999). Mothers' singing to infants and preschool children. *Infant Behavior and Development, 22*(10), 51–64.

Bredekamp, S., and Copple, C. (Eds.). (2009). *Developmentally appropriate practice in early childhood programs serving children from birth through age 8.* Washington, DC: National Association for the Education of Young Children.

Cronbach, L. (1951). Coefficient alpha and the internal structure of tests. *Psychometrika, 16*, 279–334.

Custodero, L. A. (2008). Harmonizing research, practice, and policy in early childhood music: A chorus of international voices (Part I). *Arts Education Policy Review, 109*(2), 3–5.

Custodero, L. A., Britto, P. R., and Brooks-Gunn, J. (2003). Musical lives: A collective portrait of American parents and their young children. *Journal of Applied Developmental Psychology, 24*(5), 553–72.

Custodero, L. A., Britto, P. R., and Xin, T. (2002). From Mozart to Motown, lullabies to love songs: A preliminary report on the Parents Use of Music with Infants Survey. *Zero-to-Three Bulletin, 25*(1), 41–46.

Custodero, L. A., and Chen-Hafteck, L. (2008). Harmonizing research, practice, and policy in early childhood music: A chorus of international voices (Part 2). *Arts Education Policy Review, 109*(3), 3–7.

Custodero, L. A., and Johnson-Green, E. A. (2003). Passing the cultural torch: Musical experience and musical parenting of infants. *Journal of Research in Music Education, 51*, 102–14.

Custodero, L. A., and Johnson-Green, E. A. (2008). Caregiving in counterpoint: Reciprocal influences in the musical parenting of younger and older infants. *Early Child Development and Care, 178*(1), 15–39.

Dai, Y. D., and Schader, R. (2001). Parents' reasons and motivations for supporting their child's music training. *Roeper Review, 24*(1), 23–26.

Glascoe, F. P. (1998). The value of "parents' evaluations of developmental status" in detecting and addressing children's developmental and behavioral problems. *Diagnostique, 23*(4), 185–203.

Gratier, M. (1999). Expressions of belonging: The effect of acculturation on the rhythm and harmony of mother-infant vocal interaction. *Musicae Scientiae, Special Issue: Rhythm, Musical Narrative, and Origins of Human Communication, 1999–2000*, 93–122.

Griffith, C., and Valerio, W. H. (2008). *Autism, reciprocal communication, and a child-directed, relationship-based music approach: A case study.* Paper and poster presented at the Twenty-eighth ISME World Conference: Music for All Ages, Bologna, Italy.

Henderson, L. W., and Meisels, S. J. (1994). Parental involvement in the developmental screening of their young children. *Journal of Early Intervention, 18*(2), 141–54.

Ireton, H. (1996). The child development review: Monitoring children's development using parents' and pediatricians' observations. *Infants and Young Children, 9*(1), 42–52.

Ireton, H., and Glascoe, F. P. (1995). Assessing children's development using parents' reports. *Clinical Pediatrics, 34*(5), 248–55.

Johnson, D. E. (1998). *Applied multivariate methods for data analysis.* Pacific Grove, CA: Duxbury Press.

Nardo, R. L., Custodero, L. A., Persellin, D. C., and Fox, D. B. (2006). Looking back, looking forward: A report on early childhood music education in accredited American preschools. *Journal of Research in Music Education, 54*(4), 278–93.

Overland, C., and Reynolds, A. M. (in press). Early childhood music education in the United States from 1980–2007: The role of the Music Educators National Conference. *Journal of Historical Research in Music Education.*

Papousek, M. (1996). Intuitive parenting: A hidden source of musical stimulation in infancy. In I. Deliege and J. A. Sloboda (Eds.), *Musical beginnings: Origins and development of musical competence* (pp. 88–112). New York: Oxford University Press.

Persellin, D. C. (2007). Policies, practices, and promises: Challenges to early childhood music education in the United States. *Arts Education Policy Review, 109*(2), 54–61.

Preston, A. L. (2007). *Five parents' descriptions of their preschool children's music behaviors.* Master's final project, Temple University, Philadelphia, PA.

Rencher, A. C. (1998). *Multivariate statistical inference and applications.* New York: Wiley.

Robb, L. (1999). Emotional musicality in mother-infant vocal affect, and an acoustic study of postnatal depression: Rhythm, musical narrative, and origins of human communication. *Musicae Scientiae, 1999–2000,* 123–51.

Rudzinski, M. (2009). *Social-music interactions: A six-month case study of a 20–26-month-old toddler.* Masters final project, Temple University, Philadelphia, PA.

Squires, J., Bricker, D., Heo, K., and Twombly, E. (2001). Identification of social-emotional problems in young children using a parent-completed screening measure. *Early Childhood Research Quarterly, 16,* 405–19.

Squires, J., Bricker, D., and Twombly, E. (2002). *Ages and stages questionnaire: Social-emotional: A parent-completed, child-monitoring system for social-emotional behaviors.* Baltimore, MD: Paul H. Brookes.

Trehub, S. E. (1999). Singing as a parenting tool. *Early Childhood Connections, 5*(2), 8–14.

Trehub, S. E., Unyk, A. M., Kamenetsky, S. B., Hill, D. S., Trainor, L., Henderson, J. L., and Saraza, M. (1997). Mothers' and fathers' singing to infants. *Developmental Psychology, 33*(3), 500–507.

BIBLIOGRAPHY

Burton, S. (2002). An exploration of preschool children's spontaneous songs and chants. *Visions of Research in Music Education, 2,* 7–16. Retrieved from www.rider.edu/~vrme/articles2/vrme.pdf.

Custodero, L. A. (2006). Singing practices in 10 families with young children. *Journal of Research in Music Education, 54*(1), 37–56.

Cutietta, R. (2001). *Raising musical kids: A guide for parents.* New York: Oxford University Press.

DeNora, T. (2000). *Music in everyday life.* Cambridge: Cambridge University Press.

Fox, D. B. (2000). An analysis of the pitch characteristics of infant vocalizations. *Psychomusicology, 9*(1), 21–30.

Gilbert, J. (1979). Assessment of motoric music skill development in young children: Test construction and evaluation procedures. *Psychology of Music, 7*(2), 3–12.

Gordon, E. E. (2003). *A music learning theory for newborn and young children.* Chicago: GIA.

Gromko, J. E., and Poorman, A. S. (1998). Developmental trends and relationships in children's aural perception and symbol use. *Journal of Research in Music Education, 46*, 16–23.

Hicks, W. K. (1993). An investigation of the initial stages of preparatory audiation. *Dissertation Abstracts International, 540A*, 1277.

Honig, A. S. (1995). Singing with infants and toddlers. *Young Children, 50*(5), 72–78.

Kelley, L., and Sutton-Smith, B. (1987). A study of infant musical productivity. In J. G. Peery, I. W. Peery, and T. W. Draper (Eds.), *Music in child development* (pp. 35–53). New York: Springer-Verlag.

Krumhansl, C. L., and Jusczyk, P. W. (1990). Infants' perception of phrase structure in music. *Psychological Science, 1*(1), 70–73.

Littleton, D. (1998). Music learning and child's play. *General Music Today, 12*(1), 8–15.

Marsh, K. (1995). Children's singing games: Composition in the playground? *Research Studies in Music Education, 4*, 2–11.

MENC. (1994). *Opportunity-to-learn standards for music instruction: Grades preK–12.* Reston, VA: Author.

Miranda, M. (2000). Developmentally appropriate practice in a Yamaha Music School. *Journal of Research in Music Education, 48*(4), 294–309.

Moog, H. (1976). *The musical experiences of the preschool child* (C. Clarke, Trans.). London: Schott Music.

Moorhead, G. E., and Pond, D. (1941). *Music of young children: 1 Chant.* Santa Barbara, CA: Pillsbury Foundation for the Advancement of Music Education.

Murphy, J. M. (1979). The use of non-verbal and body movement techniques in working with families with infants. *Journal of Marital and Family Therapy, 5*(4), 61–66.

O'Hagin, I. B., and Harnish, D. (2003). Reshaping imagination: The musical culture of migrant farmworker families in northwest Ohio. *Bulletin of the Council for Research in Music Education, 151*, 21–30.

Pflederer, M. (1964). The responses of children to musical tasks embodying Piaget's principle of conservation. *Journal of Research in Music Education, 12*, 251–68.

Reynolds, A. M. (1995). An investigation of movement responses performed by children 18 months to 3 years of age and their caregivers to rhythm chants in duple meter. *Dissertation Abstracts International 5604A*, 1283.

Reynolds, A. M. (2006, Spring). Vocal interactions during informal early childhood music classes. *Bulletin of the Council for Research in Music Education, 168*, 1–16.

Reynolds, A. M., Long, S., and Valerio, W. H. (2007). Language acquisition and music acquisition: Possible parallels. In K. Smithrim and R. Upitis (Eds.), *Listen to their voices: Research and practice in early childhood music.* Research to Practice: A Biennial Series, 3 (pp. 211–27). Toronto: Canadian Music Educators Association.

Rock, A. M. L., Trainor, L. J., and Addison, T. L. (1999). Distinctive messages in infant-directed lullabies and play songs. *Developmental Psychology, 35*(2), 527–34.

Rutkowski, J. (1990). The measurement and evaluation of children's singing voice development. *Quarterly: Center for Research in Music Learning and Teaching, 1*(102), 81–95.

Trehub, S. E. (2001). Musical predispositions in infancy. In R. J. Zatorre and I. Peretz (Eds.), *The biological foundations of music* (pp. 1–16). New York: New York Academy of Sciences.

Trehub, S. E., and Nakata, T. (2001–2002). Emotion and music in infancy. *Musicae Scientiae, 6*(1), 37–61.

Trehub, S. E., and Trainor, L. J. (1998). Singing to infants: Lullabies and play songs. In H. Hayne (Ed.), *Advances in infancy research 12* (pp. 43–77). Stamford, CT: Ablex.

Trevharthen, C. (1999). Musicality and the intrinsic motive pulse: Evidence from human psychobiology and infant communication. *Musicae Scientiae, 1999–2000,* 155–215.

Valerio, W. H., Reynolds, A. M., Bolton, B. M., Taggart, C. C., and Gordon, E. E. (1998). *Music play: Guide for parents, teachers, and caregivers.* Chicago: GIA.

Valerio, W. H., Seaman, M. A., Yap, C. C., Santucci, P. M., and Tu, M. (2006). Vocal evidence of toddler music syntax acquisition: A case study. *Bulletin of the Council for Research in Music Education, 170,* 33–46.

Walters, D. (2000). *Harmonic development: Music's impact to age three.* Pittsburgh, PA: Pittsburgh Symphony.

Young, S. (2002). Young children's spontaneous vocalizations in free play: Observations of two-to three-year-olds in a day care setting. *Bulletin of the Council for Research in Music Education, 152,* 43–53.

Chapter Eleven

Music Play Zone: An Online Social Network Site Connecting Parents and Teacher in an Early Childhood Music Class

Lisa Huisman Koops

In this study, the researcher examined the experience of parents who participated in a private, online social network documenting their children's musical experiences and development. Nine parents of children participating in an early childhood music program engaged in weekly blog posts and other forms of interaction on the social network site for seven weeks. Data included posts by participants on the social network and transcripts of exit interviews regarding the experience. The researcher coded and analyzed data for emergent themes. There was a mixed response to the use of the social network site in this study; parents seemed to recognize and identify benefits or possible benefits, but participation was tempered by a lack of time. The greatest benefits described by the parents were that the project increased parental awareness, education, and reflection on musical development; participation also facilitated connections among parents, teacher, and children in the early childhood music program. A final benefit was increased awareness by the teacher of forms of music making in the home.

Researchers and early childhood educators have described the importance of parent education within early childhood music programs (Ilari, 2005; Kenney, 2007). Parent education is important in light of research findings that parent behaviors (Berger and Cooper, 2003), perceptions (Cardany, 2004; Custodero, 2006), involvement (Custodero, Britto, and Brooks-Gunn, 2003), and attitudes (Ilari, 2005; Mallett, 2000; Wu, 2005) impact children's musical development and musical experiences. McPherson (2009) summarized a body of research on the role of parents in older children's music development. Based on this research, McPherson proposed a model that identifies a feedback loop of a child's self-beliefs, self-regulation, and motivation that affect *and* are affected by a parent's goals, behaviors, and parenting style to ultimately influence a child's musical achievement, identity, and goals. The parent is clearly a key player when it comes to a child's music education.

EARLY CHILDHOOD MUSIC AND PARENTS

Understanding what is happening in the home is crucial to developing ways to educate parents to be musically supportive of their young children. A recent study by deVries (2009) investigated parent-child musical interaction in the home through a survey of parents at three preschools in Australia. Parents reported on the frequency of playing music, singing, encouraging musical play, playing instruments, and encouraging children's musical creativity in the home. Following the survey, the researcher held two focus-group discussions in order to elicit ideas on the underlying reasons for survey answers. Parents cited lack of time as a reason for not engaging in music more often in the home, along with lack of music knowledge. Many of the parents also expressed the belief that music was taught in preschool and was, therefore, not a necessary part of the education in the home. Parents' use of commercial recordings was evident in the discussion, as was their emphasis on extramusical uses and benefits of music (such as for calming or learning). Responses on the survey and in focus groups suggested that parents do "value [music] in the home environment" (p. 403) but faced those obstacles listed above.

In a recent study, Koops (2011) found that parents described their current involvement in early childhood music instruction as marked by modeling, exploring varying roles between parent and child, and interacting with a cohort of parents and children. Several of the parents interviewed indicated satisfaction with their roles within the class and did not desire increased involvement in the class; others expressed a desire for more information about children's musical development and the teaching method used. The perceptions that seemed to contribute to parents' involvement, both current and desired, were the enjoyment that comes from musical interaction, the recognition of multiple roles of music in children's lives, and the view of acquiring musical skill and knowledge as developmental.

Finding ways to communicate with parents is central to the task of educating and engaging parents musically. Kenney (2007) describes an example of such communication: The Young Musicians program at Brigham Young University encourages communication between parents and teachers with weekly parental reports of children's musical behaviors at home during the week, including singing, playing instruments, and moving. Parents also report on children's musical preferences, including preferences for materials such as recordings, music kits, and instruments checked out from the program.

These reports are intended to help parents "focus on musical play with their children" (p. 45) as well as provide valuable information for the teacher.

SOCIAL NETWORKING

One possibility for parent communication and education is through online systems, such as social networking sites. Social network sites are defined by boyd and Ellison (2007) as

> web-based services that allow individuals to (1) construct a public or semi-public profile within a bounded system, (2) articulate a list of other users with whom they share a connection, and (3) view and traverse their list of connections and those made by others within the system. The nature and nomenclature of these connections may vary from site to site. (para. 4)

The authors noted that "social network sites (SNSs) such as MySpace, Facebook, Cyworld, and Bebo have attracted millions of users, many of whom have integrated these sites into their daily practices" (para. 1).

Online social support systems have been used in settings other than music education, as in a system designed and established by nursing faculty to support single, low-income, African American mothers (Hudson, Campbell-Grossman, Keating-Lefler, and Cline, 2008). The online system offered articles and information, chat boards, and e-mail to an advanced practical nurse at the participating university, who responded to health and support questions. Further research is being conducted to explore the benefits of using the system. Another example of the use of social network sites is among members of groups such as the Up Side of Downs, an organization that "provides support, education & advocacy for people with Down syndrome, their families & communities" (Up Side of Downs, n.d., para. 1). Family members and friends can share questions, concerns, stories, photos, encouragement, and support online through the use of blogs, discussion questions, wall postings, event calendar, and e-mails. A mother who participated in both the current study and the Up Side of Downs social network sites explained,

> This forum really helps parents feel connected and that they are not alone in their struggles. There is a sense of unconditional support and understanding which really helps a parent build confidence in their parenting skills. It also is a great way to be in the know about best practices in raising a child with Down syndrome. (Participant 5, personal communication, August 4, 2009)

The current project builds on research described above by exploring a means for (a) providing information on children's musical development,

(b) enhancing enjoyment of the early childhood music experience, and (c) interacting with a cohort of parents and children using an online forum convenient for parents. With the intent of facilitating musical development of children enrolled in early childhood music courses, the purpose of this research was to describe the development of a community of learners of parents and teacher in an early childhood music course using an online social networking site. *Community of learners* here refers to a group of people engaged in a common learning task (Smith, 2001). Following are the specific research questions: (a) How do parents describe the experience, including challenges, personal growth and recommendations for future work, of building a community of learners between parents and teacher in an early childhood music class using an online social networking site? (b) What are the perceived benefits of participation in the online community of learners for participants' children, as reported by parents? (c) What are the perceived benefits of participation to the participants themselves? (d) What forms of information and types of questions about children's musical development do parents share with the teacher and one another as a result of participating in the online social network? (e) How does the participation of the parents in the online community affect the early childhood music teacher's understanding of students, delivery of instruction, and communication with parents?

METHODOLOGY

This research was a qualitative study of the use of an online social network by parents and teacher of children in an early childhood music program at a midwestern community music school. Data consisted of weekly narrative blog posts and some file sharing by participants throughout the nine-week study, as well as exit interviews with participants. Participants were chosen through a purposeful sample of parents who had participated in early childhood music instruction for at least one nine-week session prior to the nine-week study (N = 9). The ages of the participants' children ranged from thirteen months to two years eight months at the beginning of the study. The early childhood classes took place for forty-five minutes once a week and fit the following description:

> The early childhood music classes in which participants in this study were enrolled were based on Gordon's Music Learning Theory (Gordon, 2003; Valerio, Reynolds, Bolton, Taggart, and Gordon, 1998). The *Music Play* approach to early childhood music instruction features immersing children in a playful musical environment that includes songs and chants performed by the teacher with and without words in a variety of tonalities and meters, as well as tonal

and rhythm patterns (two- and three-note patterns sung or chanted with space following). The teacher seeks to create a learning environment in which children are free to experience the music at their own level, often using props such as scarves and beanbags as well as small rhythm instruments. Typical behaviors in class include children sitting and listening; wandering around the room; using instruments or props in similar or dissimilar ways to the teacher; and responding to tonal and rhythm patterns with random or purposeful responses.

SOCIAL NETWORK SITE

The social network site used in the study was designed and customized by a computer programmer using the open source program ELGG (www.elgg. org). I named the site *Music Play Zone*, referring to a concept I am developing that refers to music play centers or zones in the home and classroom as well as a conceptual space for music learning. The popularity of existing social network sites and the way in which participants may have already made social network sites a part of their daily routines led me to explore the use of the site with this population. While similar to Facebook (www.facebook. com), a social networking system familiar to many of the participants, Music Play Zone (MPZ) was used instead of Facebook or any other social network system in order to maintain strict control over the research data. The site was private, available only to participants and researcher, and included only information and postings on musical development. The features of MPZ included *on the wire*, a place to post brief updates or thoughts by a participant (similar to the status feature of Facebook); a main blog and member blogs; calendar; file uploading (text, video, audio, photo); surveys; and questions to the group. Participants attended one of several training sessions to become familiar with the site; a secondary benefit of these sessions was the opportunity to get to know some of the other participants in the study.

Participant Activity on MPZ

Participation in the social network varied among participants. The total number of weekly posts for the nine participants ranged from two to seven, with an average of 4.4. Several participants indicated the lack of time as an obstacle to full participation; one participant's son began full-time day-care after two weeks and, as a result, the participant no longer attended class nor participated in the site; another parent completed two posts but did not choose to continue due to family visits and a lack of satisfaction with social networking in general. In addition to the weekly postings, three participants took advantage of the *on the wire* update on several occasions, a space to share a brief description of what the participant was doing or thinking at that time. Three participants posted pictures, one posted two video clips of musical events in the home, and one participant included several personal blog entries that provided additional examples of home music making that occurred during the study.

Posts on MPZ

Each week I posted a three- to five-paragraph post describing a topic in early childhood music education and raising questions for participants. The seven main blog posts covered the following topics: (a) Gordon's (2003) stages of preparatory audiation and tonal and rhythmic musical development; (b) movement, including the Laban elements (described with suggestions for use in early childhood music instruction as found in Valerio, Reynolds, Bolton, Taggart, and Gordon, 1998); (c) vocal development; (d) use of songs with and without words; (e) listening to recorded music; (f) surprises in children's musical development; and (g) attending live musical events. Participants responded to the blog post questions that asked specifics about their children's musical behaviors, preferences, and skills using a response feature on the blog.

At the conclusion of the study I retrieved all postings from the website and created a document for each participant containing each individual's activity on the site. I then conducted exit interviews with the participants; five participants chose phone interviews, which were recorded and transcribed, and ranged from five to fifteen minutes in length. The remaining four participants chose to respond to the same questions over e-mail. I transcribed the phone interviews and sent the transcripts to participants to check for accuracy and offer the opportunity for them to make any changes.

DATA ANALYSIS

To analyze the data, I read through all of the data multiple times, including the data from the site and interview transcripts. Using the software Hyper-Research (ResearchWare, n.d.), I proceeded to review each individual file, separating information into sentences or paragraphs and assigning a code, such as *parental awareness* or *child-directed music activity* to each segment of text. I used a total of forty-six codes for this process, fourteen for data from the site and thirty-two for data from parent interviews; the codes were both external (drawn from literature) and internal (arising from the data). Through reports on HyperResearch, I reviewed code frequency and prominence, building emergent themes based on centers of importance in the coded data. This analysis follows the protocol laid out in Creswell (2009). Trustworthiness was established through methodological triangulation (Denzin and Lincoln, 2000) of examining multiple forms of data and by member checking, or submitting the transcripts and data analysis to participants for review and suggestions (Creswell, 2009). One parent clarified her interview transcript.

FINDINGS

Categories and Themes of MPZ Posts

The most common categories of postings were detailed descriptions of musical activities and behaviors and notes on how children's musical behaviors were changing. Three themes arose among the material posted on the MPZ site: (a) the centrality of enjoyment, (b) the importance of family relationships to music making, and (c) the prevalence of child-directed musical activities. Parents asked few questions on the site, responding instead to the questions posed in the weekly prompts.

Categories of Postings: Detailed Descriptions and Areas of Change

Many of the postings included detailed descriptions by parents of children's musical behaviors, often in response to specific questions posed in the instructor's weekly posting. These detailed descriptions often led to statements in which the parent interpreted the child's behavior. This provided an opportunity for reflection on the part of the parents and helped me as an instructor understand more of the parents' perceptions about musical development and activities. This increased reflection was perhaps the most valuable result of this project both in parents' growth of musical developmental knowledge and interpretation as well as my resulting understanding. For instance, one parent described using the activities from class at home in various situations:

> Although [my son] is still a bit shy to participate in class, he frequently responds to the same activities if they are presented at home. For example, we recently purchased a microphone like those used in class and [he] has been starting to echo some sounds (no patterns yet). . . . In fact, this activity is often used on the changing table when he's fussing. Getting him to concentrate on the songs and trying to imitate patterns often calms him. (Participant 7)

Another main category of parent postings was descriptions of how their children's musical involvement and abilities had changed over time, both in singing, movement, and response to recorded music. Several parents wrote about notable *firsts*—the first time a child had given a purposeful response to a chanted pattern, the first time a child sang songs from class by himself at home, or the first time a child initiated the "move and freeze" game during play at home. One parent described her son's progress:

> [My son] surprised me in class last week by echoing [the teacher] and another child at different times with a similar chant and in the proper pitch/tone. That was the first time he did that and I noticed that [the teachers] picked up on it (before I did!). He has been tapping his legs in the car to songs lately and seems to be going with the pacing of the song. (Participant 4)

Theme of Postings: Enjoyment, Family, and Child-Directed Activities

Many postings evidenced the enjoyment that parents found both in experiencing music with their child and in writing about it, an idea described by one participant in her exit interview as she commented on reading the other posts:

> It was also very nice to be able to see people enjoy their children for what they could do, as opposed to what they should be doing. That's always the nicest part, too—watching people really enjoy being with their kids and what their kids can do. (Participant 6)

The centrality of enjoyment was a theme found in an earlier study of parental perceptions of early childhood music instruction (Koops, 2011).

References to family relationships came up frequently in participants' posts. Participants wrote about the importance of family interaction during musical activities at home, such as a girl wanting her parents and brother to watch her while she was dancing, or a boy listening and moving to music with his father. Older siblings and parents were influential as role models for several participants' children. Extended family was included as well, as in the case of one mother who wrote about teaching her son's cousins the songs from music class and then having everyone sing together. Several participants' descriptions indicated that music was a way for their children to interact with other family members.

Parents also described child-directed musical activities that occurred at home; occasionally these included a highlighting of the fact that children's at-home musical behavior often surpassed the musical expressions offered in class. Some of these child-directed activities mirrored class activities, but others were spontaneous, as in the case of this student:

> Later that day, while waiting for our food at [a restaurant], [she] was pretending that her crayons were people and they were singing to each other. Mostly "la la la la." It was cute because the crayons were taking turns singing. (Participant 3)

A few parents mentioned shyness or fatigue as occasional dampers to participation in class; feeling more comfortable in the home, their children opened up to greater musical expression.

Benefits and Drawbacks Identified in Exit Interviews

In exit interviews, parents identified clear benefits and drawbacks to the social networking site and the study. Themes from the interviews with participants about benefits included increased awareness of musical development; parent education; reflection; and connections to others. Lack of time, mixed views on social networking, and the desire for more face-to-face interactions were identified as drawbacks.

Benefits: Awareness, Education, Reflection, and Connection

Parents described one of the greatest benefits of participation in the social network as the increased awareness of their children's musical development and activities. They identified this awareness as beneficial to them as parents as well as to their children, as the awareness enabled the parents to respond to their children's musical behaviors more knowledgeably. One participant spoke of the effect of this increased awareness on the entire family:

> We were very aware of music, more so than we normally are. There was that overall awareness. We were hyperaware of what was going on in class, and then during the week we would look for it outside of class. I felt like I was doing it more because I was looking for things to write each week, keeping track of them. I'm sure she was doing a lot of the same things, but I might not have been so in tune to what she was doing in relationship to the class. My other kids were listening for things she was doing, and it got the whole family involved; we were part of a project. (Participant 3)

Another theme that arose from the interviews was the use of the social network as a form of parent education. Participants seemed to appreciate the weekly blogs that provided information about children's musical development and the methods used in the class. Two parents described how they felt as though they were experiencing a separate class, as reflected in this comment:

> I felt like I was taking a brief and subtle, but influential, music education class. I really loved it because, in a busy life, I don't have time to take a serious class. It was nice to get a little dose, be educated a little bit more each week. (Participant 2)

Additional participant comments indicated that this form of parent education seemed to support the awareness described in the previous paragraph to provide parents with additional tools to interact with their children musically.

Several participants also identified the opportunity for reflection as central to a positive experience in the project. One parent said,

> And taking the time to reflect—it's so hard to do in a busy schedule, but it's so beneficial. As a [former elementary school] teacher, I was always encouraging my students to do that, because I saw the benefits. . . . So I really liked that this site created that opportunity for me. (Participant 2)

Reflection seemed to be a thread that tied the awareness and education together for some parents and provided connections between class and home: "For me, I felt a lot more connected to the class in terms of what I was thinking about" (Participant 3).

Several of the social network participants indicated that their participation in the network helped them feel more connected to other members of the class, both the other children and the parents. As one mother described,

> I think more than anything I felt like I knew the other kids better than I would just seeing them on Thursday. I was aware of what they were doing away from class and that made me more connected to the children. (Participant 3)

Another participant stated that, when she read about something new another child was doing musically, she would watch for that the following week. Many participants indicated that they enjoyed reading what the other parents wrote each week as a way to get to know the other families, to hear what other children were doing, and to see their development. One participant identified this as the most important part of the project:

> I was extremely interested in what other people had to say. For me, that was the biggest benefit—seeing what other people did. . . . Not necessarily what I had to say about my children, but what other people had to say about their own. (Participant 6)

The connection to other parents described by participants seemed to fill an existing gap in the program. Several participants spoke of their desire for interaction with other parents but recognized the limitations of the forty-five-minute class period. In her exit interview, one parent described the connection to other parents facilitated by participation in the social network.

> And it also let me see how other parents were handling similar concerns. In class you don't have a lot of time to talk about it, it's not the appropriate place—we're

not there to socialize. So that kind of reflective piece and self-assessment piece is very useful. . . . It definitely made my experience with the other parents more enjoyable—you really felt like you were in it together. (Participant 6)

Another parent expressed a similar sentiment: "For me personally, I think the biggest thing was introducing me to the other parents and giving us a prompt to talk to each other, which could transfer to the class as well, which I think is important" (Participant 7).

A final connection that arose from the interviews was the connection of parents with teacher. Four participants mentioned this connection, three stating that it was a helpful part of the program and one asking for more interaction between parents and teacher with increased dialogue on the site. As a teacher, I appreciated the connection I felt with parents as they described their children's musical experiences. Reading their weekly posts aided me both in planning sessions and in processing what occurred during classes, helping me design instruction for the following week. For instance, after one mother wrote of her daughter's love of rhythm sticks, I was sure to carefully observe this student the next time we used them in class to watch for the ways she used the sticks and her rhythmic accuracy during the activity.

Drawbacks: Lack of Time, Comfort with Social Networking, Desire for Face-to-Face Interaction

Parents cited lack of time as one of the barriers to participation in the social network. The study ran from mid-April to early June, a busy time for families, several of whom had older children finishing school programs. Several participants stated that they would have liked to spend more time with the project, and recognized they would have benefited from doing so, but simply did not have the time. They noted that they were not using the full range of features of the site, such as communicating with other participants or posting audio, video, or photo files. Participants suggested that not fully using the site was due to lack of time and, in some cases, not knowing all of the other participants.

Another barrier was lack of interest or comfort using social networking, mentioned by three of the participants. In the words of one mother, "I'm not really into social networking and try not to sit in front of the computer too long . . . it's not my thing" (Participant 5). These participants expressed an appreciation for face-to-face interaction instead. More interaction, both on the site and in person, was also requested by several of the participants who expressed overall satisfaction with the project. Participants wished that people would have asked and responded to more questions online as well as use features of the site such as audio, video, and photo sharing. Concerning face-to-face encounters, participants suggested getting together socially with others outside of class and meeting other participants for an end-of-study discussion. It seems a certain level of familiarity and contact was important in order to facilitate the participation in the online network, and this level was not reached for all participants.

Two participants in the study had been previously enrolled in the early childhood music classes but were not enrolled in the class at the time of the study. These two participants had noticeably different experiences: One was very positive about the project, sharing that it was a way to learn more about her child's musical development and helped her continue to provide her child with musical experiences while away from the class. The other parent expressed her feeling of disconnection from the class experience; while she appreciated reading the information on musical development, she felt the posts did not enhance her musical interactions with her child at home or inspire her to connect with others through the site. This difference could be in part due to interaction preferences, as the second participant stated she preferred not to use social networks as a means for interaction.

CONCLUSION

There was a mixed response to the use of the social network site in this study, but there were a greater number of positive comments than negative comments about the experience. Parents seemed to recognize and identify benefits or possible benefits, but participation was tempered by a lack of time. The greatest benefits described were that the project increased parental awareness, education, and reflection on musical development, with a possible increased ability to guide music instruction with their children in some cases. The project also seemed to facilitate connections among the parents, teacher, and children in the early childhood music classes, as well as to facilitate communication and share anecdotes or updates that otherwise may not have been shared.

The issue of lack of time might be addressed by continuing the study during the school year when parents may have more time; also, during times of cooler weather, the parent may have more time at the computer. More important, though, the system could be streamlined to require less time in navigation. For instance, instead of using a social networking system, a simpler blog (such as those created at blogspot.com) could be used as a communication tool and reflection opportunity for parents. This may lack some of the interaction potential of the social networking site, but the payoff in participation and ease of use may make up for this. Another possibility is to invite parental participation as time allows, without a requirement or assignment, in the hope that parents will see the intrinsic benefits and choose to use the system in a way that is helpful to themselves and their children.

I found the information in the blog posts helpful to me as a teacher in forming a more complete picture of children's musical lives. In several posts, parents described children's musical preferences, and I was able to include some of these preferences in the class in the form of musical selections for movement activities and the choice of props used in rhythm activities. I was also able to have brief, meaningful interactions with children before or after class with reference to something a parent had written about on the site, such as with one student who had learned to sing "Tomorrow" from the musical *Annie*.

In regard to the development of a community of learners through the social networking site, the results did not indicate that this project facilitated a strong community in which all members felt they knew one another and were working together toward a common goal. Small steps forward were evident, though, especially in the comments by some participants about connecting with other children and parents. The idea of a community within the classroom could be further expanded both in online and face-to-face forums, and researchers could focus on the effect of developing this community on music instruction and children's responses and musical growth. Future researchers may also focus on the use of a social network site over a longer period of time and the use of blogs instead of the social network because of the possible benefits cited above. Finally, researchers should continue to examine the effects of parental education and communication on early childhood music instruction and children's musical development, given the important role parents play in children's musical growth.

REFERENCES

Berger, A. A., and Cooper, S. (2003). Musical play: A case study of preschool children and parents. *Journal of Research in Music Education, 51*(2), 151–65.

boyd, d. m., and Ellison, N. B. (2007). Social network sites: Definition, history, and scholarship. *Journal of Computer-Mediated Communication, 13*(1), article 11. Retrieved from http://jcmc.indiana.edu/vol13/issue1/boyd.ellison.html.

Cardany, A. A. (2004). Music education for preschool children: Perspectives and experiences of parents. *Dissertation Abstracts International, 65*(11), 4141.

Creswell, J. W. (2009). *Research design: Qualitative, quantitative, and mixed methods approaches* (3rd ed.). Thousand Oaks, CA: Sage.

Custodero, L. A. (2006). Singing practices in 10 families with young children. *Journal of Research in Music Education, 54*(1), 37–56.

Custodero, L. A., Britto, P. R., and Brooks-Gunn, J. (2003). Musical lives: A collective portrait of American parents and their young children. *Journal of Applied Developmental Psychology, 24*(5), 553–72.

Denzin, N. K., and Lincoln, Y. S. (Eds.). (2000). *Handbook of qualitative research* (2nd ed.). Thousand Oaks, CA: Sage.

deVries, P. (2009). Music at home with the under fives: What is happening? *Early Child Development and Care, 179*(4), 395–405.

Gordon, E. E. (2003). *A music learning theory for newborn and young children.* Chicago: GIA.

Hudson, D. B., Campbell-Grossman, C., Keating-Lefler, R., and Cline, P. (2008). New mothers network: The development of an internet-based social support intervention for African American mothers. *Issues in Comprehensive Pediatric Nursing, 31*(1), 23–35.

Ilari, B. (2005). On musical parenting of young children: Musical beliefs and behaviors of mothers and infants. *Early Child Development and Care, 175*(7–8), 647–60.

Kenney, S. (2007). Young musicians: Preschool children make music. In K. Smithrim and R. Upitis (Eds.), *Listen to their voices: Research and practice in early childhood music* (pp. 33–46). Waterloo, Ontario: Canadian Music Educators' Association.

Koops, L. H. (2011). Parental perceptions of current and desired involvement in early childhood music instruction. *Visions of Research in Music Education, 17.*

Mallett, C. A. (2000). An examination of parent/caregiver attitudes toward music instruction, the nature of the home musical environment, and their relationship to the developmental music aptitude of preschool children. *Dissertation Abstracts International, 61*(4), 1335.

McPherson, G. E. (2009). The role of parents in children's musical development. *Psychology of Music, 37*(1), 91–100.

ResearchWare [web page]. (n.d.). Retrieved from http://researchware.com/.

Smith, B. L. (2001). Learning communities: A convergence zone for statewide education reform. In B. L. Smith and J. McCann (Eds.), *Reinventing ourselves: Interdisciplinary education, collaborative learning, and experimentation in higher education.* Boston: Anker.

The Up Side of Downs [website]. (n.d.). Retrieved from http://community.theupsideofdowns.org/.

Valerio, W. H., Reynolds, A. M., Bolton, B. M., Taggart, C. C., and Gordon, E. E. (1998). *Music play: The early childhood music curriculum guide for parents, teachers, and caregivers.* Chicago: GIA.

Wu, S.-M. (2005). A survey of Taiwanese parents' attitudes toward early childhood music education and their participation in music activities at home. *Dissertation Abstracts International, 66*(6), 2098.

Chapter Twelve

Twenty-First-Century Parenting, Electronic Media, and Early Childhood Music Education

Beatriz Ilari

Recent studies have shown an ever growing presence of electronic media in the lives of very young children. While many parents now rely on these media to provide musical experiences for their children at home, these experiences vary enormously and are related to the anxieties, values, and beliefs of our society. For music educators, questions that stem from such experiences are important, as they relate directly to practice. How much electronic media should be used in early childhood music education practice? How can educators work with parents in ways that may diminish anxieties regarding musical experiences in the early years? The purpose of this philosophical inquiry then is to address some of these questions by opening a debate on electronic media, twenty-first-century parenting, and early childhood music education, especially in respect to children aged zero to three. The chapter is informed by recent studies in music education, parenting, early childhood education, media studies, and child psychology, and by my own experiences as an early childhood music educator and researcher.

Music educators are often confronted with the dilemma of using electronic media (such as CDs, DVDs, electronic musical toys and instruments) or digital technologies (like computers and TVs) with young children. Their questions are many: How much electronic media should be used in the music class with young children? Will the use of electronic media and digital technologies in the classroom hinder music's socializing potential? What advice should we give parents in respect to acquiring and using musical CDs, DVDs, and digital technologies at home? What does research say in respect to young children learning music through electronic media? There certainly are no easy answers to these questions. Yet answers are vital in current times, more so when we consider that, from birth, children already are immersed in diverse practices that involve electronic media and digital technologies (Marsh et al., 2005; Rideout and Hammel, 2006; Rideout, Vandewater, and Wartella, 2003; Zimmerman, Christakis, and Meltzoff, 2007).

The purpose of this philosophical inquiry is to open a debate on electronic media, twenty-first-century parenting, and early childhood music education, especially in respect to children aged zero to three. I start this chapter with a brief discussion of issues concerning twenty-first-century parenting, including notions of *edutainment* and *commodified babyhood*. Then, I review several studies concerning young children, new technologies, and music learning. Two vignettes that describe different experiences that stem from my practice as both an early childhood music educator and researcher are also presented; they serve to illustrate my arguments and aid in the development of discussion. Implications for early childhood music education are drawn at the end of the chapter.

THE AGE OF ANXIETY: PARENTING
ISSUES IN THE TWENTY-FIRST CENTURY

Vignette 1: The "Late Effects" of the Mozart Effect

An excited mother of a six-month-old girl walks into a music class, holding baby Alice in one hand and a box of CDs in the other. As she sits down on the rug, she rushes to open the box and shares her newly acquired CDs with the other moms and dads, whom, by the way, she doesn't know very well. The CDs are all related to classical music and sounds from nature. She explains to the other adults that she saw a show on TV in which the host spoke of music listening as being beneficial for the development of children's attention and overall intelligence! Generous at heart, she shares her CDs will all parents and offers to make copies for those who cannot afford to buy them. I watch the scene in silence.

As an early childhood music educator, I am puzzled by the fact that, almost a decade past the dissemination of the so-called Mozart effect by the popular press,[1] parents are still hit hard by it, or, at least, by its overall concept. In spite of all the conversations we have during or after classes, it occurs to me that the "effects of the effects" are going to be felt by new parents for several years.

In 1949 the American conductor and composer Leonard Bernstein (1918–1990) wrote his Symphony No. 2 for piano and orchestra, titled *The Age of Anxiety* based on a homonymous poem by the American poet W. H. Auden (1907–1973). The essence of the poem was man's search for meaning and identity in an ever-changing industrialized world. The metaphor of the age of anxiety seems to suit well the pressures felt by parents of infants and young children of our current times (for example, see Furedi, 2002; Paul, 2009; Schoenstein, 2002). Parenting has never been an easy task, but recently, it may have become even more complex. Certainly, parents have been anxious about raising their children before, but in recent years, their anxiety has been raised to almost unbearable levels.

Many factors have contributed to this age of anxiety in parenting, including the birth of a baby culture (p. 3) in the late 1990s (Thomas, 2007). According to Thomas, a particular political event, the White House Conference on Early Childhood Development and Learning, or the "Brain Conference of 1997" (as it became known), gave rise to much discussion on the importance of early childhood. The event aimed at impressing both Congress and the general public as a means to raise awareness of and gather funds for early childhood programs. The conference relied on the expertise of neurobiologists and other early childhood experts, who explained early brain development and the importance of nurturing the developing brain to politicians, educators, policymakers, and, of course, the press (Thomas, 2007).

A massive marketing campaign also accompanied the event. Unsurprisingly, it was exactly at this moment that the myth of the first three years (i.e., the notion that the brain organizes itself for good during this time of life) emerged in the popular press (Bruer, 1999). Coincidentally or not, Julie Aigner-Clark, a stay-at-home mom, launched the first *Baby Einstein* video in the United States, approximately one month after the brain conference, and a few weeks later, Don Campbell published his controversial book *The Mozart Effect* (Thomas, 2007). Other products followed, and about five years later, Aigner-Clark sold her company to the Walt Disney Corporation for an estimated $25 million (Thomas, 2007).

As Thomas argued, *Baby Einstein*, *The Mozart Effect*, and other brands transformed the entire culture of early child parenting. Videos, TV programs, and especially crafted CDs and toys were transformed into *surrogate parents* that also were capable of developing very young brains. In less than a decade, the everyday lives of many American children were altered by a wide plethora of toys, videos, and gadgets that promised wonders to their development (Paul, 2009; Thomas, 2007). Considering that we live in a globalized world, these changes were also felt by parents of young children living in other parts of the world (Ilari, Moura, and Bourscheidt, in press).

Today in our technology- and media-dominated era, parents across the globe often feel confused about how to raise their young children (Furedi, 2002). In the music domain, many parents of today seem to believe that musical toys, CDs, and DVDs are more efficient than live renditions in delivering music and learning experiences to their children. In interview studies, for example, parents often argue that they do not know how to sing (deVries, 2007), or that these materials have been designed (and recorded) by professionals in the field (Thomas, 2007), which supposedly endows them with more educational and aesthetic qualities. The search for expert advice has been common to early parenting in the current times (Furedi, 2002) and has added to the already enormous pressure of the so-called million-dollar baby industry (Paul, 2009) on parents of young children. Catalyzed by massive marketing strategies, both the pressure on and consumerism of parents have helped to reinforce notions of *edutainment* (Buckingham and Scanlon, 2001) and *commodified babyhood* (Hughes, 2005).

EDUTAINMENT AND COMMODIFIED BABYHOOD

The term *edutainment* is not new, but has gained attention in recent years. It has been used in diverse fields, ranging from information technology and advertising to education. Buckingham and Scanlon (2001) use the term *edutainment* when referring to an amalgam of education and entertainment "that relies heavily on visual material, on narrative or game-like formats, and on more informal, less didactic styles of address" (p. 282). The authors also argue that the pedagogy found in edutainment materials is often seen as being more interactive than what one would find in formal schooling activities. Compare, for example, a children's classical music video, with aesthetically appealing and powerful images matching the sounds, to a typical listening experience of the same classical piece, without a video, images, and "the works." From the perspective of edutainment, the video would be more fun to experience and it also would promote learning, whereas the simple listening experience would be thought to be less fun, albeit promoting learning. Yet, as Resnick (2004) contended, one of the problems associated with edutainment is that many defenders of the idea and/or creators of such products often "view education as a bitter medicine that needs the sugar-coating of entertainment to become palatable" (p. 1).

The existence of edutainment products for very young children also has helped to redefine childhood in the Western world. For many large corporations of edutainment products, young children are viewed as both learners and consumers, whose learning potential is released by consuming specific products (Hughes, 2005). This forced consumerism in the early years is often referred to as *commodified babyhood* or *commodified childhood* (Hughes, 2005). Parents are pressured to consume, as if the consumption of particular goods would guarantee learning experiences that, in the long run, will make their children smarter and even secure a place in a renowned college when they grow up (Schoenstein, 2002). Pressure comes from everywhere—from advertising representations of good parenting disseminated in the popular press (Buckingham and Scanlon, 2001) to utilitarian views of music found in parenting magazines (Sims and Udtaisuk, 2008).

What lies beneath the notion of commodified babyhood are deeper moral questions. Are babies and young children agents of their own environment and capable of interacting with it, or are they helpless creatures that need to be fully protected from the potentially negative influences of the media (Marsh, 2000)? These questions puzzle parents and scholars alike and have been at the heart of recent research.

Young Children, Electronic Media, and Early Learning: What Research Tells Us

Even if research concerning the impact of electronic media on young children "has not kept pace with the marketplace" (Rideout and Hammel, 2006, p. 4), some data exist to help us understand how children under six experience it in their daily lives. The main focus of most studies has not been on early music learning, per se, but on screen viewing (through TV, videos, and DVDs) and how it affects early learning (DeLoache and Chiong, 2009). Given that most of these studies do not specify the repertoire found in these electronic sources, and that many videos, DVDs, and TV shows contain music, I will briefly review them here.

In 2003 the Kaiser Family Foundation published an important parental survey study on the uses of digital technologies and electronic media by over one thousand children in the United States. The results provided evidence of something that many of us already knew: children aged zero to six are growing up immersed in a media-rich environment (Rideout, Vandewater, and Wartella, 2003). The study revealed that, on a typical day, young American children spent on average one hour and fifty-eight minutes in front of a screen, about the same amount of time playing outside, approximately one hour listening to music, and forty minutes being read to. Interestingly, listening to music was found to be one of the most common media-related activities of children younger than six, and almost half of the children in the surveyed sample had a stereo player (cassette or CD player) in their rooms. In 2006 the Kaiser Family Foundation published another large-scale study, this time based on a survey and focus-group sessions conducted in four different parts of the continental United States (Rideout and Hammel, 2006). Results confirmed previous findings and also suggested a slight increase in screen viewing time in children aged zero to six since 2003.

The ubiquity of electronic media in the lives of young children was also found by Marsh and colleagues (2005), who investigated uses of digital technologies and popular culture by over one thousand British children from zero to six years of age. Parental reports suggested that, although the average screen viewing time in the United Kingdom was slightly higher than in the United States (average of two hours, six minutes), music listening, despite its reported importance, occupied only about thirty-one minutes of British children's time each day. Most children in the United Kingdom watched TV[2] for the first time when they were between six and twelve months of age, and the main reported activities to accompany viewing were singing and dancing. Parents also spoke of some benefits associated with children's uses of electronic media, including digital technologies, and experiences learning popular culture. These benefits were grouped by the research team into three main categories: (a) increased knowledge and understanding of the world, (b) physical development, and (c) creative development. The question that remains to be answered is whether these perceived benefits actually take place in real life. While many early-childhood-geared corporations argue that their products are highly educational, many scholars are skeptical (Wartella and Robb, 2007). Do young children really learn anything from screen viewing?

COMPREHENSION, LEARNING, AND CHILDREN'S TV SHOWS AND DVDS

Vignette 2: Daniel, the Musical Video, and the Carrot Cake

As Mom was strolling through the mall with nineteen-month-old Daniel, she couldn't help but notice a bunch of young kids standing or sitting still, eyes glued to a flat monitor in a major bookshop. The children were watching a musical DVD, in which a boy character named Julio and a group of three lively hens sang, danced, and clapped, as they were just about to eat an appetizing carrot cake with chocolate icing. Little Daniel quickly ran to join the other children and, a few seconds later, his eyes were also glued to the screen. Mom watched the musical video for a few moments and decided to buy it, since it seemed educational, well crafted, and, moreover, Daniel seemed to like it. She soon discovered that it belonged to an educational TV series that ran for almost a decade in public television, and that this particular DVD included a series of animated musical videos (and virtually no spoken dialogues), portraying the lives of the series' main characters.

Daniel was only allowed to watch the video for about one hour each day. Yet it didn't take long before the video became his favorite. He would ask to watch it during the day (especially the beginning of the video), and the songs learned became part of his routine. As tired as she was from hearing the same songs over and over, Mom memorized them, and would often sing the songs to her son as she engaged with him in routine acts, like diaper changing, bottle feeding, playing, or when riding to and from daycare. Very soon, Daniel began to identify with Julio, his favorite character. By this time, Mom had already acquired plastic dolls of Julio and the hens, children's books on the plot, and a red cap, just like Julio's. These objects went with Daniel everywhere, and Daniel, who was also an incredibly social child, was always proud to show them to whoever came his way—be it the cashier at the supermarket, the neighbors, or a family friend.

Almost six months passed by when, one day, as Mom picked him up at daycare, Daniel asked for carrot cake. Mom was puzzled. She knew that Daniel had already tried and liked cakes at birthday parties, but these were chocolate cakes. Where did the idea for carrot cake come from? She asked the educators at daycare and nobody knew. When she got home, she asked Dad. He didn't know either. So Mom decided to find a way to ask Daniel. After talking about everything that could possibly relate to carrot cake and getting almost no hints, Mom solved the puzzle. Julio ate carrot cake. The sentence "Come in boy to drink tea and eat carrot cake with hot chocolate icing" was a repeated verse in one of Daniel's favorite songs. A little over two, Daniel had presumably established a connection between the words of a song, its portrayal on video, and the desire to eat a real carrot cake.

Studies on the relationship between screen viewing and learning in preschool children have been conducted at least since the early 1970s, when Anderson and Levin (1976) began to examine four- and five-year-olds' learning experiences with *Sesame Street*. They possibly were among the first scholars to demonstrate that preschool children were not mere passive viewers, but rather were focused and alert when segments in the show had coherent plot lines and narration (Thomas, 2007). Anderson and colleagues later demonstrated that, when invited by the show's characters, preschool children would respond to them. This led Anderson to coin the term *comprehensibility effect* to designate young children's possible comprehension of TV shows if the latter were developmentally appropriate (Thomas, 2007). However, his early research did not include children younger than three. Perhaps this was because encouraging screen viewing by such young children is a more recent phenomenon.

In 1999 the American Academy of Pediatrics (AAP) released a policy statement recommending that children under the age of two avoid television viewing at all costs, as it could be harmful to their developing minds. The document also encouraged parents and caregivers to engage in interactive activities that were more likely to promote a healthy brain development, such as playing, singing, and reading. In spite of these recommendations, young children have been commonly placed in front of a screen from an early age (Wartella and Robb, 2007). In a recent survey of screen viewing by children younger than three, Zimmerman, Christakis, and Meltzoff (2007) found that by three months of age about 40 percent of 1,069 American children watched TVs, DVDs, and videos on a regular basis. By twenty-four months, this proportion had risen to 90 percent. These statistics are frightening when we consider how little is known about the effects of screen viewing on their development (DeLoache and Chiong, 2009; Wartella and Robb, 2007).

In a recent article, Anderson and Pempek (2005) discuss TV viewing in children under two years and make a distinction between foreground and background TV. While foreground TV is directed to young children, background TV is not. Anderson and Pempek review several studies and suggest that children's attention to screen contents increases as they grow older, especially at around thirty months of age, which Anderson and Pempek attribute to the "coming together of cognitive and language development" (p. 509). The researchers also discuss recent findings that suggest that young children's sustained attention to these especially designed TV shows and videos is much higher than what was found in previous investigations. On that note, DeLoache and Chiong (2009) cite, among others, a study in which twelve- to eighteen-month-olds attended to the screen for circa 70 percent of the duration of an entire video (e.g., *Baby Mozart*), suggesting that this attention shift may be indicative of early comprehension of video contents. Although videos, DVDs, and TV shows designed for very young children do catch their attention, young children seem to pay more attention to them when their contents are within their comprehensibility (Anderson and Pempek, 2005).

Comprehensibility, however, does not necessarily equate to learning. Anderson and Pempek (2005) suggest that young children, twenty-four months and under, can learn from foreground screen viewing, although comparatively less than when they go through real-life equivalent experiences. They refer to this phenomenon as a *video deficit*. Studies using diverse methodologies have demonstrated the existence of video deficit in young children (for reviews see Anderson and Pempek, 2005; DeLoache and Chiong, 2009; Wartella and Robb, 2007). Laboratory studies show that toddlers find it more difficult to imitate a demonstration on video than the same demonstration presented live. This also seems to be true when tasks of object retrieval and vocabulary learning are presented both live and on video (Anderson and Pempek, 2005). As DeLoache and Chiong (2009) argue, very young children can make some sense of videos and DVDs that are presented to them, although what they see on the screen is interpreted in reference to their current knowledge. In addition, learning might occur when there is some amount of repetition (Anderson and Pempek, 2005; DeLoache and Chiong, 2009).

However, some caution is needed when applying results from current studies to naturalistic settings. At least two issues are at stake. First, a problem with current research is that the majority of studies (if not all) conducted to date have used videos based on real-life events and not situations in which (for example) the laws of gravity are violated through the display of magic flying objects and characters, as it occurs in many children's TV shows and DVDs (DeLoache and Chiong, 2009). Second, screen viewing requires children to understand that an object presented on a DVD, video, or TV is not the object itself but a representation of it. This is a classic problem in developmental psychology, known as the problem of *dual representation* (Wartella and Robb, 2007). According to many psychologists, dual representation does not happen until children are about thirty months old, which is, perhaps not coincidentally, the same milestone discussed earlier by Anderson and Pempek (2005).

The bottom line is that current research tells us virtually nothing about children's early learning through screen viewing (DeLoache and Chiong, 2009). This is especially unsettling when we consider the plethora of commercially available videos, DVDs, and TV shows. But what about music learning through electronic media?

MUSIC LEARNING, ELECTRONIC MEDIA, AND DIGITAL TECHNOLOGIES

As noted, music seems to be omnipresent in the routine of children younger than three years in Western countries. Their musical lives also appear to be highly dominated by electronic media and digital technologies (deVries, 2007, 2009; Ilari et al., in press; Lamont, 2008; Roulston, 2006; Young, 2008, 2009). Many young children now possess stereos in their rooms (and some TVs), along with an impressive number of CDs, musical DVDs, musical toys, and instruments (deVries, 2009; Ilari et al., in press; Young, 2008). Parents often rely on these sources, not only to provide musical experiences for their little ones, but also to *take a break* from parenting, while the child is doing something presumably educational (deVries, 2009; Thomas, 2007). Nevertheless, as it happens in conjunction with general TV screening, our knowledge of early music learning through electronic media is still quite limited. Due to space constraints, I will focus on screen viewing and audio listening, as these seem to be the most common music-technological experiences of children under age three.

Within the field of music education, some researchers have examined the extent to which video performances of specific repertoires promote music learning (Geringer, Cassidy, and Byo, 1996, 1997). Comparatively fewer studies have investigated children's responses to musical videos and DVDs. Wolfe and Jellison (1995) interviewed preschool children immediately after they viewed *Sesame Street* videos with specific song performances. The children responded more accurately when questions were more explicit or direct, and few were capable of transferring information implicit in the songs to other real-life situations. What this study suggests is that one should not assume that preschool children necessarily are learning implicit messages contained in songs presented on a screen. Moreover, Wolfe and Jellison argued that, while preschool children can learn messages from songs found in videos, this learning is facilitated when a more experienced person provided them with verbal instruction prior to viewing.

In a subsequent study, Jellison and Wolfe (1999) contrasted the responses of adults and fifth-grade students to the same segments that were shown to preschool children in the previous study. The majority of children and adults reported that they had already seen the show. The researchers found significant differences in children and adult perceptions of the video song segments, especially in respect to learning implicit messages and overall preferences.

Perhaps the gap between children's and adults' perceptions and comprehension of songs presented through screen viewing is much larger than previously thought. In other words, what adults (who are usually the creators of videos and songs for children) consider appropriate for young children to learn may not, indeed, be appropriate. To that effect, McGuire (2002) investigated the recognition of songs from *Barney and Friends* by third-grade students, many of whom had watched the show when they were younger. Results suggested that most children could not recall music from the show. According to McGuire, one of the possible explanations for children's inability to recall songs was the noninteractive nature of the show.

Altogether, results from these three studies reinforce the need for an interactive nature of music learning in the preschool years. Yet they were conducted with preschool children rather than children younger than three. Studies concerning screen viewing experiences and music learning by younger children were not found to exist in the literature.

By contrast, some researchers have investigated the nature of early music learning through the examination of long-term memory for recorded music in the beginning of life. One of the most remarkable studies was conducted by Hepper (1991), who examined responses of neonates to recorded music heard in the womb. He asked pregnant women, who were fans of one out of two soap operas, to pay close attention to the daily episodes without missing the opening vignette, with its theme song, throughout the third trimester of their pregnancies. Then Hepper tested infants' recognition of the song after the children were born. Results suggested that neonates exhibited distinct behaviors when listening to the familiar soap opera tune, indicating that they recognized it. Yet when the song was played in a different version, there was no evidence of recognition. This was, perhaps, one of the first studies to substantiate human long-term memory for recorded music.

More recently, studies have shown that, in the first year of life, babies can recall recorded music that is played to them repeatedly for periods of up to a month (Trainor, Wu, and Tsang, 2004), provided that an identical version of the music is offered at the time of testing. That is, long-term memory for music in infancy appears to be piece- and performance-specific. It is only with time and experience that children and adults seem to be able to transfer musical properties from one musical version to another and still consider it to be the *same* music. Even music that is complex can be recalled by young babies (Ilari and Polka, 2006); however, they seem to pay more attention to music that is simpler and more related to humans and interactions, such as a cappella versions of a song (Ilari and Sundara, 2009), especially when it is sung directly to them (Trainor, 1996). Thus, musical preferences and memory appear to change as children mature and become exposed to different repertoire.

Taken together, these studies imply that very young children can retain and thus learn music heard on electronic media through digital technologies, more so when songs and pieces are presented repeatedly and become familiar. Music learning seems to be more effective when, along with recorded music, there is some form of human interaction, like bouncing or rocking a child to the beat of the song happening (Phillips-Silver and Trainor, 2005). Much more research is needed before it can be established what, exactly, young children are learning from experiences with electronic media and how those experiences will affect their overall development. But what is known so far allows us to ponder some pragmatic issues concerning electronic media and digital technologies in early childhood music education.

FROM THEORY TO PRACTICE: COMING TO TERMS WITH ELECTRONIC MEDIA AND DIGITAL TECHNOLOGIES IN EARLY CHILDHOOD MUSIC EDUCATION

Defining the Role of Technology in Early Childhood Music

If young children learn better through interactions with other humans, does this mean that electronic media and digital technologies should be completely eliminated from their lives? I do not think so. After all, as Upitis (2001) suggested, we can no longer live without technology, and I would add, without electronic and digital media (e.g., CDs, digital players and cameras, and computers). As a profession, we need to come to terms with these forms of communication.

To start, it is necessary that we adopt a clear definition of *technology*, which is a complex term with many different meanings. For some persons, *technology* refers to the ways in which different species use tools and crafts as a means to control their environment. For others, *technology* refers to material objects including different tools, utensils, machines, and hardware, or specific systems and techniques. In Heidegger's (1977) view, these two definitions are complementary, as technology is a human endeavor. "The manufacture and utilization of equipments, tools and machines, the manufactured and used things themselves, and the means and ends that they serve, all belong to what technology is" (Heidegger, 1977, pp. 4–5). Thus, technology (including digital technology) can be understood as a human endeavor that is both a means and an end, and capable of transforming culture.

In the case of early childhood music education and, moreover, in the case of children younger than three, digital technologies and electronic media should be more of a means than an end. Digital technologies and electronic media have transformed early childhood music practice in a good way. The instruments we use and the CDs, DVDs, digital players, digital cameras, and other innumerous gadgets that help us deliver beautiful renditions of songs and pieces in our classes, as well as document them, are all products of technology.

The many powerful episodes of young children's engagement with recorded music that we hear about from the parents of the children we teach, or those that we experience in our programs attest to this—from the young baby who suddenly moves her body in response to a particular recorded selection to the toddler who joins in and sings along with a musical DVD or toy, even when he cannot speak. Later on, these episodes may include karaoke machines, digital music players, and fancy cell phones that deliver recorded music, which young children listen to and often share with grown-ups or one another (Young, 2009). Recorded music has existed for quite a long time now and is easy to take for granted. Yet, when it was new, aversions to it were also common (Upitis, 2001). Like Upitis (2001, p. 53), I believe that technology can be best integrated into music classrooms (and into our daily lives) when it enhances music making and allows us to become more human and artistic.

In respect to electronic media, a widespread concern lies in its content. The multimillion-dollar baby industry of our times has produced a plethora of CDs, DVDs, and musical toys that are directly linked to themes and characters from popular culture.[3] Although an in-depth analysis of popular culture in the early years obviously is beyond the scope of the present chapter, it must be mentioned as it is directly linked to digital technologies and electronic media. Early in life, a toddler like Daniel (vignette 2) can already identify his favorite characters, which are a constant in his life, and appear not only in CDs and DVDs but also in books, on T-shirts, and as plastic action figures that he has at home. While there is an obvious commercial and consumerist appeal to this large exposure to characters from popular culture (Thomas, 2007), Daniel seems to have also developed a preference and appears to have learned some things with them. After all, in spite of Daniel's exposure to other DVDs and CDs, none of them received such a strong response from him. Of course, his situation was unique in that he was only allowed to watch his favorite DVD (or any other) for a limited time each day. The rest of his time he spent playing, singing, and interacting with others, with and without show-related gadgets.

Thus, it may be possible to have a positive take on popular culture content learned through electronic media and digital technologies, granted that parents, caregivers, and educators expand these experiences into live, playful, and interactive activities that take place in real life. In early childhood music education, an example could be to sing a preferred popular song suggested by a parent or child, but with a new arrangement, new words, or new gestures that parents can do at home, with or without the original version, while not compromising popular contents and electronic media as a means, not an end.

One of the main problems associated with digital technologies, electronic media, and their primary content is when they become a substitute for other vital activities in the early years. For example, in several studies, parents say that they truly believe in the educational potential of electronic media, especially videos designed for young children (deVries, 2009), despite the fact that no research to date has substantiated these claims (DeLoache and Chiong, 2009; Wartella and Robb, 2007). Many parents would blame their actions on the pressures of the massive marketing campaign of the baby industry, the same one that has helped to produce and reinforce notions of commodified babyhood and edutainment.

No doubt, this large-scale marketing is a major reason for their behavior. But there is also another one. As noted, parenting is a challenging task, and the representations of parenthood by which we live are much more romanticized than the reality of sleep-deprivation, worries about doing the "right thing," constant feelings of guilt and fear, and so on. In this sense, many parents seem to rely on products like DVDs, CDs, electronic toys, and other gadgets, not only because they are socially accepted but also because "someone potentially more experienced said so" (Furedi, 2002). This is a vicious cycle that is hard to break. But as parents become better informed, this cycle can be broken.

Mediatic Learning and Early Childhood Music Educators

As early childhood music educators, it is our role to welcome questions from parents and caregivers, to provide information concerning research on children's mediatic music learning experiences, and to discuss how the use of media may enhance their lives. It is also vital that we help parents and caregivers select electronic media appropriately, suggest how they might use it in an interactive way, and help them understand that even the most developmentally appropriate DVD or toy is not a learning agent in itself, but can be educational and interactive.[4] We can help parents and caregivers understand the limitations of these resources and that there are many individual differences among children in a same age group. This is why we, early childhood music educators, need to be *tuned in* to what is going on in young children's lives. Instead of denying or simply ignoring that young children's lives are becoming more technological and mediatic each day, we need to be proactive and knowledgeable about what exists in terms of electronic media, digital technologies, and popular culture in order to develop critical eyes and ears.

We also need to conduct extensive research that addresses these issues, which are likely to continue to be at the heart of our practice: Do babies learn anything from watching musical videos? Can parents and caregivers truly make a foreground screen viewing experience an interactive one? Should children younger than two or three spend many hours in front of TV screens when research suggests that they learn much more from engaging with real people in real-life events (DeLoache and Chiong, 2009)? And on a deeper level, are babies and toddlers agents or passive receptors of media content? These questions need to go under urgent scrutiny, particularly since future studies will help bridge theory and practice and develop much-needed policies regarding the role of technology in the music education and lives of young children (Young, 2008).

CONCLUSION

By tuning in to what is happening in young children's "real" musical worlds, as opposed to the musical worlds we would like them to live in, early childhood music educators have much to gain; this is the only way we will be able to reach out to parents and help them overcome their anxieties and enjoy their precious time with their children. Our classes are also likely to be enhanced if we provide opportunities for parents to discuss and share thoughts, materials, and experiences with their children and digital media. By doing this, we will be able to position ourselves against the belief that early childhood music programs are a product of twenty-first-century pressure on parents (Thomas, 2007).

With the frenzy created by the so-called Mozart effect a few years back, Duke (2001) argued that music education was receiving a lot of attention, but perhaps not for the right reasons. He was probably right. I believe that many parents, like the mother in vignette 1, are experiencing *late effects* of the so-called Mozart effect. In our early childhood music classes, there are parents who believe that music classes will make their infants and toddlers smarter, as well as those who conceive of early childhood music education as purely recreational or something that they cannot miss, because it has become a commodity of some sort (Ilari et al., in press). But, as Thomas (2007) and Furedi (2002) emphasized, parents are very competent in disseminating information among themselves. Therefore, it is our duty not only to bring the best musical experiences that we can conceive to our classes but also to inform parents about the real meanings of early childhood music education for young children, which are, to me, intrinsically related to bonding, interacting, learning, belonging, and enjoyment.

On a personal note, as an expectant mother, I would not like for my daughter to spend most of her time in the company of a screen or digital music player, no matter how high-tech or developmentally appropriate its programs are. As an early childhood specialist and researcher, I know too well that babies learn from interacting with people and that play is fundamental to their development (DeLoache and Chiong, 2009; Hirsh-Pasek, Golinkoff and Eyer, 2003). I am also a firm believer in music's prosocial potential, especially in the early years (Kirschner and Tomasello, 2009), so I intend to make lots of music with her. Yet, as I wrote this chapter, I became much more aware of the pressures that are likely to impinge on me and affect the musical behaviors of this first-time parent in the forthcoming years. As I anxiously dream about spending a lot of time with her when she is ready to explore the world (with and without the aid of digital technologies, electronic media, and popular culture), I also maintain my hopes that I will do the "right thing."

REFERENCES

American Academy of Pediatrics. (1999). Media education. *Pediatrics, 104*, 341–42.

Anderson, D. R., and Levin, S. R. (1976). Young children's attention to *Sesame Street. Child Development, 47*, 806–11.

Anderson, D. R., and Pempek, T. A. (2005). Television and very young children. *American Behavioral Scientist, 48*(5), 505–22.

Buckingham, D., and Scanlon, M. (2001). Parental pedagogies: An analysis of British "edutainment" magazines for young children. *Journal of Early Childhood Literacy, 1*(3), 281–99.

Burton, S. L. (2009). Music and the math connection: An interview with Dr. Frances Rauscher. *Perspectives: A publication of the Early Childhood Music and Movement Association, 4*(1), 4–8.

Bruer, J. T. (1999). *The myth of the first three years.* New York: Free Press.

DeLoache, J., and Chiong, C. (2009). Babies and baby media. *American Behavioral Scientist, 52*(8), 1115–35.

deVries, P. (2007). The use of music CDs and DVDs in the homes with the under fives: What parents say. *Australian Journal of Early Childhood, 32*(4), 18–21.

deVries, P. (2009). Music at home with the under fives: What is happening? *Early Child Development and Care, 179*(4), 395–405.

Duke, R. A. (2001). The other Mozart effect: An open letter to music educators. *Update: Applications of Research in Music Education, 19*(1), 9–16.

Furedi, F. (2002). *Paranoid parenting.* London: Allen Lane.

Geringer, J., Cassidy, J., and Byo, J. (1996). Effects of music with video on responses of nonmusic majors: An exploratory study. *Journal of Research in Music Education, 44*(3), 240–51.

Geringer, J., Cassidy, J., and Byo, J. (1997). Nonmusic majors' cognitive and affective responses to performance and programmatic music videos. *Journal of Research in Music Education, 45*(2), 221–33.

Heidegger, M. (1977). *The question concerning technology and other essays.* New York: Harper and Row.

Hepper, P. G. (1991). An examination of fetal learning before and after birth. *Irish Journal of Psychology, 12*(2), 95–107.

Hirsh-Pasek, K., Golinkoff, R. M., and Eyer, D. (2003). *Einstein never used flash cards.* New York: Rodale Press.

Hughes, P. (2005). Baby, it's you: International capital discovers the under threes. *Contemporary Issues in Early Childhood, 1*(6), 30–40.

Ilari, B., Moura, A., and Bourscheidt, L. (in press). Between interactions and commodities: Musical parenting of infants and toddlers in Brazil. *Music Education Research.*

Ilari, B., and Polka, L. (2006). Music cognition in early infancy: Infants' preferences and long-term memory for Ravel. *International Journal of Music Education, 24*(1), 7–20.

Ilari, B., and Sundara, M. (2009). Music listening preferences in early life: Infants' responses to accompanied versus unaccompanied singing. *Journal of Research in Music Education, 56*(4), 357–69.

Jellison, J. A., and Wolfe, D. E. (1999). Video songs from *Sesame Street*: A comparison of fifth graders' and adults' opinions regarding messages for preschool children. *Journal of Research in Music Education, 47*(1), 64–77.

Kirschner, S., and Tomasello, M. (2009). Joint drumming: Social context facilitates synchronization in preschool children. *Journal of Experimental Child Psychology, 102*(3), 299–314.

Lamont, A. (2008). Young children's musical worlds: Musical engagement in 3.5-year-olds. *Journal of Early Childhood Research, 6*, 247–61.

Marsh, J. (2000). Teletubbytales: Popular culture in the early years language and literacy curriculum. *Contemporary Issues in Early Childhood, 1*(2), 119–33.

Marsh, J., Brooks, G., Hughes, J., Ritchie, L., Roberts, S., and Wright, K. (2005). *Digital beginnings: Young children's use of popular culture, media, and technology.* Research report, Literacy Research Center, University of Sheffield, UK. Retrieved from www.digitalbeginnings.shef.ac.uk/.

McGuire, K. M. (2002). The relationship between the availability of a children's television program and song recognition. *Journal of Research in Music Education, 50*(3), 227–44.

Paul, P. (2009). *Parenting Inc: How the billion dollar baby business has changed the way we raise our children.* New York: Times Books.

Phillips-Silver, J., and Trainor, L. J. (2005). Feeling the beat: Movement influences infant rhythm perception. *Science, 308*(5727), 1430.

Resnick, P. (2004). Edutainment? No thanks. I prefer playful learning. *Associazione Civita Report in Edutainment.* Retrieved from http://web.media.mit.edu/~mres/papers/edutainment.pdf.

Rideout, V. J., and Hammel, E. (2006). *The media family: Electronic media in the lives of infants, toddlers, preschoolers, and their parents.* Menlo Park, CA: Kaiser Family Foundation.

Rideout, V. J., Vandewater, E. A., and Wartella, E. A. (2003). *Zero to six: Electronic media in the lives of infants, toddlers and preschoolers.* Washington, DC: Kaiser Family Foundation. Retrieved from www.kff.org/entmedia/3378.cfm.

Roulston, K. (2006). Qualitative investigation of young children's music preferences. *International Journal of Education in the Arts, 7*(9). Retrieved from http://ijea.asu.edu.

Schoenstein, R. (2002). *Toilet trained for Yale.* New York: Perseus Press.

Sims, W., and Udtaisuk, D. B. (2008). Music's representation in parenting magazines. *Update: Applications of Research in Music Education, 26*(2), 17–26.

Thomas, S. G. (2007). *Buy, baby buy: How consumer culture manipulates parents and harms young minds.* New York: Houghton Mifflin.

Trainor, L. J. (1996). Infant preferences for infant-directed versus non-infant-directed playsongs and lullabies. *Infant Behavior and Development, 19*(2), 83–92.

Trainor, L. J., Wu, L., and Tsang, C. (2004). Long-term memory for music: Infants remember tempo and timbre. *Developmental Science, 7*(3), 289–96.

Upitis, R. (2001). Spheres of influence: The interplay between music research, technology, heritage, and music education. *International Journal of Music Education, 37*, 44–58.

Wartella, E., and Robb, M. (2007). Young children, new media. *Journal of Children and Media, 1*(1), 35–44.

Wolfe, D. E., and Jellison, J. A. (1995). Interviews with preschool children about music videos. *Journal of Music Therapy, 32*(4), 265–85.

Young, S. (2008). Lullaby light shows: Everyday musical experience among under twos. *International Journal of Music Education, 26*(1), 33–46.

Young, S. (2009). Towards constructions of musical childhoods: Diversity and digital technologies. *Early Child Development and Care, 179*(6), 695–706.

Zimmerman, F. J, Christakis, D. A., and Meltzoff, A. N. (2007). Television and DVD/ video viewing in children younger than 2 years. *Archives of Pediatrics and Adolescent Medicine, 161*(5), 473–79.

NOTES

1. For more information, see Burton (2009).

2. The authors do not make it clear that, if by TV viewing, they also include watching children's DVDs. Yet excerpts taken from parental reports seem to suggest that this was the case.

3. Popular culture is defined here as the cultural texts, artifacts, and behaviors that are generally produced on a very large scale and disseminated across the globe (for a discussion, see Marsh et al., 2005).

4. A few months ago, a major video/DVD company recalled some of its products and offered refunds for dissatisfied customers due to the unverified claim that their products would make babies and young children smarter.

Part IV

BENEFITS OF
EARLY MUSIC INSTRUCTION

Chapter Thirteen

The Effect of an Age-Appropriate Music Curriculum on Motor and Linguistic and Nonlinguistic Skills of Children Three to Five Years of Age

Joyce Jordan-DeCarbo and Joy Galliford

The purpose of the study was to investigate the effect of an age-appropriate music curriculum on music and movement tasks and linguistic and nonlinguistic skills of three- to five-year-old children. Four hundred sixty-four three-, four- and five-year-old children enrolled in two low-income preschool centers in south Miami-Dade County, Florida, participated, with one school randomly selected for the music treatment (N = 217) and the other for the control group (N = 247). Researchers designed twenty weeks of thirty-minute lessons that (a) had simple activities for nonmusic preschool teachers to deliver, (b) were easily integrated into a preschool schedule, and (c) involved parents in the home. Researchers randomly selected 20 percent of the total population (N = 92) for testing; forty-three children received the music treatment and forty-nine were in the control group. The Musical Movement Test (MMT) was used to measure motor abilities. Eight subtests of the Woodcock-Johnson Tests of Cognitive Ability–Revised (WJ-R) were used to evaluate relative development of linguistic and nonlinguistic skills before and after the music intervention. Results indicated that two tasks associated with beat competence showed significantly increased gains for the treatment group. Out of eight tasks related to the cognitive measure, four of the five linguistic subtests and two of the three nonlinguistic subtests showed significant gains for the treatment group.

In the last decade, an ongoing debate has persisted regarding the question, "Why should music be included in the preschool curriculum?" Should music educators try to justify music in the curriculum based on its own merits or for how well it can support other academic areas of development? Most educators would agree that they want children to be successful in a range of academic pursuits, including the arts. A preschool curriculum that includes

215

musical exposure may not only improve music and movement skills but may also have an effect on a child's linguistic and nonlinguistic skills, as it relates to the recognition of sound patterns, phonemic awareness, or word comprehension. Thus, a research study that measures young children's motor and linguistic development may uncover important reasons for the inclusion of music in the preschool curriculum.

CONNECTIONS BETWEEN MUSIC AND OTHER SKILLS

Connections between music and language seem obvious, since both are auditory-based systems. Evidence to support auditory similarities between music and language skills has been found in the way children process musical sounds and speech (Lamb and Gregory, 1993) and in children's recognition of phonemes and melodic or rhythmic clusters (Lerdahl and Jackendoff, 1983; Saffran, Johnson, Aslin, and Newport, 1999). While some of the structural features of music and language may require formal training, Baruch and Drake (1997) suggest that some of the features of both can be absorbed by mere exposure in the environment, which may be explained by evidence that speech and music share some cortical areas and mechanisms in the brain (Patel and Peretz, 1997)

The visual processing of written language is only one of the factors essential to reading acquisition (Goswami, 1990). The ease with which children attain reading skills has been linked with phonemic awareness, and music perception skill is reliably related to phonological awareness and early reading development (Anvari, Trainor, Woodside, and Levy, 2002). Children who are able to hear individual sound categories within words have an easier time associating these phonemes with the written representation of these sounds (Bruck and Treiman, 1990). The vestibular system, which provides a sense of balance and an awareness of the body in space, directs basic motor behaviors and listening behaviors as well (Madaule, 1994). Music is one key to the development of the vestibular system and helps to prepare the brain to process split-second changes in sounds and tones used in speech, which is necessary for learning to read. Children who are poor readers tend to be insensitive to rhyme and alliteration (Bradley and Bryant, 1983).

Developing a sense of rhythm is considered to be an important factor in learning and performing motor tasks (Zachopoulou, Tsapakidou, and Derri, 2004). Whereas Metz (1989) found no significant differences related to the use of music on the synchronization of body movement in children of two to fours years of age, Schleuter and Schleuter (1985) found that movement with a rhythmic stimulus improved as children developed the ability to synchronize their body parts: walking rhythmically was a more difficult task for preschool children than for primary-age children.

EARLY CHILDHOOD TEACHER EDUCATION

The field of early education remains characterized by teachers with minimal training. This disconnect between the average preparation of preschool teachers and the growing expectations of the profession, parents, and policymakers not only continues in today's society, but has reached a dramatic climax (National Scientific Council on the Developing Child, 2005). Research studies show that professional development is positively related to family home care (Kontos, Machida, Griffin, and Read, 1992) and to improved programs in childcare settings (Kontos, Howes, and Galinsky, 1996). Research on teaching effectiveness demonstrates that teachers deal with the complexity of their environments by relying on their own beliefs, experience, and priorities (Ball and Cohen, 1996). Thus, teachers can be reluctant to adapt new, research-based ideas unless they fit within their schema of beliefs (Kennedy, 1997).

One of the strategies resulting in positive improvement and change in teacher behaviors is modeling. Jacobs (2001) describes modeling as a means of scaffolding in early childhood teacher preparation programs. While little research has been done on teacher training regarding the delivery of music content, Burton (2005) suggests that music educators should focus on developing positive attitudes in preschool teachers and in creating a higher comfort level for leading music activities through actual experiences in the classroom.

HOME ENVIRONMENT AND MUSIC

The quality of the home environment is tied to the degree of poverty in that home (Garrett, Ng´andu, and Ferron, 1994). These researchers noted that, as the income-to-needs ratio increased, the quality of the home environment increased. In addition, early development is dependent on supportive materials, uninterrupted time, and adult support for exploratory play (Bruner, 1974).

Parent attitudes toward the school play a role in early childhood education. Surveys collected from twenty-two preschools in the Midwest indicated that the attitudes of parents/caregivers were positive toward music education (Mallett, 2000). Yet deVries (2009) found that Australian parents with children under five had little time for music, believed that music should be provided by preschools, and relied on CDs and DVDs in the home.

Galliford (2003) investigated the relationship between the amount of young children's music exposure and their socioeconomic characteristics. A sample of 307 children, three to five years of age, drawn from six different SES categories ranging from $20,000 to over a million dollars, were measured on linguistic and nonlinguistic skills (Woodcock and Johnson, 1992). Findings indicated that the linguistic and nonlinguistic skills were related significantly to the amount of time children were exposed to musical experiences, rather than to the SES category.

Summary

There is evidence indicating that music and language development are similar in the way the brain processes auditory stimulation (Saffran et al., 1999). Music experience has been shown as an effective means to increase ratings of disadvantaged preschooler children for overall developmental domains, as well as select movement abilities (Jordan-DeCarbo and Galliford, 2001). While depressed socioeconomic factors can be detrimental to children's development, there is evidence that music is powerful enough to override some of the debilitating effects. Based on the studies reviewed, both preschool teachers and parents value music but need more information on how to support children's musical development.

PURPOSE AND RESEARCH QUESTIONS OF THE STUDY

The purpose of this study was to investigate the effect of an age-appropriate music curriculum on preschool children's music and movement task performance and linguistic and nonlinguistic skills, engaging both preschool teachers and parents in the process. The researchers investigated the following questions:

1. Will preschool children, ages three to five, receiving twenty weeks of an age-appropriate music intervention significantly improve their
   (a) music and movement skills ($p = .05$) from pretest to posttest, as measured by the Music and Movement Test (MMT) (Jordan-DeCarbo, 2001) compared to the same age children in a control group? and
   (b) linguistic and nonlinguistic skills ($p = .05$) as measured by the *Woodcock and Johnson Tests of Cognitive Ability–Revised* (1992) compared to the same age children in a control group?
2. Will classroom preschool teachers in the music treatment group achieve a 90 percent rate of implementation of weekly curricular activities by the last unit of the music study?

3. Will parents return music homework during the four units of the music treatment at a level high enough to receive small rhythm instruments for the home as a reward?

PARTICIPANTS

Participants were children enrolled at two low-income childcare centers in south Miami-Dade County run by Catholic Charities of the Archdiocese of Miami. One school served as the experimental group (music treatment) and the other functioned as the control group (no music treatment). The total consenting population was 464 children aged three to five years with 217 children in the treatment group and 247 of the same ages in the control group. A total of 92 three-, four-, and five-year-olds from both schools were selected randomly to be tested. The treatment group (N = 43) had 18 three-year-olds (nine males and nine females), 16 four-year-olds (eight males and eight females), and 9 five-year-olds (four males and five females); the control group (N = 49) had 20 three-year-olds (eleven males and nine females), 21 four-year-olds (eleven males and ten females), and 8 five-year-olds (five males and three females).

CURRICULUM

The researcher-designed curriculum was based on a two-year pilot project in which one of the researchers worked with preschool children and classroom teachers. Through student observation and post hoc discussions with teachers, it was determined that the music curriculum, which also met standards set forth by the music profession (MENC, 1995) should include singing, fine and gross movement tasks, focused listening, and dramatic play. The curriculum reflected the following characteristics: (a) musical content had to be simple and fun; (b) a typical preschool schedule was followed to promote integration throughout the day; and (c) best practices for implementing the music curriculum were drawn from Developmentally Appropriate Practice (DAP) as defined by the National Association for the Education of Young Children (NAEYC) (Copple and Bredekamp, 2009).

The structure of the activities fell into the following categories: welcome, circle time, literacy, transitional, free movement/structured dance, early math, and song of the week. The connection with literacy primarily focused on rhythmic poems and ten rhymes (Copple and Bredekamp, 2009). These activities and content reinforced rhythmic speech, comprehension, and dramatization of the stories, and were enhanced by the accompaniment of rhythm instruments and other manipulatives.

To guide the practice of training, the lead preschool teachers and their paraprofessionals learned to use DAP techniques and strategies in a musical context; modeling was used as the primary instructional method (Jacobs, 2001). Professionally recorded CDs were produced to support all of the musical activities that the teachers would use on a daily basis. The twenty-week curriculum was organized into four five-week units.

Every classroom in the treatment group was given twenty-five pairs of rhythm sticks, jingles, egg shakers, scarves, and hoops for movement activities. Additional materials included two sets of tone bells (D and A) to be played with mallets and a large drum that could be played by four to five children at a time.

METHOD

Procedures

Each classroom had a thirty-minute block for music class one day a week. The music specialist modeled all the activities for that week with participating children, teachers, and assistants. Each lead teacher was expected to implement the activities on the other four days of that week for units 1 and 2 (eight weeks). During unit 3, the music specialist and the teacher worked as a team with the specialist leading new material and the teacher reinforcing the activities. Starting with unit 4, teachers had to read the step-by-step manual to determine how to conduct the music activities for the remaining five weeks of lessons. Teachers were observed by the music specialist and were provided with feedback.

The teachers were given checklists of all the music activities for each day of the week. Implementation of the music activities for each week was determined by obtaining a percentage of activities that were actually practiced, compared to the maximum number of activities that could be done in a five-day period of time doing each activity once a day. The expectation set for unit 1 lessons was an implementation rate of 25 percent; unit 2, 50 percent; unit 3, 75 percent; and unit 4, 90 percent. This was to encourage the teachers to practice the activities as the year progressed and as they developed more confidence through the weekly modeling. If the teachers met the established implementation rate, they were rewarded with children's books for their classrooms. The overall goal was to stimulate repetition of the various activities at a level high enough to effect growth in listening and movement skills among the children.

The homework assignments were simple activities drawn from the previous week's lessons. Sample activities were for parents to play a song and do the motions with the child, read a poem and add movements, or color a listening map sent home with the child. Directions were constructed in simple, sequenced steps in both English and Spanish.

Criterion Measures

Musical Movement Test

The Musical Movement Test (MMT) (Jordan-DeCarbo, 2001) consists of a series of seven movement tasks that produce scores on beat competency, motor flow, motor coordination, and expressive responses. A physical therapist and an occupational therapist verified descriptor criteria for all components of the overall measure. Both were familiar with characteristics of children with developmental delays. Two tasks were used to measure the beat competence ability of the participant—tapping the beat bilaterally on the lap to a rhyme and keeping the beat with rhythm sticks to an instrumental excerpt. Three tasks concerning motor flow ability were used: walking to a rhyme, walking to a musical excerpt, and starting and stopping to a drumbeat played by the researcher. A jumping task indicated the child's ability to coordinate the upper and lower parts of the body, as well as the ability to synchronize jumping with a musical excerpt. The final task required each child to demonstrate the ability to move a pair of scarves expressively to music that begins in a slow *legato* style and changes to a more energetic *staccato* style.

Researchers tested each child individually, and all movement responses were videotaped. Each of the seven tasks had four descriptors that were sequenced from easy to complex, numbered 1–4, as determined by the physical and occupational therapists who constructed the tool. An example of the four descriptors for the task, *Taps beat to a rhyme*, is shown below:

1. Both hands/arms move freely without tension or rigidity;
2. Adequate space is used to perform the movement task;
3. Both hands/arms move in synchrony with each other; and
4. Both hands/arms move in synchrony with the beat of the spoken rhyme and this is constant throughout.

If the child met the criteria of the descriptor, she was given the value of that descriptor number. If the child met all four descriptors, she received a total of ten points (1+2+3+4). In every case, the easiest task was the first in the sequence and the most difficult task was the last. For analysis, the seven tasks were broken into four major construct categories—beat competence (twenty points), motor flow (thirty points), coordination (ten points), and expressive movement (ten points).

Judges were asked to give an overall musicality score based on the child's awareness of the music throughout the performance of all seven motor tasks. Scoring was determined if the child demonstrated (a) little evidence, (b) some evidence, or (c) exemplary evidence of musical awareness through the movement test. Two graduate musicians with elementary teaching experience were trained as judges.

Woodcock-Johnson Tests of Cognitive Ability–Revised

The researchers were interested in the impact of auditory music stimulation on right- and left-brain functioning. Therefore, eight subtests of the *Woodcock-Johnson Tests of Cognitive Ability–Revised* (WJ-R) (1992) were used to evaluate relative development of linguistic and nonlinguistic skills before and after the music intervention. WJ-R was selected because of its excellent test-retest reliability and because the focus of the study was to use a normative test measure for evaluating relative development of linguistic and nonlinguistic skills. Subtests were chosen based on auditory development and the similar discrimination skills used in both language and music patterning.

Five linguistic subtests were chosen based on consultation with a neuropsychologist at the University of Miami: (a) Visual-Auditory Learning (a visual-auditory association task between new visual symbols and familiar words) and Delayed Recall-Visual-Auditory Learning (able to recall symbols presented in the previous subtest after a delay of thirty-five to forty-five minutes) to measure long-term retrieval; (b) Incomplete Words (identifying aurally a word with one or more phonemes missing) and Sound Blending (ability to integrate and recognize a whole word after hearing just syllables and/or phonemes of the word) to measure auditory processing; and (c) Listening Comprehension (hearing a short, recorded passage, and supplying the missing word at the end of the passage), to measure language comprehension.

The nonlinguistic subtests selected for this study were as follows: (a) Visual Closure (to visually identify a drawing altered in one of several ways), to measure visual processing; (b) Sound Patterns (to aurally identify if pairs of complex sound patterns were the same or different), to measure aural discrimination; and (c) Spatial Relations (to visually match complex shapes), to measure visual processing and applied problem solving.

Subtests were scored using the standardized criteria outlined in the WJ-R scoring manual. The nature of the test is that, as long as the child provides correct answers, the test continues with items in that subtest. Given that the time involved in testing each individual could range from fifteen to seventy-five minutes, 20 percent of the total population of participants in each school were randomly selected for the administration of both WJ-R and MMT.

RESULTS

To establish interjudge reliability, correlations between the two judges on the scores of the five categories of beat competence, motor flow, motor coordination, expression, and overall musicality for both the pretest and posttest are shown below (see table 13.1).

Means and standard deviations for the music and movement pretests and posttests are presented in table 13.2 for the 20 percent sample of the treatment and control groups.

To determine differences between the two groups, a mixed ANOVA was conducted with the within-subject factor of time (pretest vs. posttest) and the fixed between-subject factor of treatment. Results indicated that the treatment group scored significantly higher than the control group, $F(1, 90) = 5.550$, $p = .021$ on beat competence. Results of the motor flow, coordination, and expressive tasks, as well as the overall musicality scores yielded a nonsignificant interaction of site; thus, pretests/posttests are not reported (see table 13.3).

The eight subtests of the WJ-R were analyzed separately since the skills measured for each test were different. To determine differences between the two groups between pretest and posttest scores of the five linguistic and the three nonlinguistic measures, descriptive statistics for the treatment and control groups are presented, as well as the difference between pretest and posttest scores. See table 13.4 for the linguistic scores and table 13.5 for the nonlinguistic scores.

For all eight analyses, a mixed ANOVA with the within-subject factor of time (pretest vs. posttest) and the fixed between-subject factor of treatment was used to test if gains from pretest to posttest differed for the two groups. The treatment group displayed a significantly larger gain than the control

Table 13.1.   Correlations of Judges' Pre- and Posttest Scores

Measures	Correlations (Pretest)	Correlations (Posttest)
Beat Competence	.811	.836
Motor Flow	.766	.712
Motor Coordination	.752	.660
Expression	.800	.560
Overall Musicality	.761	.648

Table 13.2. Means and Standard Deviations for the Seven Movement Tasks for the 20 Percent Sample of Three-, Four-, and Five-Year-Old Children in the Treatment (T) and Control (C) Groups

	n	Mean	SD	Time	Mean	SD
Beat Competence						
Pretest T	43	11.07	5.69	Post T	14.58	4.48
Pretest C	49	12.37	5.55	Post C	13.05	5.37
Total	92	11.76	5.63	Total	13.66	5.02
Motor Flow						
Pretest T	43	12.75	6.87	Post T	15.55	4.95
Pretest C	49	11.83	6.72	Post C	13.64	6.84
Total	92	12.26	6.77	Total	14.53	6.25
Motor Coordination						
Pretest T	43	4.41	2.53	Post T	5.10	2.94
Pretest C	49	3.75	2.27	Post C	4.47	2.82
Total	92	4.06	2.41	Total	4.77	2.88
Expression						
Pretest T	43	4.38	3.04	Post T	5.69	2.89
Pretest C	49	4.41	2.89	Post C	5.40	2.86
Total	92	4.40	2.94	Total	5.54	2.86
Overall Musicality						
Pretest T	43	1.89	.58	Post T	2.13	.58
Pretest C	49	1.98	.65	Post C	2.01	.90
Total	92	1.94	.62	Total	2.07	.65

group on Visual/Auditory Learning ($p = .043$), Incomplete Words ($p = .002$), and Sound Patterns ($p = .000$). There were no significant differences in gains between the two groups for Sound Blending ($p = .148$). The treatment group displayed significantly larger gains than the control group on Listening Comprehension ($p = .004$), and Spatial Relations ($p = .000$). There was no significant difference in gains between the groups on Visual Closure ($p = .235$).

The results related to nonmusic teacher implementation of the music curriculum during the music intervention period showed that 75 percent of the teachers/paraprofessionals met the unit 1 rate of 25 percent implementation,

Table 13.3. The Effect of the Music Treatment on Pretest-to-Posttest Gains for Beat Competence Skills of a Random 20 Percent Sample of Three- to Five-Year-Old Children in the Treatment Group

Source	df	MS	F	P
Beat Competence				
Pretest/Posttest	1	182.41	9.61*	.003
Pretest/Posttest x Site	1	105.27	5.55	.021
Error	90	(18.96)		

Note: *$p < .05$.

Table 13.4. Means and Standard Deviations for Pretest and Posttest Linguistic Scores for Three- to Five-Year-Old Children in the Music Treatment Group (T) Compared to the Nonmusic Treatment Group (C)

WJ-R/Linguistic	Groups	n	Mean			SD		
			Pretest	Posttest	d	Pretest	Posttest	d
Visual/Auditory	T	43	456.09	468.91	12.81	17.33	7.02	14.45
	C	49	457.02	464.49	7.46	14.21	12.34	10.35
Total		92	456.59	466.55	9.96	15.66	10.39	12.65
Incomplete Wds	T	43	444.33	463.51	19.18	17.33	14.29	11.38
	C	49	443.27	454.05	10.77	15.62	14.21	13.81
Total		92	443.76	458.47	14.70	16.36	14.94	13.35
Sound Blending	T	43	440.23	457.56	17.32	15.65	7.37	13.17
	C	49	436.71	449.67	12.95	16.73	13.23	15.23
Total		92	438.36	453.36	15.00	16.24	11.53	14.40
Listening Comp.	T	43	422.12	438.35	16.20	18.11	16.57	13.63
	C	49	427.06	434.90	7.83	18.32	19.79	13.56
Total		92	424.76	436.51	11.75	18.29	18.44	14.16
Delayed-Vis.Aud.	T	43	467.70	483.67	15.97	16.05	8.75	11.65
	C	49	467.12	476.57	9.44	15.27	12.37	11.61
Total		92	467.39	479.89	12.50	15.55	11.35	12.02

Table 13.5. Means and Standard Deviations for Pretest and Posttest Nonlinguistic Scores for Three- to Five-Year-Old Children in the Music Treatment Group (T) Compared to the Nonmusic Treatment Group (C)

Nonlinguistic	Groups	n	Mean			SD		
			Pretest	Posttest	d	Pretest	Posttest	d
Visual	T	43	458.00	468.51	10.51	12.64	9.54	7.15
Closure	C	49	456.51	464.55	8.04	16.40	10.41	11.76
Total		92	457.21	466.40	91.9	14.70	10.15	9.91
Sound	T	43	449.14	473.33	24.18	15.65	24.12	17.30
Patterns	C	49	448.04	456.39	8.34	18.06	19.55	12.46
Total		92	448.55	464.30	15.75	16.89	23.29	16.83
Spatial	T	43	449.63	476.40	26.76	24.81	13.25	17.47
Relations	C	49	451.92	462.18	10.26	24.30	19.87	18.10
Total		92	450.85	468.83	17.97	24.43	18.43	19.55

80 percent met the unit 2 rate of 50 percent implementation, 87 percent met the unit 3 rate, and 100 percent met the unit 4 overall outcome rate of 90 percent, with several of the teachers implementing all music activities at a rate of 100 percent. The composite rate for all teachers during unit 4 was 92 percent.

Out of 217 families, 193 parents returned homework assignments at a level high enough to receive a rhythm instrument as a reward. Parent compliance with the weekly homework had a slow beginning. Only 15 percent of parents received instruments following the first unit of lessons. Following unit 1, children pressured parents to comply and rates increased steadily over the three remaining units to surpass the overall outcome rate of 85 percent and achieve a final rate of 89 percent participation.

DISCUSSION

Results indicated that children in the experimental group, compared to the control group, showed significant gains for the motor construct, beat competency. These results are consistent with previous findings (Weikart, 1987); there were no significant interactions with regard to age level, which is consistent with Metz (1989).

Motor flow—walking to a rhyme (basic beat pattern) and changing to a running motor task (subdivision beat pattern) to external musical excerpt—was difficult for these children, similar to findings by Schleuter and Schleuter (1985). While raw treatment scores were higher than the control group, increases were not significant.

The jumping task may have been too difficult for this age level. Clark and Phillips (1985) believe that the basic coordination for jumping develops slowly and generally does not stabilize until around the age of seven.

The interjudge reliabilities for the music and movement tasks were acceptable but posttest comparisons were lower than pretests, with the exception of beat competency. Posttest comparisons were especially low for the expressive task. Given the high number of judgments for seven movement tasks, each with four levels of difficulty, plus three levels for an overall musicality score for ninety-two participants, discrepancies due to fatigue or lack of focus or concentration could easily have been a factor in the judges' ratings.

Gains on Sound Patterns and Spatial Relations demonstrated a large effect size; Visual-Auditory, Delayed Visual-Auditory, Listening Comprehension, and Incomplete Words showed moderate effect sizes (Keppel and Wickens, 2004). Researchers had anticipated significant findings for those tasks related to nonlinguistic ability, since these are nonverbal skills and more closely related to music. Significant gains for sound patterns (Jordan-DeCarbo, 1990) and spatial relations (Rauscher et al., 1997) have been previously documented for children in school settings.

The Visual Closure subtest, however, yielded nonsignificant results, which is consistent with the findings of Galliford (2003). In addition, Jordan-DeCarbo (1982) found that using a visual discrimination model did not transfer to an aural discrimination model, indicating that visual processing may not be affected by musical exposure.

Researchers did not anticipate the level of growth found for children's nonlinguistic functioning. Of the five subtests, four—Visual/Auditory, Incomplete words, Listening Comprehension and Recall Delayed Visual-Auditory—produced significant pretest/posttest results for the music treatment group as compared to the control group. All four of these tests depended primarily on auditory skills, even if some visual stimulation was involved. These results support the theory that the basic learning processes may be similar for music and language (Saffran et al., 1999) and that daily exposure to auditory sounds may enhance learning in both areas (Lamb and Gregory, 1993).

Sound Blending—the task of recognizing whole words from disassociated parts—did not produce significant gains, which could have been due to the fact that the majority of the sample was Hispanic in ethnicity. Not having a familiar vocabulary of English words may have inhibited children from making sense of the sound fragments.

As shown by the gain in implementing instructional materials, the training procedures for the lead teachers and the paraprofessionals worked well. Distribution of instrument rewards for parents returning homework pages led to a remarkable change in parent participation in the study. Anecdotal results of the teacher meetings following each unit reinforced the successful components of developing a triangular framework of students, teachers, and parents, the incremental expectations for compliance, and patience with the growing confidence of the teachers.

CONCLUSION

This study documents that an age-appropriate curriculum, delivered by nonmusic preschool teachers, significantly increased linguistic and nonlinguistic skills on six out of eight subtests for a 20 percent mixed sample of children selected from a total of 464 children receiving daily music experiences. This long-term study demonstrates the effectiveness of music in contributing to the growth of children's cognitive ability with language as related to auditory recognition and in motor development associated with beat competence.

REFERENCES

Anvari, S. H., Trainor, L. J., Woodside, J., and Levy, B. A. (2002). Relations among musical skills, phonological processing, and early reading ability in preschool children. *Journal of Experimental Child Psychology, 83,* 111–30.

Ball, D. L., and Cohen, D. K. (1996). Reform by the book: What is—or might be—the role of curriculum materials in teacher learning and instructional reform? *Educational Researcher, 25,* 6–8.

Baruch, C., and Drake, C. (1997). Tempo discrimination in infants. *Infant Behavior and Development, 20,* 573–77.

Bradley, P., and Bryant, L. (1983). Categorizing sounds and learning to read: A causal connection. *Nature, 301,* 419–21.

Bruck, M., and Treiman, R. (1990). Phonological awareness and spelling in normal children and dyslexics: The case of initial consonant clusters. *Journal of Educational Child Psychology, 50,* 156–78.

Bruner, J. S. (1974). The organization of early skilled action. In M. P. M. Richards (Ed.), *The integration of a child into a social world.* New York: Cambridge University Press.

Burton, S. L. (2005, Winter). Children's musical worlds: Considering the preparation of early childhood educators. *Early Childhood Connections, 11*(1), 23–28.

Clark, J. E., and Phillips, S. J. (1985). A developmental sequence of the standing long jump. In J. E. Clark and J. H. Humphrey (Eds.), *Motor development: Current selected research* (Vol. 1, pp. 73–85). Princeton, NJ: Princeton Book Company.

Copple, C., and Bredekamp, S. (Eds.). (2009). *Developmentally appropriate practice in early childhood programs* (Rev. ed.). Washington, DC: National Association for the Education of Young Children.

deVries, P. (2009). Music at home with the under fives: What is happening? *Early Child Development and Care, 179*(4), 395–405.

Galliford, J. (2003). *The effects of music experience during early childhood on the development of linguistic and non-linguistic skills.* Doctoral dissertation, University of Miami, Miami FL.

Garrett, P., Ng´andu, N., and Ferron, J. (1994). Poverty experience of young children and the quality of their home environments. *Child Development, 65*(2), 331–35.

Goswami, U. (1990). A special link between rhyming skill and the use of orthographic analogies by beginning readers. *Journal of Child Psychology, 31,* 301–11.

Jacobs, G. M. (2001). Providing the scaffold: A model for early childhood/primary teacher preparation. *Early Childhood Education Journal, 29*(2), 125–30.

Jordan-DeCarbo, J. (1982). The effect of same/different discrimination techniques, readiness training, pattern treatment, and sex on aural discrimination ability and singing ability of tonal patterns with kindergartners. *Journal of Research in Music Education, 30,* 237–46.

Jordan-DeCarbo, J. (1990). The effect of aural discrimination training and vocal training on the vocal performance ability and aural discrimination ability of four- and five-year-old children. *Psychomusicology, 9,* 111–12.

Jordan-DeCarbo, J. (2001). *Music and movement test.* (Unpublished).

Jordan-DeCarbo, J., and Galliford, J. (2001). The effects of a sequential music program on the motor, cognitive, expressive language, social/emotional, and musical movement abilities of preschool disadvantaged children. *Early Childhood Connections, 7*(3), 30–42.

Kennedy, M. (1997). The connection between research and practice. *Educational Researcher, 26*(7), 4–12.

Keppel, J., and Wickens, T. D. (2004). *Design and analysis: A researcher's handbook* (4th ed.). Upper Saddle River, NJ: Prentice Hall.

Kontos, S., Howes, C., and Galinsky, E. (1996). Does training make a difference to quality in family childcare? *Early Childhood Research Quarterly, 11*, 427–445.

Kontos, S., Machida, S., Griffin, S., and Read, M. (1992). Training and professionalism in family day care. In D. L. Peters and A. R. Pence (Eds.), *Family day care: Current research for informed public policy* (pp. 188–208). New York: Teachers College Press.

Lamb, S. J., and Gregory, A. H. (1993). The relationship between music and reading in beginning readers. *Educational Psychology, 13*, 13–27.

Lerdahl, F., and Jackendoff, R. (1983). *A generative theory of tonal music.* Cambridge, MA: MIT Press.

Madaule, P. (1994). *When listening comes alive.* Norval, Ontario: Moulin.

Mallett, C. A. (2000). *An examination of parent/caregiver attitudes toward music instruction, the nature of the home musical environment, and their relationship to the developmental music aptitude of preschool children.* Doctoral dissertation, University of Nebraska, Lincoln.

MENC: The National Association for Music Education. (1995). *Prekindergarten music education standards* [brochure]. Reston, VA: Author.

Metz, E. (1989). Movement as a musical response among preschool children. *Journal of Research in Music Education, 37*, 48–60.

National Scientific Council on the Developing Child. (2005). *Helping young children succeed: Strategies to promote early childhood social and emotional development.* Retrieved from www.ncsl.org/programs/cyf/childhood report0905.htm.

Patel, A. D., and Peretz, I. (1997). Is music autonomous from language? A neuropsychological appraisal. In I. Deliege and J. Sloboda (Eds.), *Perception and cognition of music* (pp. 191–215). Hove, UK: Psychology Press/Erlbaum.

Rauscher, F. H., Shaw, G. L., Levine, L. J., Wright, E. L., Dennis, W. R., and Newcomb, R. L. (1997). Music training causes long-term enhancement of preschool children's spatial-temporal reasoning. *Neurological Research, 10*, 2–8.

Schleuter, S. L, and Schleuter, L. J. (1985). The relationship of grade level and sex differences to certain rhythmic responses of primary grade children. *Journal of Research in Music Education, 33*(1), 23–29.

Saffran, J. R., Johnson, E. K., Aslin, R. N., and Newport, E. L. (1999). Statistical learning of tone sequences by human infants and adults. *Cognition, 70*, 27–52.

Weikart, P. S. (1987). *Round the circle.* Ypsilanti, MI: High/Scope Educational Research Foundation.

Woodcock, R. W., and Johnson, M. B. (1992). *Woodcock-Johnson tests of cognitive ability* (Rev. ed.). Rolling Meadows, IL: Riverside.

Zachopoulou, E., Tsapakidou, A., and Derri, V. (2004). The effects of a developmentally appropriate music and movement program on motor performance. *Early Childhood Research Quarterly, 19*, 631–42.

Chapter Fourteen

The Impact of a Music and Movement Program on School Readiness

Lili M. Levinowitz

The purpose of the study was to understand how music instruction supports the attributes that young children need for school success. Specifically, the problems of the study were to evaluate the effects of a comprehensive early childhood music program on development of school readiness and literacy skills in urban preschool children. The subjects of this study were preschool children from a northeast urban school district representing a substantially disadvantaged population in terms of academic development. Over three years, an early childhood music and movement curriculum model was phased into twenty public elementary preschool classrooms. The authors concluded that both the content and the process of the music and movement program do positively affect the attributes that young children need for school success.

At the inception of music education into public education, music education was considered an important support for other nonmusical values. In a petition to the Boston School Committee in 1837, Lowell Mason and the Boston Academy of Music suggested that the introduction of vocal music be tried against the gold standard of education at that time: Is it intellectual—is it moral—is it physical? (Boston School Committee, 1837).

Music educators, of course, recognize that music is a way of knowing (Gardner, 1983; Levinowitz, 1998) and therefore prefer to focus on music performance and music literacy instruction in their subject-specific classrooms. Nevertheless, perhaps based on recent federal mandates, content specialists—music teachers included—are being invited to supplement reading and other literacy-based instruction in their classrooms. Fortunately, music educators exhibit favorable attitudes toward the teaching of these other skills, particularly language and reading skills, in their subject specific music classrooms (Gerber and Gerrity, 2007).

Since the turn of the twenty-first century, there has been an explosion of research that sheds light on the functional origin and biological values of music (Mithen, 2006; Peretz and Zatorre, 2004). This research confirms that music education is intrinsically valuable (Elliott, 1995) but also supports other types of learning. It seems reasonable to suggest that Hetland's (2000) suggestion that "cognitive processes normally associated with music share neural networks with other kinds of mental activity" is now being confirmed (p. 238).

Most recently, the Dana Arts and Cognition consortium (Gazzaniga, 2008) gathered the work of cognitive neuroscientists and reported the following: (a) interest in a performing art leads to a high state of motivation that produces the sustained attention necessary to improve performance that leads to improvement in other domains of cognition (Posner, Rothbart, Sheese, and Kieras, 2008); (b) specific links exist between high levels of music training and the ability to manipulate information in both working and long-term memory (Jonides, 2008); (c) in children, there appear to be specific links between the practice of music and skills in geometrical representation (Spelke, 2008); and (d) correlations exist between music training and both reading acquisition and sequence learning (Wandell, Dougherty, Ben-Schachar, Deutsch, and Tsang, 2008). Much of this more recent research has confirmed previous research that suggests that music may enhance spatial-temporal reasoning, which has a positive impact on reading development (Bilhartz, Bruhn, and Olson, 2000; Rauscher, Shaw, and Ky, 1993; Rauscher et al., 1997).

Standley (2008) reported, in a meta-analysis of thirty studies using a variety of music interventions to affect reading skills, that music activities do have a moderately strong, significant, overall effect size when the activities incorporate specific reading skills matched to the needs of children. Furthermore, it was found that, when contingent music is used to reinforce reading behavior, benefits are great.

Similarly, in meta-analyses of six experimental studies using standardized measures of reading performance following music instruction, Butzlaff (2000) found a "strong and reliable association between music instruction and standardized measures of reading ability" (p. 170). More recently, Register, Darrow, Standley, and Swedberg (2007) reported in a study of the use of music to enhance reading skills that second-grade students with reading disabilities improved significantly on word decoding, word knowledge, and reading comprehension when an intensive short-term music curriculum was designed to target reading comprehension and vocabulary skills. Finally, researchers examining the effects of music training on brain and cognitive development undertaken with underprivileged three- to five-year-old children inferred that music instruction supports gains in language of those underprivileged children (Neville et al., 2008).

Learning to read and write are ongoing processes that begin in infancy (Strickland and Riley-Ayers, 2007). Successful readers are usually those children who, during early childhood, had developmental and reading readiness and experienced rich oral language, phonological awareness, print awareness, and alphabet knowledge that constitutes emergent literacy experience (Goldman, Aldridge, and Russell, 2007). In the book, *Language and Literacy Supports for Struggling Readers: Meeting the Goals of No Child Left Behind*, Goldman and colleagues (2007) note the importance of music to support these struggling readers.

There is currently evidence that suggests that music has influence on children's acquisition and mastery of the aforementioned literacy skills. Standley and Hughes (1997) investigated the effects of an early intervention music curriculum on the prereading and prewriting of four-year-old children in an early intervention classroom. They found that music enhanced print concepts and prewriting skills of the children in the study. In several follow-up studies by Register and colleagues (2007) those findings were substantiated.

Accordingly, in a study undertaken in an urban school system to evaluate the impact of utilizing the music and movement model in the present study, Cohen and Frank (2009) found that four-year-old children who participated in the *Music Together*[1] program made significantly greater gains in problem solving, language development, and physical development than those children in the control group.

Scripp (2002) asserts that, despite solid research findings, "the comprehensive, sequential study of music has yet to be accepted as a core ingredient of public education. . . . Significant, positive correlations between high quality musical training and math/language achievement reported in the research constitute evidence sufficient to support the integration of music into the core curriculum of public education" (p. 133). Considering the aforementioned grounding research, the purpose of the present study was to understand how music instruction supports the attributes that young children need for school success. Does the inclusion of music activities within early childhood curricula actually lower student test scores because less time is spent on subjects that address specific test content?

Specifically, the problems of the present study were to evaluate the effects of a comprehensive early childhood music program on (a) development of school readiness and (b) long-term literacy skills in urban preschool children.

METHOD

This three-year study was designed and implemented through collaboration among (a) an urban school district, (b) an urban nonprofit community music school, and (c) an international, research-based early childhood music and movement program. The project was funded through the U.S. Department of Education: Arts in Education Innovation Grant (U.S. Department of Education, OMB No. 1890-0004). The external evaluator for the study was a non-profit firm with a mission to improve public education and social services through documentation, evaluation, research, and technical assistance.

Subjects

The subjects for this study were preschool children representing a substantially disadvantaged population in terms of academic development. Compared to national norms, the children in this urban school district enter kindergarten one year behind in academic skills and over one and one-half years behind in communication skills. In addition, "22% of their parents never finished high school and 51% have had no education beyond the high school level" (Trenton Board of Education, 1999).

The participating urban school district had approximately 13,230 students enrolled at the time of the study, with two-thirds eligible for free or reduced lunch. The students are 68 percent African American, 26 percent Hispanic, and 6 percent other. On the language arts subtest of the district-administered *Terra Nova* test in spring 2003, 59 percent of first-grade students and 57 percent of second-grade students scored at or above grade level. On a spring 2003 state-level eighth-grade proficiency test, only 30 percent of students passed in Language Arts.

Procedures

Over three years, an early childhood music and movement curriculum model was phased into twenty public elementary preschool classrooms. Eleven of the district's eighteen elementary schools housed the twenty preschool (four-year-old) classrooms during the last year of the project. The participating elementary schools are clustered into feeder groups for four middle schools. The selection of classes in these schools was based on this cluster pattern. The student populations in these schools were similar in both socioeconomic and cultural characteristics through the grade levels. Because all twenty preschool classes were in the study by the end of the three project years, randomization in selection was not an issue.

The conceptual framework for this project was based on the participating school districts' State Department of Education's mandate that *Early Childhood Program Expectations: Standards of Quality* be implemented in all preschools. Although presented in eight discrete learning domains, including creative arts, the instructional program is delivered as an integrated process. The *Creative Arts Expectations* require that preschool children "express themselves and develop appreciation for music" (expectation 1) and "develop an appreciation for dance and movement" (expectation 2). These *Early Childhood Program Expectations: Standards of Quality* reflect goals of federal initiatives such as *No Child Left Behind* (P.L.107-110).

The music and movement curriculum model used in this study is based on the concept that all children are musical. Its music and movement activities are designed to help children develop their innate music aptitude and achieve basic music competence: "the ability to sing in tune, keep a beat and participate with confidence and pleasure in the music of our culture" (Levinowitz and Guilmartin, 1989, p. 1). In addition to musical growth, the enriched musical environment encouraged language development. Rhyming, phonemic awareness, patterning, repetition, sequencing, and prediction—concepts contained in the varied song repertory—are building blocks of emergent literacy. Use of the songbook during the music sessions reinforced proper use of books and encouraged children to invent stories from the pictures that accompany the songs. The children also began to identify music notation and left/right visual tracking through musical activities. For non-English-speaking children, the English-language songs provided a gentle bridge to their new language.

The experimental music and movement curriculum that was introduced into the twenty classrooms included professionally trained early childhood music specialists who provided weekly thirty-minute music and movement classes for preschool children and their teachers. The specific activities incorporated during these classes were singing, moving, rhythmic and tonal matching and improvising, and instrument play. The music repertory was multicultural and exposed the children and teachers to a rich variety of musical styles, modes, and meters. Songbooks were used during the lessons to develop associations between music making and music notation. Attractive wood-block illustrations served as storytelling vehicles and other prereading activities.

Instruction was organized in fifteen-week semesters, or cycles, with a different song collection utilized in each cycle. All teachers and paraprofessionals were expected to participate during these sessions and serve as music-making models for the children. To engage classroom teachers and parents in the musical education of their children, professional teacher development and parent education were important components of the program. Special teacher editions of the CDs and songbooks were provided for each classroom for each new song collection. Also, each class was supplied with basic rhythm instruments that remained in the classrooms. To facilitate continued music making at home, each semester every family received the same CD and songbook used by their children in school.

As part of the preschool literacy initiative included in this study, teachers were encouraged to pair music activities with literacy development. To facilitate the academic impact of pairing reading and singing, the participating school district supplied each school in the project with ten pattern, rhyming, and nursery rhyme books that relate through their content or theme to the song literature. The music curriculum songbook was used during music sessions to model proper use of books and to encourage children to invent stories from pictures that accompany the songs. Teachers were asked to keep a log of successful activities for collection and future dissemination.

The experimental treatment also included a professional development component, such as introductory workshops and songs workshops for classroom professionals, specialist training for music teachers, and parent education and opportunities for involvement. These components are presented in detail below.

Introductory Workshops

Prior to the start of each group of classes, teachers and paraprofessionals attended an intensive, half-day introductory workshop titled "How Children Learn Music and What You Can Do to Help," presented by the Center for Music and Young Children.[2] The participants received continuing education credits and training stipends for all of these professional development workshops. Workshops included an introduction to the pedagogy and philosophy of the *Music Together* early childhood music and movement curriculum used in this study and practices for using music activities during the school day (such as for transitions and classroom management and as part of core curriculum). Participants learned the importance of providing a rich musical environment during this particularly fertile, music-learning time of children's lives and how to track students' musical development. Through teacher training, teachers and music specialists collaborated on developing extensions of the music activities into literacy teaching, such as sociodramatic-play and language development.

Songs Workshops

At the start of each new semester, all participating classroom teachers gathered with the early childhood music and movement specialists to learn new song cycle repertory during highly interactive, three-hour songs workshops. These events provided unusual opportunities for preschool teachers to interact with their counterparts from other schools in a fun, mutually supportive, educational, and inspiring environment.

Early Childhood Music Specialist Training

Elementary school music teachers assigned to participating preschool class-rooms had the option of receiving professional early childhood music specialist training. This was a three-day intensive training provided by the Center for Music and Young Children. Every effort was made to engage these important resource teachers in the project and to encourage them to reinforce the specialized music and movement curriculum model in their elementary schools.

Parent Involvement and Education

A basic tenet of the *Music Together* curriculum model used in this study is that participation and modeling by parents or other caregivers, regardless of their musical ability, are essential to a child's musical growth. Prior to the start of programs in each school, parents completed a home music engagement survey that provided baseline data on the type and amount of music making at home. Family editions of CDs and songbooks used in the classroom were sent home with each child for each new song cycle so that music making could continue at home. (Spanish translations were available for all parent materials.)

Each semester, two family music events were conducted at the school to provide opportunities for family music making, for parents to learn about their children's musical development, and to help parents develop new tools with which to actively engage in their children's education. Often these "family-music parties" attracted multiple generations, with grandparents and siblings as well as parents participating.

Evaluation

Evaluating student outcomes was done through use of a set of assessment scales that measure the attainment of literacy skills. The assessment scales identified to measure student outcomes included two already used by the district.

The participating school district's Office of Early Childhood Programs administered the *Brigance K and 1 Screen* (2006) in the spring to all five-year-old children as part of their regular screening process to assess readiness for kindergarten. The *Brigance K and 1 Screen* is used to assess a sampling of a child's learning, development, and skills in a broad range of areas including language, motor ability, number skills, body awareness, and visual discrimination. To administer the scale requires that a trained examiner ask students questions about body parts, as well as the use of objects, colors, numbers, and picture identification, and also that the examiner observe gross-motor, visual-motor, and other motor skills.

The district also administered the *Terra Nova* Achievement Test (CTB/McGraw Hill) to the students in the kindergarten through tenth grade as part of their regular spring screening process. The *Terra Nova* is a standardized achievement test designed to provide achievement scores that are valid for most types of educational decision-making; it was developed through numerous revisions with specific focus on relevance to actual curricular practice. Areas that are assessed are reading/language arts, mathematics, science, and social studies. *Terra Nova* has longstanding and thorough data on reliability and validity. Only the reading/language arts subtest was used because that subtest was relevant to the purpose of the study—long-term literacy. The mathematics, science, and social studies subtests were not relevant to the purpose of the study.

DESIGN AND ANALYSIS

The project commenced in ten preschool classrooms while the remaining thirteen classrooms served as the control. For the second project year, eighteen classrooms (ten from the first year and eight new classrooms) participated in the experimental music and movement treatment, and the remaining five preschool classrooms served as the control group. Finally, in year 3 all twenty preschool classrooms participated in the experimental music and movement treatment. This design allowed the implementation of the music and movement experimental treatment in all preschool classrooms—with accompanying training of these teachers—by the end of the three-year project. Furthermore, the environments in terms of music integration in nontreatment classrooms were held constant, as regular music teachers spend only one session per week with the students in preschool classrooms.

All preschool and kindergarten students' scores (identification numbers were used to protect their privacy) were kept on a district database that was made available to the external evaluators, although the school district did not make individual scores by students available to the external evaluators for confidentiality reasons. *Brigance K and 1 Screen* scores were analyzed in several ways. The scores from the preceding spring prior to the onset of the study were used as baseline data. Using the average score (90.3, N = 147) from the baseline data, gain scores were calculated for each of the first two years of the study for all classes in the comparison and treatment groups; those gain scores served as data for years 1 and 2 of the project. The data were organized into a two-by-two design (group x year), and a two-way analysis of variance (ANOVA) was calculated using these data. Because there were no comparison groups in year three of the project, a one-way design to compare means for the baseline group and the treatment group was used; a *t*-test for independent means using the raw scores was calculated.

Only the reading and language arts subtests of the *Terra Nova* achievement test were used as data for this study. The *Terra Nova* scores that were reported by the school district were average percentile ranks, by school. Because these data are not continuous or normally distributed, only parametric descriptive statistics are reported to compare treatment and control group difference for this performance measure.

RESULTS

Brigance K and 1 Screen Performance Measure

Means and standard deviations for years 1 (treatment: $M = 4.2124$, $SD = 12.4869$; control: $M = 2.0375$, $SD = 11.7552$) and 2 (treatment: $M = .3437$, $SD = 10.7962$, control: $M = .1246$, $SD = 11.7552$) of the project showed little observed mean difference and hence, the difference was not found to be statistically significant. As expected, based on the means presented above, the researchers failed to find a statistically significant interaction ($F (1, 479) = .1.201$) or main effect for group ($F (1, 479) = .802$). A main effect for year, however, was found to be statistically significant ($F (1, 479) = 9.461$).

As in years 1 and 2, the researchers failed to find statistically significant differences between the baseline group ($M = 90.3082$, $SD = 12.021$) and the third-year treatment groups ($M = 88.0647$, $SD = 13.567$). All children received the experimental treatment in the third year of the project.

Terra Nova Performance Measure

Mean percentile ranks for treatment versus comparison groups are presented in table 14.1. Student achievement in reading and language arts was assessed with the *Terra Nova* Standardized Achievement Test for first-grade students. Scores for all first-grade students by school in 2004–2005 were used as baseline data for students who were in preschool classes in 2003–2004, the first year of the project.

The average spring 2005 NCE score for all first-grade students in the fifteen schools that are part of this study was 54.7 in reading and 53.6 in language arts. It is also important to note that the average spring 2005 NCEs for schools that were in the treatment group in 2003–2004 were 55.4 in reading and 54.7 in language arts. The average NCE scores for comparison schools

Table 14.1. Summary Descriptive Statistics for Terra Nova Scores

	Reading	Language Arts
2004–2005		
Baseline	54.7	53.6
Treatment	55.4	54.7
Comparison	46.9	50.2
2005–2006*	56.3	54.9
2006–2007	56.2	54.4

*One-half were in treatment schools in 2003–2004

were 46.9 in reading and 50.2 in language arts. Treatment schools' scores were slightly higher. The average scores for first-grade students in 2005–2006, about half of whom had been in the MVY program in 2003–2004, were 56.3 in reading and 54.9 in language arts. In 2006–2007, the average scores for first-grade students in reading were 56.2, and in language arts the average scores were 54.4.

These parametric descriptive statistics indicate a positive change from the baseline average scores. While these increases were minimal, they represent an upward trend in first-grade reading and language arts test scores, an outcome that is not typically the case in these schools. However, with new emphasis on literacy in Trenton (as in districts around the country), it is not possible to attribute improvements in test scores directly to the MVY program.

DISCUSSION

Based on the data derived from this study, it cannot yet be concluded that the music and movement model used in this study enhanced the outcomes for either school readiness or for long-term literacy. Because the school district did not make individual scores by student available to the external evaluators of the study, it is quite possible that a Type II error was committed. That is, it seems reasonable to suggest that the researchers failed to find a statistically significant difference in the *Brigance K and 1* outcome (school readiness) because only groups could be followed based on the confidentiality requirements of the school district. Because there is considerable student transience among the district schools, the analysis could have been stronger if individual scores for each student were available. Perhaps a statistically significant difference between comparison and treatment group may have been found.

That there was a main effect for year between year 1 and 2 is interesting. During year 2 (but not year 1 and 3) of the study, the school district administered both the preschool *Brigance Screen* in the fall and the *Brigance K and 1 Screen* in the spring. Thus, some inferences regarding growth over this academic year can be made. The mean for the students constituting that fall screening was relatively low (78.9) compared to the average performance score for students in the district prior to the study (86.2). Because low scores at the onset of year 2 were found, it is speculated that improvement did occur. This can be ascertained by examining the gain scores on the *Brigance K and 1 Screen* in the spring of the second year of the study and comparing them to the average scores that were used as the baseline.

Furthermore, if individual student standard scores were made available by the school district rather than only percentile trends by school for the *Terra Nova*, an inferential statistic could have been calculated to better understand the contribution of the music and movement model on long-term literacy.

Noteworthy is the fact that the dependent variables, the *Brigance K and 1 Screen* test and the *Terra Nova* test, were used because they were administered by the school district as part of their regular screening process. Although these tests have psychometric reliability and validity, it could be that other tests that measure the outcomes incorporated in this study could be used and differing results may occur. Therefore, further research is needed using different measurement tools to determine whether the music and movement model utilized in this study enhances school readiness and long-term literacy.

CONCLUSION

Regardless of the aforementioned, it seems that both the content of the preschool music and movement model program, including weekly contact through music classes taught by an early childhood music specialist and the process for inclusion of home and classroom materials that engage parents and caregivers in music making *support* the attributes that young children need for school readiness, although they do not appear to enhance it. Furthermore, the fact that scores did not go down, which typically is the case in this educational setting, counters the rationale behind the current trend in schools to reduce or eliminate music and other arts programs from school curricula to make time for extra reading and math.

REFERENCES

Bilhartz, T. D., Bruhn, R. A., and Olson, J. E. (2000). The effect of early music training on child cognitive development. *Journal of Applied Developmental Psychology, 20*(4), 615–36.

Boston School Committee. (1837). Report of special committee in music education. In M. L. Mark (Ed.), *Source readings from ancient Greece to today* (pp. 70–74). New York: Routledge.

Brigance K and 1 Screen. (2006). North Billerica, MA: Curriculum Associates.

Butzlaff, R. (2000). Can music be used to teach reading? *Journal of Aesthetic Education, 34*(3), 167–78.

Cohen, M., and Frank, M. (2009). *Total learning initiative research summary: Formative research summary, preschool Music Together, embedded professional development program.* Action for Bridgeport Community Development Inc. New York: Michael Cohen Group.

Elliot, D. J. (1995). *Music matters.* New York: Oxford University Press.

Gardner, H. (1983). *Frames of mind.* New York: Basic Books.

Gazzaniga, M.(2008). *Arts and cognition: Findings hint at relationships.* New York: Dana Press.

Gerber, T., and Gerrity, W. (2007). Attitudes of music educators toward the teaching of language reading skills in the music classroom. *Bulletin of the Council for Research in Music Education, 173*, 71–88.

Goldman, R., Aldridge, J., and Russell, K. A. (2007). *Language and literacy supports for struggling readers: Meeting the goals of No Child Left Behind.* Birmingham, AL: Seacoast.

Hetland, L. (2000). Learning to make music enhances spatial reasoning. *Journal of Aesthetic Education, 34*(3–4), 179–238.

Jonides, J. (2008). *Musical skill and cognition.* New York: Dana Press.

Levinowitz, L. M. (1998). The importance of music in early childhood. *General Music Today, 12*(1), 4–7.

Levinowitz, L., and Guilmartin, K. K. (1989). *Music and your child: A guide for parents and caregivers.* Princeton, NJ: Center for Music and Young Children.

Mithen, S. (2006). *The singing Neanderthals.* Cambridge, MA: Harvard University Press.

Neville, H., Andersson, A., Bagdad, O., Bell, T., Currin, J., Fanning, J., et al. (2008). *Effects of music training on brain and cognitive development in underprivileged 3–5 year old children.* New York: Dana Press.

Peretz, I., and Zatorre, R. (Eds.). (2004). *The cognitive neuroscience of music.* New York: Oxford University Press.

Posner, M., Rothbart. M. K., Sheese, B. E., and Kieras, J. (2008). *How arts training influences cognition.* New York: Dana Press.

Rauscher, F. H., Shaw, G. L., and Ky, K. N. (1993). Music and spatial task performance. *Nature, 365*, 611.

Rauscher, F. H., Shaw, G. L., Levine, L. J., Wright, E. L., Dennis, W. R., and Newcomb, R. L. (1997). Music training causes long-term enhancement of preschool children's spatial-temporal reasoning. *Neurological Research, 19*, 2–8.

Register, D., Darrow, A., Standley, J., and Swedberg, O. (2007).The use of music to enhance reading skills of second grade students and students with reading disabilities. *Journal of Music Therapy, 44*(1), 23–37.

Scripp, L. (2002). Essay: An overview of research on music and learning. In R. J. Deasy (Ed.), *Critical links: Learning in the arts and student academic and social development* (pp. 132–36). Retrieved from www.aep-arts.org/cllinkspage.htm.

Spelke, E. (2008). *Effects of music instruction on developing cognitive systems at the foundations of mathematics and science.* New York: Dana Press.

Standley, J. M. (2008). Does music instruction help children learn to read? *Update: Applications of Research in Music Education, 27*(1), 17–29.

Standley, J., and Hughes, J. (1997). Evaluation of an early intervention music curriculum for enhancing pre-reading/writing skills. *Music Therapy Perspectives, 15,* 79–86.

Strickland, D. S., and Riley-Ayers, S. (2007). *Literacy leadership in early childhood: The essential guide.* New York: Teachers College Press.

Terra Nova Achievement Test. (n.d.). New York: McGraw-Hill.

Trenton Board of Education. (1999). *Needs assessment of early childhood programs in the Trenton public schools.* Trenton, NJ: Author.

Wandell, B., Dougherty, R. F., Ben-Schachar, M., Deutsch, D., and Tsang, G. J. (2008). *Training in the arts, reading, and brain imaging.* New York: Dana Press.

NOTES

1. *Music Together* is a music and movement approach to early childhood music development for infant, toddler, preschool, and kindergarten children and their parents, teachers, and other primary caregivers.

2. The Center for Music and Young Children (CMYC), developer of *Music Together*, was founded in 1985. CMYC is committed to helping families, caregivers and early childhood professionals rediscover the pleasure and educational value of non-formal musical experiences. Rather than emphasizing traditional music performances, CMYC encourages family participation in spontaneous musical activity occurring within the context of daily life.

Chapter Fifteen

The Role of Early Childhood Music Class Participation in the Development of Four Children with Speech and Language Delay

Cynthia Crump Taggart, Jenny Alvarez,
and Kathy Schubert

This case study explored two questions. What role, if any, does participation in an early childhood music class play in the language development of young children with speech and language delay; and how do these children respond and develop musically in the class? Participants were four speech- and language-delayed children, ages seventeen to thirty months. The researchers attended classes, took field notes, and then discussed what they had observed. These discussions were transcribed for analysis. Also, each of the researchers kept an e-mail journal.

The musical interactions of the children appeared to follow a similar developmental sequence. First, the children watched, listened, and explored. Then they began to imitate, first without correctness, then with delay, and eventually with accuracy. Eventually some were able to anticipate musically and demonstrate an understanding of musical context. Participation in class appeared to facilitate linguistic development. The children attended better in music class than in other settings. Music class elicited spontaneous vocalization, and vocalizations incorporated a progressively larger vocabulary. In addition, there were many language "firsts" that occurred during class. Several other themes emerged. The use of manipulatives elicited response, as did the teacher's imitation of a child's vocalization. Repetition appeared to facilitate imitation, whereas novelty resulted in higher levels of attention. Early childhood music classes appeared to be beneficial for the children's musical development, which is not surprising, as facilitating music development was the stated goal of the instructional program. However, participation in early childhood music classes also seemed to stimulate language development.

Parents enroll their children in early childhood music classes to support their children's development musically, socially, and cognitively (Gingras, 2009), and early childhood music programs make strong claims that participation in their programs will provide this developmental support. Yet the research base supporting these claims is limited, at best. Too often, they are made based on extrapolations from research with older children or from research on a specific therapeutic music intervention. Little is known about whether the results of these studies transfer meaningfully to early childhood music class settings, and especially to classes offered to infants and toddlers.

The purpose of this research was to examine the role that participation in an early childhood music program plays in the language and music development of four young children. The study grew out of a partnership between the Early Childhood Music Program at Michigan State University and the Early On Program of the Ingham Intermediate School District in mid-Michigan, which is an early intervention program for children with developmental delays or who have established conditions associated with delays in development from birth through age three. After Early On faculty had observed their children participating in the early childhood music program over the course of several years, they reported that the children seemed to benefit in several ways. They observed that the children seemed to participate as musical equals to the typically developing children in the class. In addition, they reported that the classes seemed to facilitate both language and social development as well. Yet these were "hunches" rather than conclusions drawn as a result of systematic observation designed to answer specific research questions. The faculty at Early On was particularly interested in the role that music class participation played in the language development of the children identified as having speech and language delays, as these children represented much of their client population. With this in mind, two Early On faculty members and the director of the Early Childhood Music Program embarked on this study.

REVIEW OF LITERATURE

Because music and language are both aurally and orally based, researchers and theorists have recognized that music and language learning share similar processes and have relationships with one another (Anvari, Trainor, Woodside, and Levy, 2002; Atterbury, 1985; Gordon, 2003; Lamb and Gregory, 1993; Saffran, Johnson, Aslin, and Newport, 1999). In fact, Chen-Hafteck (1998), in discussing early sound perception, early vocalizations, and the emergence of speech and singing, claimed that music and language learning structures are nested when children are very young and are only distinguishable as children get older. Additionally, Patel, Peretz, Tramo, and Labrecque (1998) found that music and language share some cortical areas in the brain.

Researchers have begun to investigate the effects of specific music interventions on language skill development. Wade (1996) and Helfrich-Miller

(1984) found that melodic intonation therapy, which combines melody, slowed tempo, and exaggerated rhythm and stress with speech, helped improve initial consonant production in a child with language delay. Gromko (2005) studied kindergarten children and found that music instruction improved children's phonemic awareness. Similarly, Anvari and colleagues (2002) studied four- and five-year-old children and found that music perception skills were related to phonemic awareness and contributed uniquely to predicting children's reading ability. Other researchers have concluded that music is related to or supports the development of reading skills (Atterbury, 1985; Douglas and Willats, 1994; Lamb and Gregory, 1993). In a meta-analysis of thirty studies, Butzlaff (2000) found a strong association between music instruction and reading ability as measured by standardized tests. Schraer-Joiner (2009) studied the impact of music activities on three- and four-year-old children with cochlear implants, many of whom are language delayed because of their hearing loss early in life. She found that singing activities promoted children's use of the voice and reinforced vocabulary. They also built confidence in the children. Yet few researchers have studied the effect of music instruction on the language development of infants and toddlers. Likewise, there is a paucity of research on the role that music plays in the language emergence of very young children with speech and language delay.

RESEARCH QUESTIONS

This study explored the participation of young children with speech and language delays in an early childhood music class in which the primary curricular goal was to support and enhance music development. The guiding questions were as follows:

1. What role, if any, does participation in an early childhood music class play in the language development of very young children with speech and language delay?
2. How do very young children with speech and language delay respond and develop musically in an early childhood music class?

METHOD

Participants

The primary participants in this case study were four children from the Early On program. These children were selected purposefully by the Early On program staff as those who might benefit from a group musical experience. All four were identified as having speech and language delay. Noel (all child-participant names are pseudonyms) was seventeen months old at the start of the study after receiving a cochlear implant at fourteen months as a result of a congenital profound bilateral sensory neural hearing loss from birth. He babbled but was not accurately imitating sounds except for "mom" and "ee" for "please." He also recognized his name when spoken. Brady was twenty-five months old and was diagnosed with Down syndrome. He had an early history of ear infections and received ear tubes at about six months. His verbal behaviors were imitations of consonant and vowel combinations, and he could speak approximations of ten single words. Phil was seventeen months old at the start of the study and had few language skills. He babbled and explored sounds, but did not imitate sounds or approximate words. Daryl was thirty months. His speech and language delay related primarily to articulation. In addition, his Early On teachers expressed concern regarding his attention and impulsivity.

The three researchers served as participant observers, participating in the classes while taking field notes and watching the primary participants. Two of the researchers, Jenny and Kathy, worked for Early On and regularly saw the four participants outside of music class, and the third, Cindy, directed the early childhood music program. The teacher of the class, Denise, was an experienced early childhood music teacher.

Design and Procedures

The ten-week early childhood music class had ten children enrolled, ranging in ages from birth to age three, with a caregiver attending for each child. The classes met weekly for forty-five minutes, beginning in late January and ending in early April. Children were immersed in a rich musical environment of singing, chanting, and movement and were allowed to explore that environment with no expectations of correctness. Sometimes the children participated, sometimes they watched, and sometimes they engaged in exploration that was not related to the activities of the class. The musical repertoire consisted of songs and chants in a wide range of tonalities and meters. Approximately two-thirds of the repertoire was presented without text, using a neutral syllable such as "la" or "bum," and one-third of the songs were performed with text. This was typical in the early childhood music classes at Michigan State University, as it allows the children to focus on the tonal, rhythmic, and expressive elements of the music rather than the meaning of the song texts. The teacher regularly modeled continuous, fluid movement for the children as she sang. The teacher and children often used manipulatives, such as beanbags, scarves, and pompons.

Data were collected in several ways. All three researchers attended each class and took rich field notes. In every class period, Jenny and Kathy each focused on two of the four participants, concentrating on their language and social behaviors, and Cindy observed all four, concentrating on their musical behaviors. In addition, Denise observed the behaviors of the children as she taught. Immediately following each class, the researchers and the teacher discussed what they had seen in the class. These discussions were audio-recorded and transcribed for analysis. In addition, each researcher sent an e-mail journal that reflected the contents of their field notes to one another before the next class period. In this way, the data reflected the lenses of four early childhood specialists and were collected in multiple forms, providing triangulation and contributing to trustworthiness. Following data collection, the transcripts and e-mail journals were coded and analyzed for emerging themes, using the lens of the research questions to guide the analysis.

RESULTS

Musical Response and Development

Musical responses developed as the semester progressed. Noel rarely responded at the beginning of the semester. However, by the middle of semester, he was engaging in activities, and by the end of the semester, he was demonstrating beat competency occasionally and making sustained vocal sounds.

Early Observation:

Jenny: Noel was very watchful and cautious at first. His gaze was directed at his mom and accompanying Early On teacher for the first portion of the class and at others in general. Gradually his gaze was directed at Denise as he watched as others participated. Very active watching. (E-mail journal entry, January 28)

Midway Observation:

Kathy: Last week he was just kind of taking it all in to see what was going on, but now he remembers. There was a lot of imitation when Denise used the sticks.

Cindy: And, as the activity went on, he started working toward correctness, not in terms of being on the beat but in terms of doing the same category of activity, waving the sticks and tapping where we were waving and tapping. (Discussion transcript, March 3)

Late Observation:

Jenny: He's doing more and more, and he especially loves the sticks . . . I did see him raise his hands and lower his hands with the sticks [with the teacher], which was new. Last week he didn't do that.

Cindy: I actually saw him doing some of this with beat competence, so it was accurate, but not for long. I also heard him do "ah ahhhhhhhhh" [in response to a dominant/tonic pattern from the teacher], but it was not quite accurate. It had the pitch direction but was not quite on the right pitches. (Discussion transcript, April 7)

At first, Brady's responses were primarily movement responses, and those responses were delayed. He began to vocally explore as the semester progressed, and by the end of the semester he was singing the dominant pitch accurately and was able to demonstrate stylistic understanding through movement. He also learned to predict what was coming next musically so that he could participate in time.

Early Observation:

Jenny: . . . what I noticed was that he was imitative, which I know he can be. Sometimes it was immediate, if the movement was large or very familiar. But, often it was delayed. (Discussion transcript, January 28)

Midway Observation:

Cindy: I even heard him sing dominant today. He was waving a big stick in the air singing "ahhhh!" He didn't go down to tonic [as did the teacher], but the dominant was on pitch. That was right on cue. It wasn't a beautiful singing voice. It was more like a holler. But, it was a pitched holler and was right in the key that we were working in. (Discussion transcript, February 25)

Late Observation:

Cindy: One thing that I really saw change in Brady is his ability to anticipate. He was doing lots of anticipatory behavior today, rather than waiting until after everyone did it and then imitating it. So, he was at the time the rest of the class was doing it, particularly with moving his arms for V and I. He wasn't delayed at all on that, which is new.

Jenny: So, to say it again, he was with you.

Denise: Well, right off the bat with the sticks today, I ended the tune and he put his sticks up before I said anything or modeled. (Discussion transcript, April 7)

Phil began the semester making spontaneous vocalizations. Partway through the semester, he began to sing tonic in response to the music in the classroom, and, by the end of the semester, he was accurately singing tonic and dominant pitches to all of the songs and in every class.

Early Observation:

Cindy: Lots of spontaneous vocalizations: "Woo," "Eee" vocal slides," ah" and "ow." (E-mail journal entry, January 28)

Midway Observation:

Kathy: I wasn't even watching him and I heard him.

Cindy: That was amazing. It made me want to cry!

Denise: He hit tonic dead on like everything, and I heard a couple of more V to I responses that were up and down but not directly hitting. A lot of up and down but always back to that accurate tonic.

Jenny: Up to this point, he has been visual and not auditory. And today his imitations were auditory, even with some of the novel activities. His ears were turned on. (Discussion transcript, March 17)

Daryl demonstrated correctness from the beginning of the semester, accurately echoing four-beat rhythm patterns, singing tonic, and moving to beat. This continued, and he began to explore using his singing voice in a more sustained way.

Early Observation:

Cindy: From week one Daryl was tapping his foot accurately to patterns and singing tonic on the V to I final cadences (E-mail journal entry, January 28)

Midway Observation:

Cindy: He's starting to explore the upper registers; he's starting to explore his head voice. And boy, he is very rhythmically strong. He was tiptoeing to macrobeat and microbeat [being played] on the drum with accuracy today. His four-beat patterns were accurate. (Discussion transcript, March 10)

The musical interactions and responses of the children seemed to follow a similar developmental sequence, although different children began at different points in the sequence. Noel began at the start of the developmental sequence, whereas Daryl had highly developed musical skills for his age level when he first entered the classroom. At first children got comfortable in the setting by watching, listening, and gradually exploring. Then students began to imitate, first without correctness, then with delay, and eventually with accuracy. Eventually some of the children were able to anticipate musically and demonstrate an understanding of musical context. This sequence parallels and supports the stages of preparatory audiation as outlined by Gordon (2003). In the stages of preparatory audiation, first children observe, listen, and absorb. Next, they respond randomly, and then they connect their responses to the musical sounds in the environment. Eventually they learn to imitate correctly and then give the imitations syntactical meaning, making it possible for them to anticipate musically. Although all of these children exhibited speech and language delay, those without hearing loss did not demonstrate developmental delays musically.

Language Response and Development

In terms of language skills, Noel began by attending to class but making few sounds.

> *Jenny:* As a child who has just been activated with the implant, he's trying to figure things out. He really watched his familiar people to begin with. And then about halfway through, he attended to Denise, and then she was his primary person to attend to. He was in a general taking-it-in mode. And, his eyes are his primary mode of taking things in, and I just think that so many sounds just are not known to him. They're not meaningful. (Discussion transcript, January 28)

Eventually he said the words "no" (Discussion transcript, February 25) and "me" (Discussion transcript, March 3) for the first time during music class.

Brady explored many sounds vocally during class. As with Noel, several language firsts occurred during class. He strung different syllables together for the first time and answered a question with a new word: "there."

> *Cindy:* He did lots of both "buh" and "bah," a couple of different vowel sounds with the same consonants.
>
> *Kathy:* I mean, it wasn't just one syllable. There were several.
>
> *Denise:* There were several in a row, yeah!
>
> *Jenny:* That's the first time he's EVER put syllables together of any sort.
>
> *Kathy:* You mean string them? Wow! (Discussion transcript, February 25)
>
> *Kathy:* When Denise was pulling the scarf off his head and singing "Where is Brady?" [sung on the dominant] and replying, "There he is," [sung on tonic}, he went "deh," trying to say "there."

Jenny: He did it twice, and the first time I just wrote "vocalized" but when he did it again, it was clearly a "dah."

Kathy: Yes, and it was with the same inflection that Denise had. It makes me think, because it's harder for kids with Down Syndrome to imitate words and sounds, that movement and inflection like that must be very helpful for his speech development. (Discussion transcript, March 3)

The following week Brady's "dah" and "deh" had changed to "dere," which was recognizable as the word "there."

As the semester progressed, Phil increased his sound vocabulary. He said his first word that was clearly recognizable—"mama" (Discussion transcript, March 13)—during music class and demonstrated understanding of verbal instructions for the first time.

Cindy: He really responded to the "no." He left the beanbag right away and walked over to her. That was neat.

Kathy: Yes, that was good for his understanding of language.

Jenny: Is she doing more at home in terms of giving him directions and expectations?

Kathy: I don't know, but she's more engaged with him here, which I'm glad about. (Discussion transcript, March 10)

By the end of the semester, he was saying "bye-bye," "hello" (Discussion transcript, March 24), and "more" during class (Discussion transcript, April 7).

Daryl began to perform entire phrases of the chants with words, which was more sustained verbal behavior than he had demonstrated previously. Kathy, who is also a speech therapist, attributed this directly to his participation in music class.

Cindy: He said, "boom, boom, boom went the giant" and he tried to say "scrub-a-dub-dubba" a little bit, but that was harder for him. But the "boom, boom, boom went the giant" was very clear.

Jenny: It really was, and longer phrases, too.

Kathy: I think it has really helped his articulation, too, because just getting those beats, the pattern of the rhythm is so good for articulation. You know, his language is good, but some of the speech sounds were a little bit off, and he's hard to understand. But, I think it's so much better now. Just being able to do it with the rhythm is really helpful. (Discussion transcript, March 10)

Overall, attention levels were better for the children in music class than was true in other group settings. These attention levels may have played a role in the linguistic development of the children, as attention has been identified as a precursor of and essential to the development of language skills (Spaulding, Plante, and Vance, 2008; Torro, Sinnett, and Soto-Faraco, 2005).

> *Jenny:* I think for Brady that he could organize himself here. . . . He was always appropriate, always appropriate with the materials, always with us, so very appropriate in this group with lots of possible distractions. So, I would have to say, that was HUGE for me. . . . He hasn't shown such focus in other settings. . . . He did very well. Just optimal for him, I would say. (Discussion transcript, April 7)

> *Jenny:* What was significant for Phil was his attention. (E-mail journal entry, February 25)

> *Kathy:* We really are concerned about his [Daryl's] attention, but I think his attention here is wonderful.

> *Cindy:* His attention here is really strong. I would never have known you were concerned.

> *Kathy:* And, I think it's getting stronger at home, too. . . . When we first started working with him . . . he just ran from one thing to the next. But here, he's very, very into everything you are doing. I think it's a wonderful thing for him. (Discussion transcript, March 10)

Participation in music class did appear to play a role in the children's linguistic development. Generally, the children attended better in music class than in other group settings. Music class also elicited spontaneous vocalizations from the three younger children, and their vocal explorations incorporated a larger vocabulary of sounds as the semester progressed. In addition, there were many "firsts" that occurred during music class, such as speaking the first word, adding new words to a child's spoken vocabulary, following verbal directions, and stringing multiple syllables and words together. All of this is evidence that the music class environment may stimulate speech and language development.

Unexpected Surprises

Several other themes emerged during data analysis that were unrelated to the original research questions. Certain teacher choices, behaviors, and initiatives elicited more response from the children.

Use of manipulatives played an important role in the learning of the children. In general, the use of manipulatives elicited response from the children, particularly when a movement with the manipulative was paired with a vocal sound.

> *Cindy:* One of the things that I am beginning to see is the use of props to elicit response, because, with Phil, it is dramatic.

Jenny: It would go with the motor piece. Kids are in the sensorimotor period of development. They get more vocal when the prop is paired with sound and . . .

Cindy: Movement.

Jenny: And today he grabbed my hands to do it. There was a point when we were doing, moving scarves, and he was moving me. He became vocal at that point also. (Discussion transcript, March 3)

Also, many of the manipulatives engaged the children more deeply in the activities, although not all manipulatives engaged all children.

Jenny: The scarves are what did it . . .

Kathy: The scarves worked for him [Noel].

Jenny: That was the time he looked really happy, and then after that he seemed happy. (Discussion transcript, March 3)

This supports the findings of Hornbach (2005), who found that the use of manipulatives often elicited children's musical responses.

The children also used props to initiate social interactions by offering them to one another to engage or prolong social interactions.

Jenny: I think Brady's interactions with the other kids are really sweet, and they're very appropriate. He uses props to say "hi." He'll give them a prop, something to engage and prolong that interaction. (Discussion transcript, March 10)

Jenny: Phil was throwing the scarves to the little girl with the barrettes. . . . As he was throwing, he was using that to interact, sing "baa, baa" [sung on dominant to tonic] as he did so.

Cindy: Every time he tried to put the scarf on her head, he'd do it with a "baa baa."

Jenny: And he used it not to repeat but to interact! (Discussion transcript, March 17)

The teacher's imitation of a child's vocalization and the incorporation of that vocalization into the music of the classroom resulted in increased response, particularly from the younger children.

Cindy: Phil had a vocal slide that carried through the entire class, starting in the middle register and going down. Near the beginning of the class, he did it all on his own . . . it did not seem to be related to what was happening in class. However, that changed when Denise brought out the scarves. She threw one up in the air and accompanied its flight path with a high to low vocal slide, imitating Phil's slide. It was as if a switch was flipped in Phil. For the remainder of the activity, he was performing vocal slides, but this time he was accompanying them with the scarf motion, as Denise did. When the activity was over, his vocal slides mostly ended as well. (E-mail journal entry, January 30)

Again, this supports Hornbach (2005), who found that imitating a child's response sometimes resulted in a chain of musical interactions.

Another theme that emerged was parent learning. Parenting skills improved during the course of the semester. As parents had the opportunity to observe a variety of different adult/child interaction, they interacted with their children more appropriately musically and in a more supportive way.

> *Jenny:* So this is good for Mom too, to see how other people interact with their kids and how other kids can sit.
>
> *Cindy:* It was interesting to see how much Phil, at the beginning of the class period, was really interacting with George [another parent].
>
> *Kathy:* The Dad, yes.
>
> *Cindy:* Very, very interactive. And that did seem to pull his Mom into interacting with him in another way than she sometimes does.
>
> *Jenny:* See, this is helpful . . . this whole setting . . . seeing how to interact perhaps differently with your kids. (Discussion transcript, March 3)

The parents learned both from watching the teacher as well as from observing the interactions of other parents with the children.

Finally, positive affect emerged as a theme. All of the children enjoyed the music class, as demonstrated by smiles and laughter during class and tears at the end of class. The class seemed to be engaging and a positive experience from the perspective of the children.

> *Kathy:* We're trying to see if there were any expressions of enjoyment: laughs and smiles.
>
> *Jenny:* Oh my gosh. That was Brady.
>
> *Kathy:* I mean, they all did. They loved it. (Discussion transcript, Jan. 28)
>
> *Jenny:* And then, as soon as you started the "Goodbye Song" [the song that signals the end of class], he [Noel] made an "ooh" sound and his voice dropped and his face got red.
>
> *Cindy:* It was the saddest face I've ever seen!
>
> *Kathy:* I didn't see his face because he was looking towards you, but I could hear what his face sounded like without seeing it! (Discussion transcript, February 25)

Cindy: And he [Noel] was really joyfully participating . . . just joy written all over his face. (Discussion transcript, March 3)

CONCLUSION

Because this is a case study, no generalizations should be made to other children or settings. However, the results may be transferable to children with similar characteristics and in similar settings. For the children in this study, early childhood music classes appeared to be beneficial for their musical development, which is not surprising, as facilitating music development was the stated curricular goal of the instructional program in which they participated. However, even though facilitating language development was not a stated goal of the program, for these children, participation in early childhood music classes stimulated language development. Children were able to attend better in music class than they were in other group settings, and the types of activities in music class elicited language responses, many that were "firsts" for individual children. In addition, the children enjoyed their participation, and the parents developed parenting skills as a result of their participation.

Parents should be encouraged to enroll their young children in developmentally appropriate music classes, first and foremost so that their children have rich musical experiences and a foundation on which to build future music learning. However, there may be other benefits from engaging in such an environment, such as enhanced language development. Researchers should continue to study the multifarious benefits of early childhood music instruction and what types of music environments are the most beneficial for young children.

REFERENCES

Anvari, S., Trainor, L., Woodside, J., and Levy, B. A. (2002). Relations among musical skills, phonological processing, and early reading ability in preschool children. *Journal of Experimental Child Psychology, 83*, 111–30.

Atterbury, B. W. (1985). Musical differences in learning-disabled and normal achieving readers aged seven, eight, and nine. *Psychology of Music, 13*, 114–23.

Butzlaff, R. (2000). Can music be used to teach reading? *Journal of Aesthetic Education, 34*(3), 167–78.

Chen-Hafteck, L. (1998). Music and language development in early childhood: Integrating past research in the two domains. *Early Child Development and Care, 130*, 85–97.

Douglas, S., and Willats, P. (1994). The relationship between musical ability and literacy skills. *Journal of Research in Reading, 17*, 99–107.

Gingras, P. (2009, January). *Who are they and why are they here? Family factors leading to enrollment in an early childhood music program.* Paper presented at Early Childhood Music Special Research Interest Group of MENC: The National Association of Music Education Conference, Learning from Young Children, Newark, DE.

Gordon, E. E. (2003). *A music learning theory for newborn and young children* (Rev. ed.). Chicago: GIA.

Gromko, J. (2005). The effect of music instruction on phonemic awareness in beginning readers. *Journal of Research in Music Education, 53*(3), 199–209.

Helfrich-Miller, K. R. (1984). Melodic intonation therapy with developmentally apraxic children. *Seminars in Speech and Language, 5*, 119–25.

Hornbach, C. M. (2005). *Ah-eee-ah-eee-yah-eee, bum and pop, pop, pop: Teacher initiatives, teacher silence, and children's vocal responses in early childhood music class.* Doctoral dissertation, Michigan State University, East Lansing.

Lamb, S. J., and Gregory, A. H. (1993). The relationship between music and reading in beginning readers. *Educational Psychology, 13*, 13–27.

Patel, A. D., Peretz, I., Tramo, J. J., and Labreque, R. (1998). Processing prosodic and musical patterns: A neuropsychological investigation. *Brain and Language, 61*, 123–44.

Saffran, J. R., Johnson, E. K., Aslin, R. N., and Newport, E. L. (1999). Statistical learning of tone sequences by human infants and adults. *Cognition, 70*, 27–52.

Schraer-Joiner, J. (2009, January). *The impact of music activities on preschool cochlear implant users' speech and language skill development: A multiple case study.* Paper presented at Early Childhood Music Special Research Interest Group of MENC: The National Association for Music Education Conference, Learning from Young Children, Newark, DE.

Spaulding, T. J., Plante, E., and Vance, R. (2008). Sustained selective attention skills of preschool children with specific language impairment: Evidence for separate attentional capacities. *Journal of Speech, Language, and Hearing Research, 51*, 16–34.

Torro, J. M., Sinnett, S., and Soto-Faraco, S. (2005). Speech segmentation by statistical learning depends on attention. *Cognition, 97*, B25–B34.

Wade, C. A. (1996). *A case study: The effects of Melodic Intonation Therapy and oral-motor treatment on initial consonant production by a child with developmental verbal dyspraxia.* Unpublished masters thesis, Kansas State University, Manhattan.

Chapter Sixteen

Examining Music Experiences with Anthony, a Child Who Has Autism

Wendy Valerio, Annabel Sy, Hannah Gruber,
and Claire Griffith Stockman

Co-researchers of this study, Annabel, Hannah, and Claire, spent four years engaging in a reciprocal, communication-based music approach with Anthony, a ten-year-old boy who has severe autism and loves music. The purpose of this research was to examine their music experiences. The specific problem of this heuristic case study was to discuss the elements of Music Play *and their adaptations that support Anthony's challenges when he is engaged 1:1 (teacher-student) in this approach. Researchers collected data via journals, videotape, notes from conversations, and interviews. Emergent themes demonstrated that, for Anthony, music play experiences provided a place for him to experience self-regulation, shared attention, and reciprocal communication. Moreover, those experiences provided opportunity for him to relax, to be himself, to express himself through music, and to connect with someone. For Annabel and Anthony, music play experiences provided peace and comfort, respite, moments to cherish, joy, and triumph. For Hannah, Claire, and Wendy, their music play experiences provided the opportunity to develop as teachers and musicians through their close, personal, musical relationships with Anthony.*

Children with autism spectrum disorders (ASDs) present a variety of sensory, motor, communication, and socioemotional deficiencies at a variety of intensities, making it difficult for them to function in society. With those deficiencies, children with autism especially experience impaired emotional sharing and social interactions that limit their abilities to develop relationships with others, and leave their families searching for ways to communicate with their children so that they may develop emotionally, socially, physically, and intellectually to the best of their abilities.

Recently, Greenspan and Wieder (1997, 1998, 2005, 2006) have developed *Developmental Individual-Difference Relationship-Based/Floortime* (DIR/

Floortime), a relationship-based intervention for children with ASDs. When engaging in the DIR/Floortime approach, parents guide children with autism through six developmental stages: (a) self-regulation, shared attention, and interest in the world; (b) intimacy, engagement, and falling in love; (c), two-way communication; (d) complex communication; (e) emotional ideas; and (f) emotional and logical thinking. Those six stages form a developmental hierarchy in which each achievement at each stage lays the foundation for achievement at subsequent stages (Greenspan and Lewis, 1999; Greenspan and Wieder, 2006). As stated by the Interdisciplinary Council on Developmental and Learning Disorders (ICDL), the understanding is that development at each of those stages is essential for children to develop "spontaneous and empathetic relationships as well as the mastery of academic skills" (Interdisciplinary Council on Developmental and Learning Disorders [ICDL], 2010a, para. 2); parents *individualize* the intervention to meet the biological challenges specific to their child. Those biological challenges include over-reactive or underreactive sensory modulation, sensory processing difficulties, and motor planning/physical sequencing difficulties. Parents who use the DIR/Floortime approach individualize their interactions with their child in emotional, affect-based, and learning *relationships* to assist their children in achieving the milestones necessary for development.

The Floortime aspect of the DIR/Floortime model refers to the sessions spent working through the six developmental stages during play activities as parents and children build relationships and focus on use of affect. Parents who use the DIR/Floortime model with children who have autism act as play partners who focus on developing skills at each developmental stage that is not yet mastered, while encouraging the development of skills at each successive developmental stage as they surface. Play activities build on the child's interests and strengths, following the child's lead, and may involve anything from physical/sensorimotor games to symbolic play. They are often performed on the floor, but can be performed during any daily routine, anytime, anywhere (Greenspan and Wieder, 2006).

In Floortime play sessions, parents act as play partners in 1:1 relationships with their child to encourage the child to respond to and initiate reciprocal communication through continuous, back-and-forth, verbal, and/or non-verbal interactions (Greenspan and Wieder, 2006). During such circles of communication, the play partner uses the child's physical and verbal cues as springboards for further reciprocal communication and creation of ideas through expanding play interactions. When using this approach, the parent nurtures the child according to his developmental stage, optimizing each moment to encourage higher developmental capacities. With supportive circles of communication, the child begins to create his own ideas, expands them, and involves his partner in the creative process. The process of how each play activity evolves, rather than the end product, gives the child the tools to strengthen his basic developmental capacities.

In their study *Review of 200 Cases of Children with Autistic Spectrum Disorders Receiving the DIR/Floortime Approach*, Greenspan and Wieder (1997) reported that children who received DIR/Floortime-based interventions for two to eight years demonstrated progress in interpersonal skills, intrapersonal skills, and cognitive skills. Some of the children shifted from the autistic to the non-autistic range (*Childhood Autism Rating Scale*) (Schopler, Reichler, and Renner, 1998) after receiving DIR/Floortime intervention. Later, Greenspan and Wieder (2005) found that many children had maintained and/or continued their gains through adolescence by demonstrating empathy and excelling in music and writing. Recently, Solomon, Necheles, Ferch, and Bruckman (2007) adapted the DIR/Floortime model in the PLAY Project Home Consultation (PPHC) program and found that children who spend fifteen hours per week in 1:1 interaction with their parents demonstrated significant increases (p < 0.0001) in Functional Emotional Assessment Scale (FEAS) scores (Greenspan, DeGangi, and Wieder, 2001).

Other researchers (Fang, 2009; Frick, 2000; Gruber, 2007; Kern, Wolery, and Aldridge, 2007; Wimpory, Chadwick, and Nash, 1995; Wimpory, Hobson, and Nash, 2006) have suggested that music interventions may help children with autism develop communication skills that allow them to establish relationships with others. Gruber (2007) employed a music learning theory/reciprocal communication–based approach (Gordon, 2003; Valerio, Reynolds, Taggart, Bolton, and Gordon, 1998) with children with autism and found that those children displayed increasing trends in vocal imitation and vocal initiation.

RESEARCH CONTEXT, PURPOSE, AND PROBLEM

The co-researchers of this study—Annabel, Hannah, Claire, and Wendy—spent four years engaging in a music curriculum based on the tenets of *Music Play* (Valerio et al., 1998), a developmental, reciprocal communication-based music approach, with Anthony, a ten-year-old boy who loves music and has severe autism. The purpose of this research was to examine our music experiences. The specific problem of this heuristic case study was to discuss the elements of *Music Play* and their adaptations that support Anthony's challenges when he is engaged 1:1 (teacher-student) in this approach.

METHOD

We chose a heuristic design for this study to (a) emphasize connectedness and relationship, (b) portray personal significance, (c) creatively synthesize findings based on intuition and tacit understanding, and (d) allow the research participants to remain visible throughout the study (Patton, 2002). To enhance triangulation and trustworthiness, multiple data sources included journals, videotape interviews, field notes and notes from multiple in-depth conversations during a four-year period (Patton, 2002). All videotaped interviews were transcribed and submitted to participants for member checks (Creswell, 1998, 2003). As recommended by Moustakas (1990), the following data presentation includes a comprehensive depiction of Anthony by Annabel, individual depictions of how Hannah and Claire used and adapted elements of *Music Play* to support Anthony's challenges, and a creative synthesis of how their experiences influenced Anthony's development and quality of life.

Anthony and Annabel

Anthony is a ten-year-old boy who was diagnosed with autism when he was twenty-two-months-old. Anthony's autism was categorized as *severe* with significant challenges in sensory, motor, communication, and socioemotional development based on the Childhood Autism Rating Scale (CARS) (Schopler et al., 1998), a standardized autism rating scale. Annabel, Anthony's mother, recalled that when Anthony was approximately eighteen months old, she began to notice his symptoms:

> Well, he used to vocalize one-word requests, and he just stopped. And I just lost eye contact [with him] and the whole engagement piece, and he was totally shut out. . . . And he started having rituals, like lining up his toys, or just really obsessing over little things. (A. Sy, personal communication, October 8, 2008)

When Annabel recognized Anthony's symptoms, she dedicated her life to educating herself about ASDs and finding the most appropriate interventions and therapies for him, including investing in a traditional behavioral program (Lovaas, 1981), and later a language-based behavioral program (Partington and Sundberg, 1998). Both programs targeted specific/discrete skills, such as vocalization on demand, using a reinforcer/reward-based approach, but neither helped Anthony with his fundamental challenges with sensory processing and self-regulation, the ability to stay calm and emotionally, mentally, and physically regulated. These challenges prevented Anthony from shared attention and meaningful, spontaneous communication that lead to personal relationships with others. Annabel described Anthony's intervention in his early years as follows:

> Talking consistently on demand, or singing along with his partner is difficult for him. We wanted him to TALK, TALK, TALK [emphasis added by Annabel]. It is difficult for Anthony to stay calm enough to talk consistently or stay engaged for extended periods of time. Any trigger can quickly cause him to get overexcited (overactive, hyperseeking, seeking more input) or overloaded (shutdown, underactive, hyposeeking, not tolerating any additional input). Anthony has difficulty moving his body in a coordinated way. Anthony would seek so much rhythm and music throughout the day. He could not seem to get *enough*—because he could not get *in sync* with an ongoing rhythm, including his own. By the time Anthony was 7 years old, the world was *too much* [for him]. His difficulty with staying calm and engaged with his world grew worse with time. (A. Sy, December 28, 2008)

Annabel is a doctor of medicine (MD) with a specialty in internal medicine and a subspecialty in allergy and immunology. She has taken an indefinite leave from her profession to fully devote her time to help rehabilitate her son Anthony. In order to find the optimum support for Anthony, Annabel has received training in various intervention approaches to help children with autism, which include Applied Behavior Analysis (ABA) (Lovaas, 1981), Verbal Behavior (VB/ABA) strategies (Partington and Sundberg, 1998), the Picture Exchange Communication System (PECS) (Frost and Bondy, 1994), Sensory Integration (SI) techniques (Kranowitz and Silver, 1998), and, later, DIR/Floortime principles (Greenspan and Wieder, 1998). Annabel acts as Anthony's primary caregiver, main interventionist, and teacher. She provides him with homeschooling and accompanies him in all daily activities.

Anthony's Challenges and *Music Play*

In 2005, when Anthony was seven years old, his family began implementing the DIR/Floortime framework to help him with his sensory challenges. In consultation with DIR/Floortime experts, they determined that Anthony's major fundamental challenge is the ability to stay calm while tolerating, processing, and exploring a full range of sensations. Anthony must expend great effort to tolerate and process almost all sensory input even during what most persons would consider a simple activity. For example, if Anthony and a partner were in a room alone, and the partner was attempting to engage Anthony in a game of rolling a ball back and forth, the partner may playfully and gently roll the ball to Anthony, expecting Anthony to pick up the ball and roll it back to him. To participate in the game, Anthony may be struggling *not* to pay attention to even the slightest of sounds outside the room, the texture of the carpet, the lights that are buzzing, the smell of something cooking in the kitchen, and/or the movement of the ceiling fan. Such things would not distract most children, but for Anthony the sensory input from those stimuli is overbearing. This makes it difficult for him to become engaged and sustain interaction with anyone.

Anthony exhibits a mixed-sensory profile, meaning he can transition quickly from hyperseeking (overactive) behaviors to hyposeeking (underactive) behaviors (and vice versa) to identical sensory input in any given time frame. Such rapid changes in his arousal state can make engagement with Anthony difficult, even in favorite activities like music. This underscores the importance of his play partner's abilities to interpret his cues and adapt as needed in order to engage him in reciprocal communication. Annabel must pay attention to Anthony's arousal state from moment to moment to determine if he is in a state of regulation or dysregulation. By understanding Anthony's unique sensory profile (e.g., how he reacts to a variety of sensations/stimuli), Annabel has developed approaches or adaptations/adjustments that help Anthony stay engaged and sustain 1:1 reciprocal communication with her.

As with many children with autism, Anthony exhibits numerous and frequent self-stimulatory behaviors (stims), such as flicking his fingers, rocking his body, and making random vocalizations, as if constantly seeking rhythm and music from within himself. Annabel believes that he tries to be in sync and to connect with the world using his body rhythms, in lieu of words. He often adopts body postures such as kneeling on all fours and rubbing the floor, or crawling in this position, sliding his palms on the floor, seeking tactile stimulation as well as proprioceptive input—that is, input to the body causing movement and spatial awareness (ICDL, 2010b). Examples of proprioceptive input include compression to the joints, such as jumping, squeezing hands, and crawling. Such input leads to improved self-regulation and a state of calmness.

When we began data collection for this study, Anthony had a vocabulary of approximately five hundred words, but he did not often initiate conversation. He made and continues to make spontaneous vocalizations mainly in the form of requests such as "I want music," and he can initiate a game using words, such as "One potato, two potato." With time, he has begun echoing more words and short phrases, and he has begun making spontaneous comments, such as "yummy" or "I love it," in response to positive experiences.

Though Annabel provides Anthony with a daily regimen of activities at home, she also provides him with opportunities for socialization with other children. In the spring of 2005, Annabel enrolled Anthony in a program for three-year-olds at the Children's Center at the University of South Carolina (USC), where he attended many activities including group music classes based on *Music Play* (Valerio et al., 1998). During the next four years Anthony, accompanied by Annabel, continued to participate in group music classes and private music classes at the Children's Center with Hannah (graduate music education student) and Claire (undergraduate/graduate music education student), under the guidance of Wendy (music education professor). We conscientiously observed Anthony and used his movements and vocalizations to encourage reciprocal communication, while being sensitive to his states of stimulation and his need to practice self-regulation in order to communicate and participate in music activities.

Hannah and Claire

Hannah holds B.M., B.M.E., M.M., and M.M.E. degrees, as well as Gordon Institute for Music Learning Mastership Early Childhood Level I and Elementary Level I Certifications. She had been teaching music play classes at the USC Children's Center for one year when she met Anthony and Annabel. During an interview, Hannah recalled her first musical surprise from Anthony:

> I was teaching music play in the 3-year-olds' classroom at the Children's Center. For several weeks, Anthony would sometimes participate, sometimes just sit there with his mom, or be off playing some game. One day I was walking in the hallway, with the other [music] teacher, and Anthony saw the two of us and started singing the hello song we used to start each class. A few days later, in class, my co-teacher and I sang "Pennsylvania Dreamin'" (Valerio et al., 1998). It was the first time that we had used that song, and as soon as we finished, he sang it back perfectly; the whole thing. Everyone [in the classroom] just stopped what they were doing and looked at him and said, "Wow, where did that come from?" And then he kept singing it over and over. (H. Gruber, personal communication, October 27, 2008)

Annabel was thrilled with Anthony's music performance for Hannah, and she was also encouraged by her observations of Anthony in music play classes. She proposed that Hannah provide individual music play sessions for Anthony in addition to the classes he attended at the Children's Center. During the next two years, Hannah and Anthony engaged in weekly music play sessions, observed by Annabel. To learn more about autism, Hannah enrolled in graduate courses that provided an overview of ASDs and research methods in special education with a focus on ASDs.

During the summer of 2007, Hannah's acceptance of a position at another university required her to move to another city and cease her work with Anthony. During the next year, however, Anthony continued to attend the prekindergarten class at the Children's Center, where he experienced weekly group music play classes and private music play sessions taught by Claire, a music education student who had completed an early childhood music methods course based on the tenets of *Music Play* (Valerio et al., 1998) and taught by Wendy. In 2008, to learn more about ASDs and how she might support Anthony's challenges, and with Annabel's financial support, Claire completed *The Basic Course on the DIR/Floortime Model for Infancy and Early Childhood* (Greenspan, 2010) taught online by Greenspan.

Music Play

The authors of *Music Play* (Valerio et al., 1998) base their developmental music curriculum on *A Music Learning Theory for Newborn and Young Children* (Gordon, 2003). When leading music play classes, teachers present songs and rhythm chants in a variety of tonalities and meters, some with words and some without words, to individual children or groups of young children, while using movements to promote breathing, body awareness, and coordination. Teachers encourage children to join in the music and movement activities, as they are ready, with the understanding that children progress through types and stages of music development. Gordon (2003) theorized that children are first acculturated to music as they absorb the music in their environment. As they begin to respond to that music through vocalization and movement, children develop musically with guidance by adults who provide music stimuli and listen and watch for children's responses, using those responses as springboards for music interactions and engaging them in reciprocal musical communication. With music guidance and scaffolding, children learn how to musically imitate, improvise, and communicate as they become coordinated with themselves and then with others (Reynolds, Long, and Valerio, 2007).

During music play classes teachers often use purposeful silences to entice children to vocalize, to allow for time to audiate, and to allow children opportunity to anticipate what might happen next (Hicks, 1993; Hornbach, 2005, 2007; Reynolds, 1995, 2006; Valerio, 1997; Valerio and Reynolds, 2009; Valerio, Seaman, Yap, Santucci, and Tu, 2006). Those teachers understand that children will most likely participate in music babble and music approximation before they imitate accurately or improvise in context with syntax (Hicks, 1993; Gordon, 2003; Reynolds, 1995, 2006; Reynolds et al., 2007). The goal for teachers who use the *Music Play* (Valerio et al., 1998) curriculum is not to teach a child to perform music activities but to engage a child in music and movement processes that allow for inaccuracies, approximations, and interactions that result in music communication. As a child begins to babble and approximate, a music teacher uses the child's sounds and movements to create music contexts that allow music conversation to develop and evolve between the teacher and the child. As a result, the teacher's guiding principle is to be involved reciprocally, in the moment-to-moment process of music making with a child, rather than the end product of music performance.

Annabel noticed that many elements of a curriculum based on the tenets of *Music Play* (Valerio et al., 1998) allowed Anthony to engage in interaction and activities with others at a pace that was beneficial to him. She commented about Anthony's experience in initial private music sessions with Hannah:

> I was thrilled to see Anthony so happy and appear to be comfortable with himself and his partner. From the start I could see that what Hannah was doing in *Music Play* meshes well with the framework we follow to support Anthony. (A. Sy, personal communication, July 8, 2008)

Music Play Elements Support Anthony's Challenges

In order to engage in activities with another human, Anthony must have a calm arousal state. That is, he must not be over- or understimulated. Because Anthony's autism often makes it difficult for him to maintain a calm arousal state, Anthony's music teachers must be sensitive to his arousal states and engage him in activities as he is ready. Annabel observed:

> The lack of complex language supports his sensory processing and regulation challenges. By engaging in music without words, he is able to carry out reciprocal communication with his partner for extended periods of time, using the medium he understands the most (pure rhythm and musical notes, without the concern to decode any words). (A. Sy, personal communication, July 8, 2008)

Anthony's music teachers use his vocalizations and movements as springboards for music interaction. By doing so, they engage Anthony in reciprocal communication through music. Annabel summarized elements of music play that support Anthony's challenges (see table 16.1).

Purposeful Silences, Fill-in-the-Blank, and Music Conversations

Annabel noticed the power of purposeful silence during music play.

> The brief pauses built in the music play exercises are beneficial to Anthony in many ways because they:

Table 16.1. Annabel's Observations of Music Play Elements That Supported Anthony's Challenges

Elements in Music Play	Example
Matching Anthony's arousal state • Adjusting activities helped Anthony gain the regulation necessary to engage in music and movement activities.	After a vigorous drum exchange with Hannah, Anthony appeared to be *overloaded* and threw himself on the floor and started crying. Hannah lay on the floor next to him and softly hummed a calming tune: *Ni, Nah, Noh* (Valerio et al., 1998). Soon Anthony recovered, got up, and was ready to play again. Hannah gradually approached him and joined him in his play.
Matching rhythm with movement and vice versa • Matching Anthony's movements helped him stay regulated (calm) enough to remain engaged in music and movement activities. • Reinforcing Anthony's movements also helped his motor planning, which in turn further sustained self-regulation.	Anthony was dribbling the basketball, one of his favorite activities. Hannah played the drum and matched the rhythm of Anthony's basketball dribbling. By doing so, Anthony maintained engagement in an activity with another person.
Encouraging circles of communication through repetition and variation • Repetition helped Anthony because he needed consistent expectations and approaches to support his motor planning development. Repetition also provided multiple circles of communication when followed in a repetitive back-and-forth pattern. • Putting variations in the repetitive pattern offered flexibility for the appropriate sensory input (to support optimal arousal state—for instance, loud or soft voice, fast or slow movements). • Variations offered opportunities for spontaneity and creativity and led to musical partners speculating on each other's thoughts, creating anticipation, and enriched engagement by expanding reciprocal communication. • Definite, solid circles of communication were established before expanding the circle; partners were engaged in repetitive, back-and-forth patterns before variations were initiated.	When beginning an activity, Wendy and Claire performed the rhythm chant, *Jump Over the Ocean* (Valerio et al., 1998), with soft, gentle voices to match Anthony's arousal state. They also matched his tempo as he bounced on a small trampoline. They repeated the rhythm chant and the bouncing several times. Anthony's arousal state soon changed as he heard a train whistle in the distance. He paused his bouncing, turned away from Wendy and Claire, dropped to his knees and began stimming with his fingers as he vocally imitated the train whistle. Wendy copied Anthony's vocal imitation of the train whistle, much to Anthony's delight, as he smiled and giggled. Wendy continued to perform Anthony's vocal train whistle pattern and then extended it to include a tonal pattern of her own as she accompanied herself with rhythmic patting on her legs. Anthony ran to the other side of the room and put his tummy on the seat of a chair as he continued to listen to Wendy's repeated and varied patterns. Then he smiled and ran back to kneel on the trampoline. Wendy and Claire sat down near Anthony. Wendy purposefully paused her singing. Soon Anthony repeated his original train whistle pattern and created other tonal patterns as he and Wendy sang in dialogue.
Using purposeful silence • Purposeful silences offered by the music teachers provided the opportunity to create an anticipatory moment to encourage partner referencing, such as looking at a partner for cues and shared enjoyment.	Hannah performed a repetitive musical pattern with an animated ending strike on the drum. In each succeeding cycle, she would perform a purposeful silence before she carried out the last strike on the drum. This would make Anthony look up at her to anticipate the coming of the "fun" part. They would exchange smiles and he would flash a gleam in his eyes.
Following the child's lead and use of a developmental approach • Treating anything Anthony did as valuable allowed the teachers to build on Anthony's thoughts and strengths, and also contributed to his ability to make meaning with others.	Anthony made a noise by puffing his cheeks with air, and Hannah, Wendy, and Anthony had a beautiful musical exchange based on that noise.

(A. Sy, personal communication, September 20, 2005; September 25, 2008)

- support Anthony's sensory challenges—no breaks could lead him more easily to experience sensory overload,
- encourage spontaneity—Anthony can get focused enough (not distracted from noise) and gets enough time to come up with his own ideas, and
- encourage intimacy when two music partners feel something together, even if they are not clearly doing anything tangible, otherwise. (A. Sy, personal communication, July 8, 2008)

Annabel recalled a scene during which Claire and Anthony shared a long moment of silence:

Anthony and Claire just finished a song—they remained sitting on the carpet, facing each other. It appeared they were both looking at their hands in front of them on the carpet floor, and they stayed very close together so that their hands were almost opposite each other. The room was very quiet; there was hardly any movement, just a feeling of serenity in the air. If I have to pick a caption to reflect Anthony's thoughts here, it would read, "Your music and presence comfort me. I stay around to be with you." . . . And then, very gradually, and in his usual subtle way, Anthony moved his head forward towards Claire, and tried to kiss her forehead with his! (A. Sy, personal communication, June 15, 2008).

Hannah and Claire also used the technique of incorporating purposeful silence into activities to entice Anthony to fill in the blank with vocalizations or patterns on the drum. Hannah wrote:

I used omissions [purposeful silences], as I did in my other music play classes. People with autism often need more time to process information, so I tried to leave a longer space for him to respond. Once I had performed a song or chant a few times, (sometimes only one time), Anthony had it in his head how the song or chant was supposed to go. If I left out parts, he would fill them in. When I first started working with Anthony, he would fill in omissions in songs, but they were often in a spoken voice. As we spent more time together, he would respond in a beautiful singing voice. (H. Gruber, personal communication, October 27, 2008)

Claire wrote:

When he crawled away I followed, and many times, he was whispering my [rhythm] chant as he was crawling. It makes me feel that, maybe before, I was assuming that he was disengaging, when really he was just taking my content into his own terms. He also sang songs when I left holes [purposeful silences]. (Griffith, 2009, p. 44)

By providing silence and waiting for Anthony's responses, Hannah and Claire allowed Anthony the opportunity to respond as he was able. When his responses were vocalizations or drum patterns, Hannah and Claire used those responses to engage Anthony in music conversations first by imitating Anthony's rhythm or tonal vocalization and then by vocalizing a rhythm vocalization or tonal vocalization that was different from Anthony's vocalization. Hannah recalled:

> We had rhythm conversations using our voices and on the drum, and we had tonal conversations using tonal patterns. . . . It took him awhile before he did any of the tonal patterns . . . and even the rhythm patterns he didn't say right away, but we did a lot [of rhythm pattern turn-taking] on the drum. (H. Gruber, personal communication, October 27, 2008)

When asked about the nature of the rhythm conversations, tonal conversations, and drum conversations, Hannah stated, "Sometimes he would imitate. Sometimes he would be different. Sometimes he would just go over to the drum and initiate [a rhythm pattern exchange on the drum]" (H. Gruber, personal communication, October 27, 2008).

Anthony's music conversations with Hannah and Claire were rewarding for everyone. They were obvious, overt interchanges that occurred because Anthony was in a calm arousal state so that he could achieve shared attention with his teachers. Hannah and Claire used Anthony's responses playfully and musically to engage him in reciprocal communication. Hannah projected:

> I think what happened is he recognized that in his world there aren't very many times when other people imitate what he does or feed off of what he does. Most of the time people are trying to get him to do something (things that will make him "fit in" to the world of typically developing children) . . . I don't know if he had a conscious realization of this, but everything he did [in music play sessions] was right and was good. He never heard, "No, do it this way." Whatever he did, I could take and turn into something [musical and communicative]. I could either say it back or change it a little bit or turn it into a song or turn it into a rhythm chant. Especially when I first started working with Anthony, these rhythmic conversations were a way to interact with him in a different way than just singing a song or chant to him. We were relating to each other and reacting to what the other person did. (H. Gruber, personal communication, October 27, 2008)

Anthony Initiates Music Communication

Because Anthony has difficulty acting on his thoughts, his initiation of interactions represented a new level of reciprocal music communication success for him. To initiate interactions requires one to act with intention. Anthony's initiation of interactions with intention caused occasions for joy and delight for all involved.

As Anthony engaged in music play with Hannah and Claire, he increasingly initiated interactions with intention and complexity. Hannah recalled:

> There wasn't a lot of [eye contact between Anthony and me] at the beginning, but I can remember one specific time when we were singing "Surprise" (Valerio, 1997). We were putting beanbags on our heads and then dumping them off during the purposeful silence. At one point, Anthony looked up at me, reached out, and took the beanbag off my head. It was a great moment when I felt like he and I really connected. (H. Gruber, personal communication, October 27, 2008)

Regarding the same beanbag scene, Annabel wrote:

> Anthony *found* his head and moved to match the beat! He moved his head to make his beanbag drop from his head to match the beat. Anthony *found* his partner (Hannah) . . . and reached out to make her beanbag drop from her head! He accomplished all these, completely unsupported! This is huge for Anthony! Motor planning is a challenge for him—it is difficult for him to locate his body parts in relation to space. You can tell that he was having difficulty, particularly putting the object on his head, but he persisted, showing intentionality, so he could stay connected with Hannah, and even initiate part of the interaction. (A. Sy, personal communication, June 12, 2005)

With support from Hannah and Claire, the frequency of those initiations increased, but they were not always predictable.

> The hardest thing for me was not to get frustrated with myself. I didn't understand why I could sing a song one day and get amazing responses and then sing it again the next day with no apparent response. It took time for me to realize that he was internalizing everything that happened in music class, whether he showed it or not. (H. Gruber, personal communication, October 27, 2008)

In time, Anthony initiated his own melodic content, singing familiar songs and creating new songs with his music play partners. Hannah recalled a time when she was singing "The Ant Dance" (Taggart, Bolton, Reynolds, Valerio, and Gordon, 2000):

> Anthony had heard this song before, but this time when I stopped singing, he started singing the song (using words I had never heard him speak) in a beautiful head voice. He sang and moved around the room for about three minutes and then somehow he morphed "The Ant Dance" into "Santa Claus Is Coming to Town." When he started singing "Santa Claus," he came over to where I was

lying on the floor and sat right on top of me and continued singing. (H. Gruber, personal communication, October 27, 2008)

Many times, Anthony's vocalizations could be interpreted as nonsensical, but Hannah and Claire imitated his vocalizations and playfully used them to create music. Annabel recalled one particular instance when Claire interpreted one of Anthony's wail-like vocalizations as a melodic pattern. With her musical interpretation of Anthony's vocalization, Claire capitalized on the opportunity to create a song, "Zo-Way-O" (see figure 16.1), with Anthony:

> Anthony and I collaborated on a new song today: "Zo-Way-O." He started singing the initial pattern, and I added the scalar answer. Then he sang the whole song! It was so awesome. We had created something together, and he not only sang his contribution, but mine as well. Talk about communication. He was definitely valuing me as an artistic peer. (C. Griffith, 2009, p. 43)

Through their sustained work with Anthony, Annabel, Hannah, and Claire observed his progress with the initiation of (a) physical contact, (b) a game, and (c) complex musical content. Because Hannah and Claire were able to meet Anthony's arousal states, to follow his lead, to interpret his vocalizations and movements musically, they were able to engage him in reciprocal communication through music.

Making Adjustments

Hannah and Claire commented that it was not always easy to read Anthony's moods or arousal states. As Annabel explained, he often transitions quickly from being overactive to underactive and vice versa, and he does not make eye contact in ways that helps one who is unfamiliar with him understand his mood or arousal state. But, by being patient and adjusting their music activity

Figure 16.1.   Song Initiated by Anthony and Created in Collaboration with Claire

pacing, Hannah and Claire learned to read Anthony's cues. They learned that reciprocal communication includes the teacher's quick and sensitive making of adjustments to match Anthony's arousal states. Claire recalled learning how to help Anthony:

> There was a point in the session, I guess about halfway through, and he started being very unresponsive and very closed off, and I now understand that he was overstimulated. . . . He kind of shut down and was quiet, and then almost abruptly, he had a full-blown meltdown. He was screaming, he was running, he was flailing. . . . So I moved and I was sitting across from him, and I was doing the rocking and soft singing that Annabel has talked to me a lot about, because if he can get rocking and get started, that will help him get acclimated, figured out, calmed down. I had my legs crossed, and so what he did, was he came at me. I didn't know what was going to happen. He came at me, flipped himself around, and plopped in my lap. [He] grabbed my arms, and that's something he's done once [previously]. (C. Griffith, personal communication, December 10, 2008)

Annabel recommended that Claire modulate her music and movement activities to help Anthony maintain an optimum arousal state. She suggested that Claire ask herself the following questions to determine how to make adjustments in her music and movement presentation.

> How can I [Anthony's partner] modulate my behavior so I can help Anthony stay calm? As I read his cues and react to what he does, I ask myself, "Is my voice too loud? Too soft? Was my movement so quick (that I startled him)? Or do I need to be animated, with brighter affect as he is needing more input to feel right enough to engage back and forth with me?" (C. Griffith, personal communication, December 10, 2008)

Annabel commented, "It was also great to watch Claire change her affect (by changing the speed and intensity of her singing) to woo Anthony to respond to her cues" (C. Griffith, 2009, p. 39).

Anthony's Benefits

Annabel observed Anthony's development during music play in terms of milestones that allowed him to regulate himself and communicate with others during music play sessions and at other times. According to Annabel, Anthony achieved milestones in personal relationships and reciprocal communication. He learned to move his body with the beat, which helped his self-awareness and regulation, and in so doing, made him more able to engage and communicate with the world around him, as in the beanbag exercise described by Hannah. He became able to be engaged with his partner for long periods of time. For example, one music play session with Hannah lasted for more than two hours without a single meltdown. Anthony learned to seek out his partner and to initiate play. Anthony's achievement at those milestones helped him at home during daily activities. After several weeks of doing drumming exchanges with Hannah, Anthony intentionally grabbed one of his caregiver's hands and led her to the drum, to start the drum exchange with her. He learned more and more to move in sync with an ongoing rhythm and beat. He learned to explore objects around him and purposefully create various patterns of rhythm with them. As Anthony learned to stay calm and engaged, and able to have more circles of back-and-forth (musical) play, he enjoyed being a co-creator (of music) in the process.

Annabel wrote the following regarding Anthony's development and its influence on his family's relationship with him:

> I felt so happy as I watched Anthony grow so much happier. He found the need to connect, using a language he can speak (music). The lack of words/complex language helped support his sensory processing and he is able to explore and enjoy himself and his world (partner) better. It is great to see him become more assertive and intentional (acting out his own intent or desires) during play. Our family's music play experience helped us appreciate the use of rhythm, music, and silence to help support Anthony's challenges. We learned to read his cues better and adjust our activity as needed. As Anthony became more calm (just right with his arousal state), he became more engaging and assertive.
>
> We learned to practice and expand opportunities for us to engage with Anthony, without the need to use words. As we got better at following his cues, we discovered how subtle Anthony's communicative intent can be, in the context of a music activity. It can be just rubbing his feet against the mat, or wiggling his fingers in the air to match a partner's ongoing beat. We also learned to give (communicative) meaning to anything he does (whether that was the original purpose or not), and in turn, and with time, his behavior has grown to be truly purposeful (to communicate), and engage in reciprocal play. (A. Sy, personal communication, January 10, 2009)

Annabel also described other benefits for Anthony from the music play sessions, and explained his inconsistency in engaging in communication, play, and demonstration of specific skills:

> Anthony tends to fragment, or disengage easily, from any activity because of his inability to stay regulated (calm and organized) and his lack of motor planning. He tends to leave the activity when challenged or if the task is too difficult for him. The elements in music play [sessions] help support his self-regulation and engagement to allow him to stay on task (focused, not fragmented). The nature of the activity (music, his strength) and tolerant approach (errorless, with no right nor wrong answer) help him feel successful all the time. This boosts his

self-confidence, leading to a positive, happy affect, which, in turn, supports his motor planning and further helps him be successful.

At times, when Anthony can achieve self-regulation, even momentarily, he demonstrates hints of complex skills, as in music creativity, representing a higher developmental capacity. Anthony can slide up and down the developmental ladder, depending on the situation, so it is not surprising that he can exhibit various specific skills inconsistently. For example, there are times that he cannot stay regulated and engaged, and therefore, he cannot exhibit the skills he possesses. Meeting Anthony where he is developmentally, moment-to-moment, is a major key to success in getting him where he needs to be in any activity. (A. Sy, personal communication, July 8, 2008)

Benefits for Hannah and Claire

As they engaged in music play with Anthony, Hannah and Claire each realized that they were benefiting from engaging in reciprocal music communication with him. Hannah commented that learning to turn Anthony's sounds and movements into opportunities for music communication was musically challenging and rewarding. Moreover, she commented that she

> became more comfortable with singing in front of others and singing in different tonalities and different meters. I didn't have to think so much about what I was doing, and I could pay more attention to what he was doing. (H. Gruber, personal communication, October 27, 2008)

Claire reflected:

> Modifying music teaching and learning strategies for children who seem to have overwhelming challenges is not a barrier to learning, but may become a joyful examination of music engagement processes. I believe that we were always pleasantly surprised by our successes because through our goals, we found unexpected positive outcomes. Those focused around interpersonal interaction, and we found [musical] ways to encourage behaviors that exemplified this. (C. Griffith, 2009, p. 50)

Developing individual relationships with Anthony helped them develop as teachers and musicians. This allowed them to respond spontaneously and required them to improvise musically and with the structure of each lesson.

Annabel's Final Thoughts

Although Anthony and I were the only ones directly involved in this research project, our entire family enjoyed the benefits of our music play experiences, which I can sum up with these key words: *peace and comfort, respite, cherish, joy and triumph.* Following is a creative synthesis of Anthony's family's experiences, summarized by Annabel.

Peace and Comfort

For me, the most painful thing about being a parent of a child with autism is the need to recruit and train people intensively to bond and play with my child—as if it takes only a certain level of expertise for a fellow human being to be able to understand and connect with him. After our experience with music play, I can breathe better. I can now think, "Oh, my child will be okay, because he can actually live and enjoy and appreciate the human experience with somebody . . . (he can be just like all of us)." And from a parent's standpoint of having been through lots of interventions and having worked with different people with various (autism) perspectives, I think this is really a very comforting experience. With music play, we felt there can be someone out there who can really appreciate him for what he is, and not have to worry about what he needs to be (A. Sy, personal communication, July 8, 2008).

Respite

When we watch Anthony in his music play, it is like slipping into a world where we do not have to worry about his autism. It is very refreshing to hear (from Hannah, Claire, and Wendy) about his special musical skills (something that he can do that is exceptional)—quite the opposite of what we are usually advised about (his deficits).

Additionally, during music play sessions, we forget about *autism rules.* Ever since Anthony's (autism) diagnosis, we have been living through an overwhelming list of things to do including specific techniques—the *DOs* of autism. But what is more overwhelming for us are the rules of *DON'Ts,* for fear of encouraging inappropriate behavior. We find that these *autism rules* can alienate and disempower family and friends—Anthony's support structure as a whole.

I also realize that more importantly, this experience (music play) is a respite for Anthony:

> I always say it's a refreshing experience for us, but really, it's a refreshing experience for Anthony—can you just imagine? You just feel like, "Wow, he's so happy!" Anthony would stay in that [music] room for 2 hours and not want to escape. (A. Sy, personal communication, July 8, 2008)

Cherish

We never realized and appreciated, to the degree that we do now, Anthony's musical creations. We are now more keenly aware of every music and rhythm he creates with anything, anytime (such as how he flips pages of a book with a beat), and in so doing helped us practice more opportunities to bond and join him in his (musical) play. We cherish his vocal stims (a *problem behavior* for others) as we turn them into joyful musical exchanges.

Joy

My life with my child brings lots of unexpected, joyous delight. I am aware how this might be difficult for other people to appreciate, so I am very happy that Anthony's partners in music play had the chance to feel the joy of *Anthony*. Witnessing this brings me joy, even more so.

Triumph

Most stories of success in autism are about losing diagnosis, or being mainstreamed, grade-level, near-typical, or indistinguishable. We would love to share our outlook of a success story. First and foremost, this is Anthony's success story in the face of severe autism.

Other Insights

One day, after meeting with Claire and Wendy to discuss questions about Anthony and how specific approaches can help him, I shared these thoughts:

> I realized that all through these years of working with Anthony, you [Wendy, Claire, and Hannah] know very little about autism and the specific nature of Anthony's challenges. Yet, you were able to relate with Anthony to the degree that was difficult for us without autism training to achieve in the past. Maybe it is because with music, and with the right approach, you touch the very *core* of his existence. (A. Sy, personal communication, October 8, 2008)

Music is the one powerful thing that can be enjoyed, shared, and exchanged in reciprocal play, without taboo, anywhere, regardless of culture, social structure, language, age, race, and gender; music transcends space and time.

As I watch each session of music play, I think about Anthony and what is in his head: what is he thinking moment to moment, what is he feeling, what is his intent . . . what makes him so happy and calm enough to engage in reciprocal play with his partner.

I thought about a poem that Anthony would write, if he could, about his music play experience:

> In music play
> I share my smiles.
> I join in laughter.

I find joy and peace.
No *right,* nor *wrong*
No threats
No rules.
I can be me!
You *wait and see*
Build on my strengths.
You match my pace
Respond to my *cues*
Dance with my *state.*
You *hear* me and we can *talk.*
In a language that does not need words.
Thank you for living a part of me.
My life is my music.
And music is *me.*

CONCLUSION

Findings from this heuristic case study should not be generalized; however, our findings may be beneficial and inspirational to families who have children with autism. For Anthony, music play experiences provided a place for him to experience self-regulation, shared attention, and reciprocal communication. Moreover, those experiences provided a place for him to relax, to be himself, to express himself through music, and to connect with someone. For Annabel, Anthony's play experiences provided peace and comfort, respite, moments to cherish, joy, and triumph. For Hannah and Claire, their music play experiences provided the opportunity to develop as teachers and musicians in close, personal, musical relationships with Anthony.

We encourage music development researchers and music teachers to document their music experiences with all children, and especially with those who have challenges due to autism. By doing so, we may continue to provide insight into the uses of music for improved interventions for children with autism, as well as improved quality of life through music making.

REFERENCES

Creswell, J. W. (1998). *Qualitative inquiry and research design: Choosing among the five traditions.* Thousand Oaks, CA: Sage.

Creswell, J. W. (2003). *Research design: Qualitative, quantitative, and mixed methods approaches* (2nd ed.). Thousand Oaks, CA: Sage.

Fang, E. R. (2009). *Music in the lives of two children with autism: A case study.* Doctoral dissertation, Retrieved from ProQuest Dissertations and Theses. (AAT 1473522).

Frick, J. M. (2000). *A qualitative study of music and communication in a musically rich early childhood special education classroom.* Doctoral dissertation. Retrieved from ProQuest Dissertations and Theses. (AAT 9940757).

Frost, L. A., and Bondy, A. (1994). *PECS: The picture exchange communication system.* Cherry Hill, NJ: Pyramid Educational Consultants.

Gordon, E. E. (2003). *A music learning theory for newborn and young children.* Chicago: GIA.

Greenspan, S. I. (2010). *The basic course on the Greenspan Floortime approach.* Retrieved from http://stanleygreenspan.com/.

Greenspan, S. I., DeGangi, G. A., and Wieder, S. (2001). *Functional emotional assessment scale (FEAS).* Bethesda, MD: Interdisciplinary Council on Developmental Learning Disorders.

Greenspan, S. I., and Lewis, N. B. (1999). *Building healthy minds: The six experiences that create intelligence and emotional growth in babies and young children.* New York: Perseus.

Greenspan, S. I., and Weider, S. (1997). Developmental patterns and outcomes in infants and children with disorders in relating and communicating: A chart review of 200 cases of children with autistic spectrum diagnoses. *Journal of Developmental and Learning Disorders, 1*, 87–141.

Greenspan, S. I., and Wieder, S. (1998). *The child with special needs: Encouraging emotional and intellectual growth.* Reading, MA: Perseus.

Greenspan, S. I., and Wieder, S. (2005). Can children with autism master the core deficits and become empathetic, creative, and reflective? A ten to fifteen year follow-up of a subgroup of children with autism spectrum disorders (ASD) who received a comprehensive developmental, individual-difference, relationship-based (DIR) approach. *Journal of Developmental and Learning Disorders, 9*, 39–61.

Greenspan, S. I., and Wieder, S. (2006). *Engaging autism: Using the Floortime approach to help children relate, communicate, and think.* Cambridge, MA: Da Capo.

Griffith, C. (2009). *Examining experiences of teaching music to a child with autism while using a music learning theory-based intervention during informal music sessions infused with DIR/Floortime strategies.* Master's thesis. Retrieved from Dissertations and Theses at University of South Carolina. (AAT 1463997).

Gruber, H. (2007). *Musical responses and collateral benefits of a music-learning-theory-based intervention for children with autism.* Unpublished master's thesis, University of South Carolina, Columbia.

Hicks, W. (1993). *An investigation of the initial stages of preparatory audiation.* Doctoral dissertation. Retrieved from ProQuest Dissertations and Theses. (AAT 9316493).

Hornbach, C. M. (2005). *Ah-eee-ah-eee-yah-eee, bum and pop, pop, pop: Teacher initiatives, teacher silence, and children's vocal responses in early childhood music classes.* Doctoral dissertation. Retrieved from ProQuest Dissertations and Theses. (AAT 3189669).

Hornbach, C. M. (2007). The use of silence in eliciting student responses in early childhood music classes. In K. Smithrim and R. Upitis (Eds.), *Listen to their voices: Research and practice in early childhood music.* Research to practice: A biennial series, 3 (pp. 228–42). Waterloo, Ontario: Canadian Music Educators Association.

Interdisciplinary Council on Developmental and Learning Disorders. (2010a). *Individual differences.* Retrieved from www.icdl.com/dirFloortime/IndividualDifferences.shtml.

Interdisciplinary Council on Developmental and Learning Disorders. (2010b). *The sensory system: How we sense any new information.* Retrieved from www.icdl.com/dirFloortime/overview/BiologicalChallenges/SensorySystem.shtml.

Kern, P., Wolery, M., and Aldridge, D. (2007). Use of songs to promote independence in morning greeting routines for young children with autism. *Journal of Autism Development Disorders, 37,* 1264–71.

Kranowitz, C. S., and Silver, L. B. (1998). *The out-of-sync child: Recognizing and coping with sensory integration dysfunction.* New York: Berkley.

Lovaas, O. I. (1981). *Teaching developmentally disabled children: The me book.* Austin, TX: Pro-ed.

Moustakas, C. (1990). *Heuristic research: Design, methodology, and applications.* Newbury Park, CA: Sage.

Partington, J. W., and Sundberg, M. L. (1998). *The assessment of basic language and learning skills: An assessment, curriculum guide, and tracking system for children with autism or other developmental disabilities.* Danville, CA: Behavior Analysts.

Patton, M. (2002). *Qualitative research and evaluation methods* (3rd ed.). Thousand Oaks, CA: Sage.

Reynolds, A. M. (1995). *An investigation of the movement responses performed by children 18 months to three years of age and their caregivers to rhythm chants in duple and triple meters.* Doctoral dissertation. Retrieved from ProQuest Dissertations and Theses. (AAT 9527531).

Reynolds, A. M. (2006). Vocal interactions during informal early childhood music classes. *Bulletin of the Council for Research in Music Education, 168,* 1–16.

Reynolds, A. M., Long, S., and Valerio, W. H. (2007) Language acquisition and music acquisition: Possible parallels. In K. Smithrim and R. Upitis (Eds.), *Listen to their voices: Research and practice in early childhood music.* Research to practice: A biennial series, 3 (pp. 211–27). Waterloo, Ontario: Canadian Music Educators Association.

Schopler, E., Reichler, R. J., and Renner, B. R. (1998). *Child autism rating scale (CARS).* San Antonio, TX: Psychological Corporation.

Solomon, R., Necheles, J., Ferch, C., and Bruckman, D. (2007). Pilot study of a parent training program for young children with autism: The P.L.A.Y. Project Home Consultation program. *Autism: International Journal of Research and Practice, 11*(3), 205–25.

Taggart, C. C., Bolton, B. M., Reynolds, A. M., Valerio, W. H., and Gordon, E. E. (2000). *Jump right in: The music curriculum, teacher's guide, book 1.* Chicago: GIA.

Valerio, W. H. (1997). Surprise! Music development means music play for adults as well as children. *Early Childhood Connections, 1*(3), 7–14.

Valerio, W. H., Seaman, M. A., Yap, C. C., Santucci, P. M., and Tu, M. (2006). Vocal evidence of toddler music syntax acquisition: A case study. *Bulletin for the Council for Research in Music Education, 170,* 33–45.

Valerio, W. H., and Reynolds, A. M. (2009). Peek-a-boo and fill-in-the-blank: Age-old games with a social music interaction twist. *Early Childhood Music and Movement Perspectives, 4*(3), 10–15.

Valerio, W. H., Reynolds, A. M., Taggart, C., Bolton, B. M., and Gordon, E. (1998). *Music play*. Chicago: GIA.

Wimpory, D., Chadwick, P., and Nash, S. (1995). Brief report: Musical interaction therapy for children with autism; An evaluative case study with two-year follow-up. *Journal of Autism and Developmental Disorders, 25*, 541–52.

Wimpory, D., Hobson, R., and Nash, S. (2006). What facilitates social engagement in preschool children with autism? *Journal of Autism and Developmental Disorders, 37*, 564–73.

About the Editors

Suzanne L. Burton received her A.A. in piano pedagogy and B.M. in music education from Spring Arbor University and M.M. and Ph.D. in music education from Michigan State University. She is associate professor of music education and director of graduate studies at the University of Delaware. As the general music specialist, Dr. Burton teaches undergraduate methods courses in early childhood and K–12 general music and graduate courses on research methods, curriculum and assessment, music psychology, and philosophy. She advises graduate theses and projects. Her scholarly interests include music acquisition, music teacher preparation and perspective consciousness, school-university partnerships, and community engagement. Known for her editorial work, Dr. Burton is the former editor of the Early Childhood Music and Movement Association publication *Perspectives*, and is on the editorial board of *Visions of Research in Music Education*. She is editor of the *Visions of Research in Music Education* special issue on early childhood music and coeditor for the *Arts Education Policy Review* issue on school-university partnerships. Her work is widely published and may be found in numerous professional journals and books. The first recipient of the College Music Society's Robby Gunstream Music in Education Award for ProjectMUSIC (a service-learning project), she is also a recipient of the Delaware Symphony Orchestra's Jessie Ball du Pont Educators Award. Dr. Burton is currently the National CMENC chair and chair of the MENC Early Childhood SRIG.

Cynthia Crump Taggart received her B.M. and M.M. in music education from the University of Michigan and her Ph.D. in music education from Temple University. Currently, she is professor and chair of music education at Michigan State University. Professor Taggart directs and teaches in the

Early Childhood Music Program of the Community Music School of Michigan State University's School of Music. As an MSU faculty member, she received the prestigious Teacher-Scholar Award. Prior to teaching at MSU, she taught for four years at Case Western Reserve University, where she won the Undergraduate Teaching Excellence Award for the Humanities and Social Sciences. She also has extensive elementary and preschool teaching experience in Wisconsin, Michigan, and Pennsylvania. In addition to being a faculty member, she is immediate past president of the College Music Society. Dr. Taggart's publications include coauthorship of *Music Play: The Early Childhood Music Curriculum* and *Jump Right In: The General Music Curriculum*, as well as coeditorship of *Readings in Music Learning Theory* and *The Development and Practical Applications of Music Learning Theory*. In addition, she has written extensively for professional journals. Her research interests are early childhood music, measurement, psychology of music, music learning theory, and music aptitude.

About the Authors

Jenny Alvarez is an early intervention teacher in the Early On Program of Ingham County Intermediate School District in Michigan. She has a certificate in infant mental health from the University of Michigan, a master's degree in child development from Syracuse University, and a B.S. in deaf education from the University of Texas.

Audrey Berger Cardany is on faculty at Peabody Conservatory of Music of the Johns Hopkins University in Baltimore, Maryland, where her research and pedagogical interests include early childhood music education and music and language literacy. She serves as the vocal and general music specialist, teaching undergraduate and graduate music education courses.

Lecia Cecconi-Roberts is an independent researcher and professional musician in Wake County, North Carolina, and a music teacher who has received several awards for her work with students ranging from preschoolers through undergraduates. Her research interests include early childhood music, middle school instrumental students, and preservice teachers.

Shelly Cooper is associate professor of music education at the University of Arizona, where her research interests include historical aspects of music education and music acquisition in early childhood. She teaches undergraduate and graduate courses in general music, early childhood music, and research methods, and serves as coordinator of music education, editor of *General Music Today*, director of a preschool music program, and director of the Desert Skies Symposium on Research in Music Education.

Diana R. Dansereau is assistant professor of music education at Boston University, where her scholarly interests include the musical capacities of young children, classroom and music teacher education, school-community collaboration, and research methods in music education. She teaches an undergraduate elementary and early childhood methods class as well as graduate psychology, sociology, and research courses.

John W. Flohr is professor emeritus from Texas Woman's University, Denton, and serves as part-time faculty with Walden University's Richard W. Riley College of Education. He currently teaches graduate courses in research, supervises doctoral research in the arts, and performs in jazz and classical mediums. Research interests include early childhood, neuroscience, assessment, and arts education.

Joy Galliford is adjunct instructor in music education at the University of Miami with research interests in early childhood development. She teaches an undergraduate technique class and supervises elementary/secondary interns. She is the administrator of a music enrichment program for children ranging from newborn to eight years old.

John Grego is associate professor of statistics and director of the Statistical Laboratory in the Department of Statistics at the University of South Carolina, conducting research in latent class models, categorical data analysis, and environmental statistics. He collaborates with researchers in a wide variety of disciplines and teaches undergraduate and graduate courses in experimental design, statistical computing, and categorical data analysis.

Hannah Gruber is assistant professor of keyboard at the Crane School of Music, SUNY Potsdam. She is active as a presenter and researcher on the effects of music on children with autism and performs regularly, collaborating with various artists, including Christopher Creviston, Joseph Lulloff, Timothy McAllister, Oskar Ruîz, David Stambler, James Umble, and members of the U.S. military bands.

Christina Hornbach is assistant professor of music and coordinator of music education at Hope College in Holland, Michigan. She specializes in early childhood, elementary general, and choral music methods and materials.

Beatriz Ilari is a music educator and researcher with main interests in the psychological and sociocultural dimensions of musical development and learning. She is currently coeditor of the *International Journal of Music Education-Research* (ISME) and an associate researcher in the faculty of music of the State University of Campinas, Brazil, where she directs graduate student work.

Joyce Jordan-DeCarbo is professor and chair of music education and music therapy at the University of Miami with research interests in general music, aural discrimination, and early childhood development. She teaches undergraduate and graduate general music methods, coordinates and supervises internships, and serves as thesis/dissertation advisor for graduate students.

Julie Derges Kastner is a graduate student at Michigan State University and an early childhood music teacher at the MSU Community Music School. Previously, she taught elementary general music and choir for Fairfax County Public Schools, Virginia, and early childhood music at the Levine School of Music in Washington, DC.

Dan Keast is associate professor of music and chair of music at the University of Texas of the Permian Basin, located in Odessa, Texas. His main research emphasis is the creation of virtual learning activities to generate higher levels of student engagement.

Lisa Huisman Koops is assistant professor of music education at Case Western Reserve University, where her research focuses on the vital role of the family in optimizing early music development and education. She teaches undergraduate methods courses in early childhood, general, and world music, and graduate courses in philosophy and advanced research, as well as early childhood music courses at the Music Settlement.

Lili M. Levinowitz is a professor of music education at Rowan University; she is jointly appointed to both the College of Fine and Performing Arts and the College of Education. She is the coauthor of *Music Together: An Early Childhood Music Program for Families and Preschool Children* and teaches infants through graduate students.

Anne McNair recently completed the Ph.D. in music education from the University of South Carolina, where her research interests included music acquisition and joint music attention. She currently directs choirs for children and youth at Shandon Presbyterian Church and is developing a new community choir for children in Columbia, South Carolina.

Diane Cummings Persellin is professor of music education at Trinity University in San Antonio, Texas, where she teaches undergraduate and graduate courses in early childhood, elementary, and secondary music education, supervises field experiences and internships, and directs the Trinity Handbell Ensemble. Her research interests include acquisition of music skills, teacher education, professional development, and assessment in early childhood music education.

Alison Reynolds is associate professor of music education at Temple University, where her research interests include music acquisition and development, professional development among experienced teachers, and movement as essential to music development. She teaches undergraduate methods courses in general music, and graduate courses in research and practice, and guides undergraduate and graduate researchers.

Kathy Schubert is a speech language pathologist with the Ingham Intermediate School District serving the birth-to-three population in the Early On Program by working with families who have concerns about their young children's speech and language development. As a strategy to increase speech, language, and overall development, Kathy facilitates the partnership between Early On and the Early Childhood Music Program at Michigan State University.

Wendy L. Sims is professor and director of music education at the University of Missouri, where she is an award-winning teacher of undergraduate through doctoral students, as well as toddlers and preschoolers enrolled in MU's Child Development Laboratory. Dr. Sims has a long history as a researcher, author, conference presenter, and leader in professional organizations including MENC: The National Association for Music Education and the International Society for Music Education, and currently is the editor of the *Journal of Research in Music Education.*

Amanda Page Smith (M.M.E., Westminster Choir College; B.M., St. Olaf College) is the director of children's music at the Brick Presbyterian Church and the Brick Church School in Manhattan. She is active as a workshop clinician through choral organizations such as Choristers Guild and the American Choral Directors Association, and serves on the faculty of the Choristers Guild Institute at the Louisville Seminary.

Claire Griffith Stockman (M.M.E., University of South Carolina) teaches prekindergarten through fifth-grade music classes in Hamilton County, Chattanooga, Tennessee. She is currently exploring the ways music instruction contributes to the fabric of school culture and climate.

Annabel Sy is a physician with training in internal medicine and allergy and clinical immunology, whose son Anthony was diagnosed with autism, dyspraxia, sensory dysfunction, seizure disorder, and multiple food allergies. She used a variety of treatment approaches to support Anthony's challenges with autism, including sensory integration techniques, picture exchange communication system, applied behavioral analysis, and later a developmental, individualized, and relationship-based (DIR/Floortime) framework for his intervention program.

Wendy Valerio is associate professor of music education and director of the Children's Music Development Center at the University of South Carolina School of Music. She teaches graduate and undergraduate courses in music learning methods and directs undergraduate and graduate researchers. Her research interests include music acquisition and development.

Krista Velez (M.M. and B.M., University of Delaware) is a music educator for students with autism in New Jersey. She teaches private flute and piano lessons and presents workshops on guiding the musical development of students with special needs.

Ching Ching Yap is the director of institutional assessment at the Savannah College of Art and Design, where her research interests include assessment in the arts, collaborative learning, and music acquisition. Before joining SCAD, Dr. Yap was a research assistant professor at the Office of Program Evaluation, College of Education, University of South Carolina, serving on advisory boards on assessment and consulting in assessment designs and measurement issues.

DATE DUE